I'm always

Cardbo

Hey!! Did you see the Narset planeswalker that was spoiled?! She's incredible!!
The abilities, the flavor, the high loyalty, every-thing about her is amaz-- what?!
Yeah, I guess I'm driving right now--why do you ask?
ONE WAY

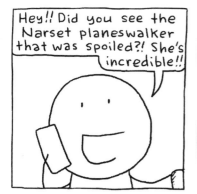

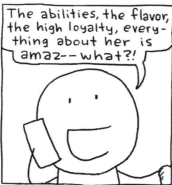

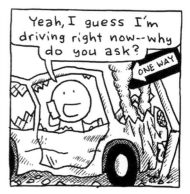

A collection of comics about the world's most addictive game.

I'm always thinking about Cardboard Crack

Copyright © 2015

Check out these other Cardboard Crack books:
Cardboard Crack
I will never quit Cardboard Crack
Cardboard Crack anytime, anywhere
Cardboard Crack until the day I die

Cardboard Crack is in no way affiliated with or endorsed by Wizards of the Coast LLC. Wizards of the Coast, Magic: The Gathering, and their respective logos are trademarks of Wizards of the Coast LLC. All rights reserved.

This book collects comics that originally appeared online between October 19, 2014 and March 7, 2015, and can also be viewed at:
cardboard-crack.com
facebook.com/CardboardCrack

For information write:
cardboardcrack.mtg@gmail.com

Printed in the U.S.A.

For Treasure Cruise.
We had fun while it lasted.

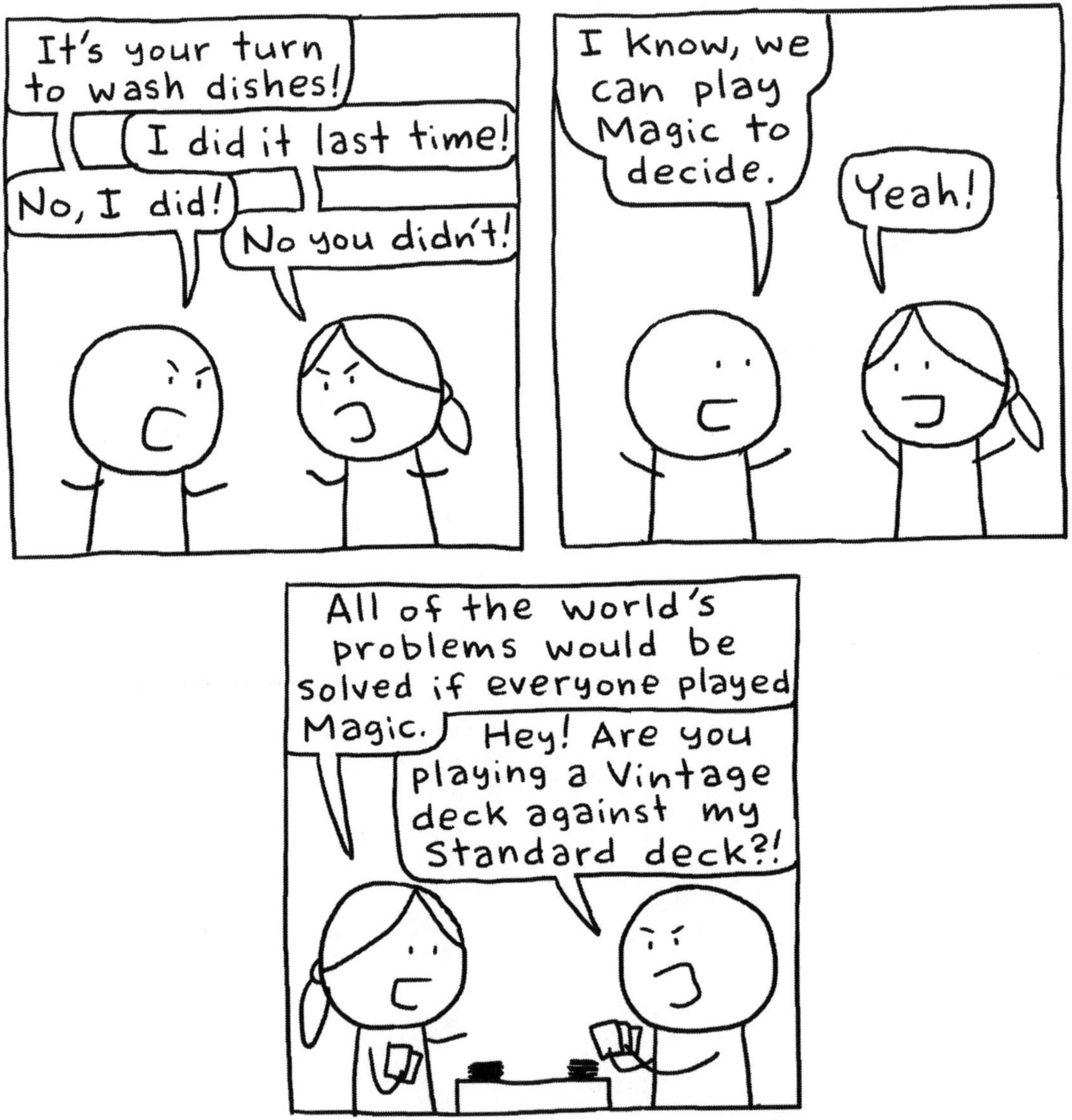
It's your turn to wash dishes!
I did it last time!
No, I did!
No you didn't!
I know, we can play Magic to decide.
Yeah!
All of the world's problems would be solved if everyone played Magic.
Hey! Are you playing a Vintage deck against my Standard deck?!

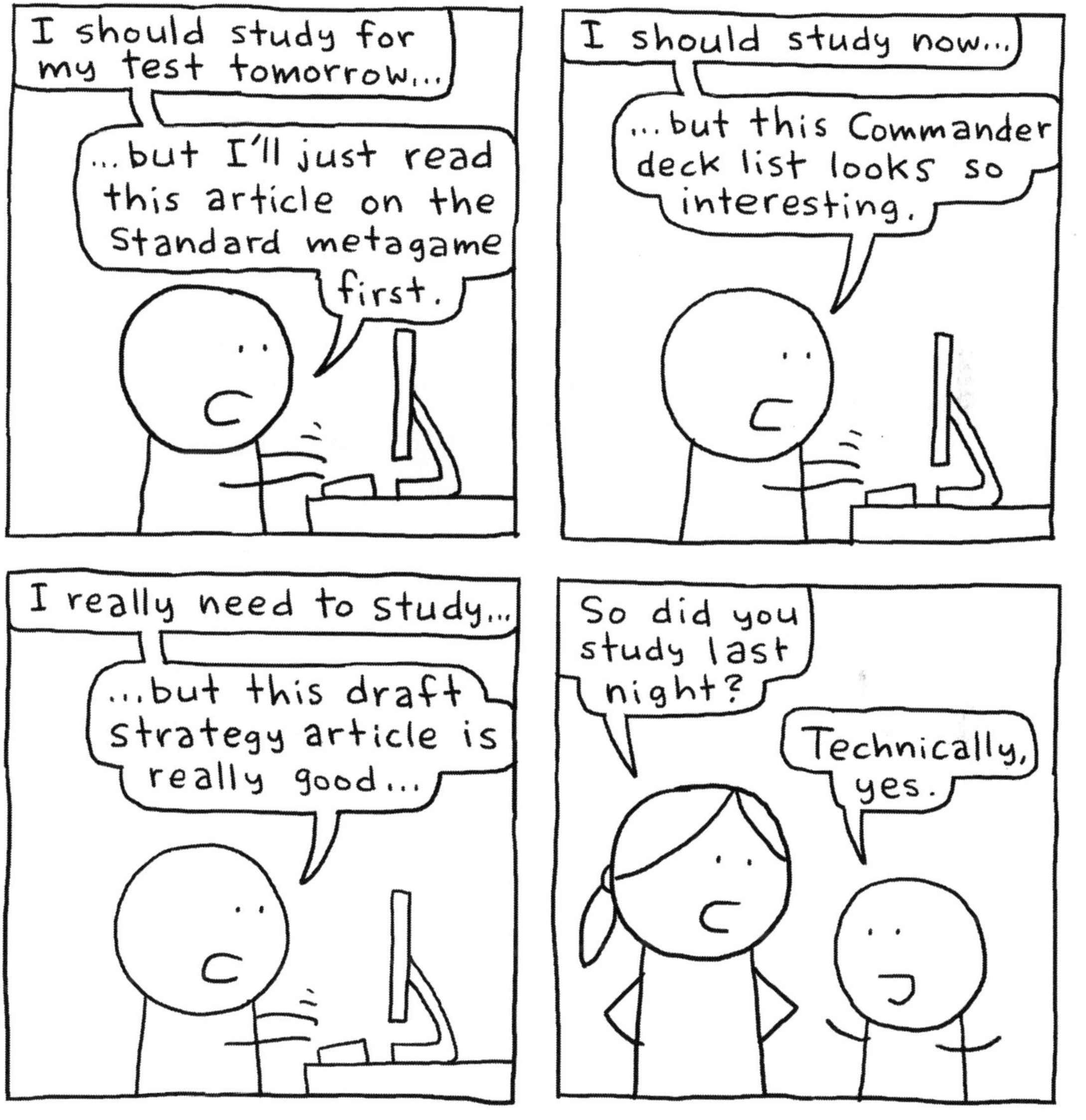
I should study for my test tomorrow...
...but I'll just read this article on the Standard metagame first.
I should study now...
...but this Commander deck list looks so interesting.
I really need to study...
...but this draft strategy article is really good...
So did you study last night?
Technically, yes.

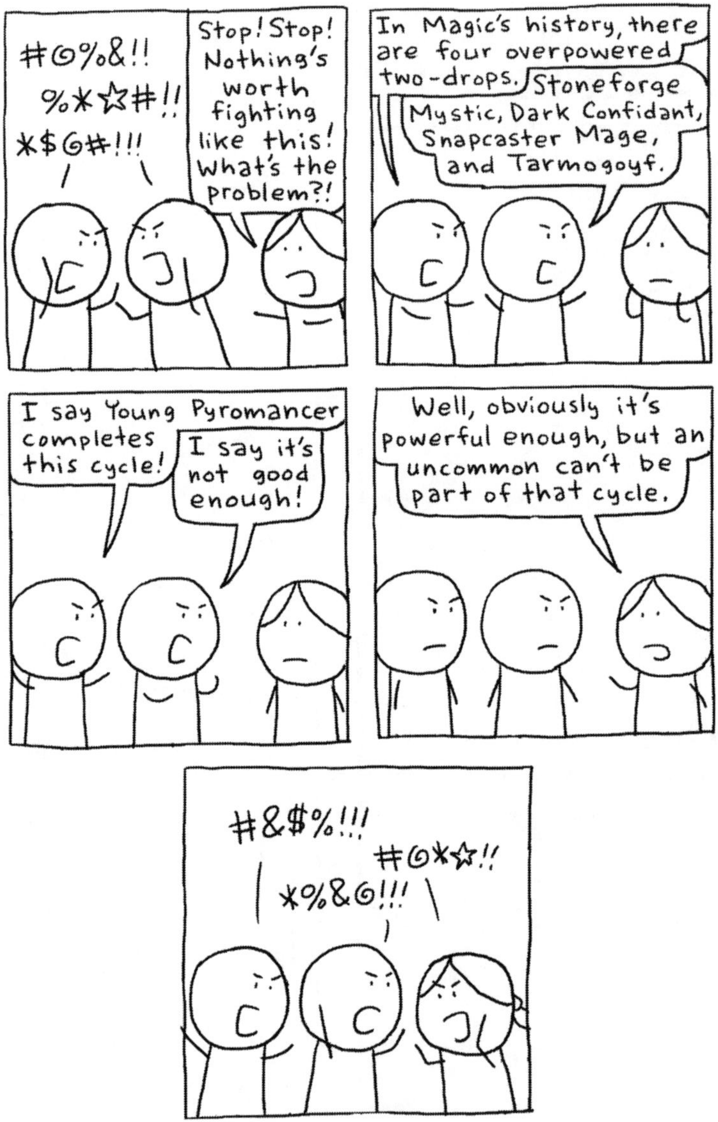
#@%&!!
%*☆#!!
*$@#!!!
Stop! Stop! Nothing's worth fighting like this! What's the problem?!
In Magic's history, there are four overpowered two-drops.
Stoneforge Mystic, Dark Confidant, Snapcaster Mage, and Tarmogoyf.
I say Young Pyromancer completes this cycle!
I say it's not good enough!
Well, obviously it's powerful enough, but an uncommon can't be part of that cycle.
#&$%!!!
#@*☆!!
*%&@!!!

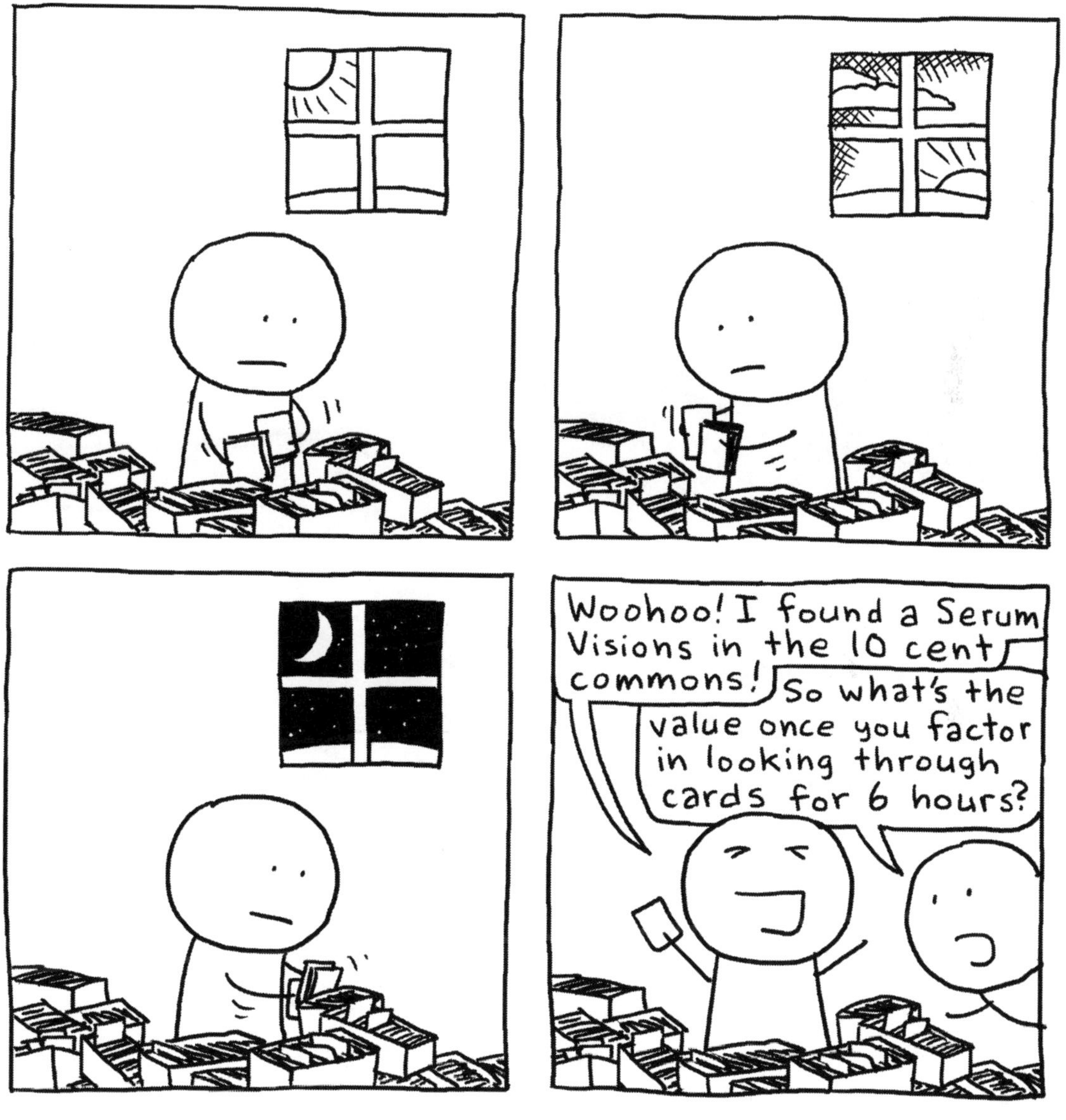
Woohoo! I found a Serum Visions in the 10 cent commons!
So what's the value once you factor in looking through cards for 6 hours?

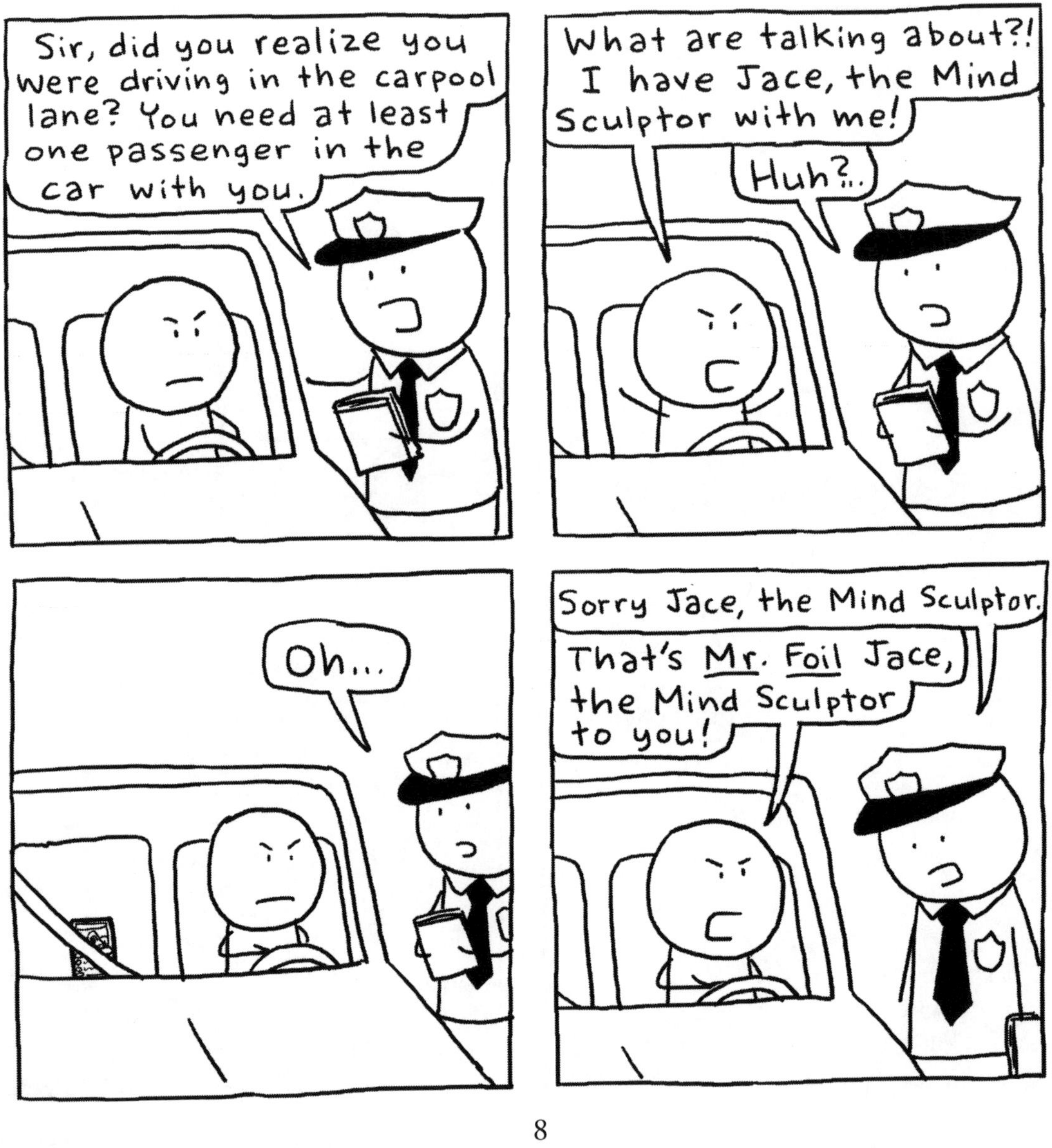
Sir, did you realize you were driving in the carpool lane? You need at least one passenger in the car with you.
What are talking about?! I have Jace, the Mind Sculptor with me!
Huh?...
Oh...
Sorry Jace, the Mind Sculptor.
That's Mr. Foil Jace, the Mind Sculptor to you!

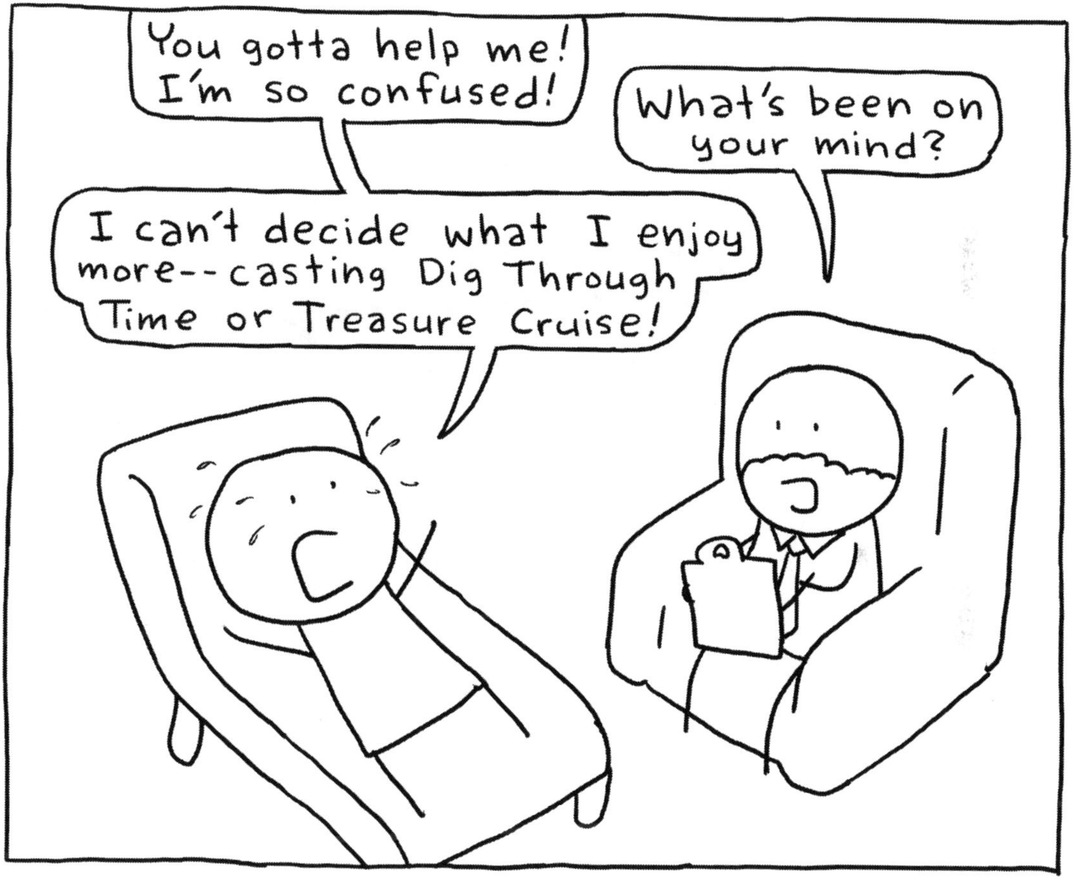
You gotta help me! I'm so confused!
What's been on your mind?
I can't decide what I enjoy more--casting Dig Through Time or Treasure Cruise!

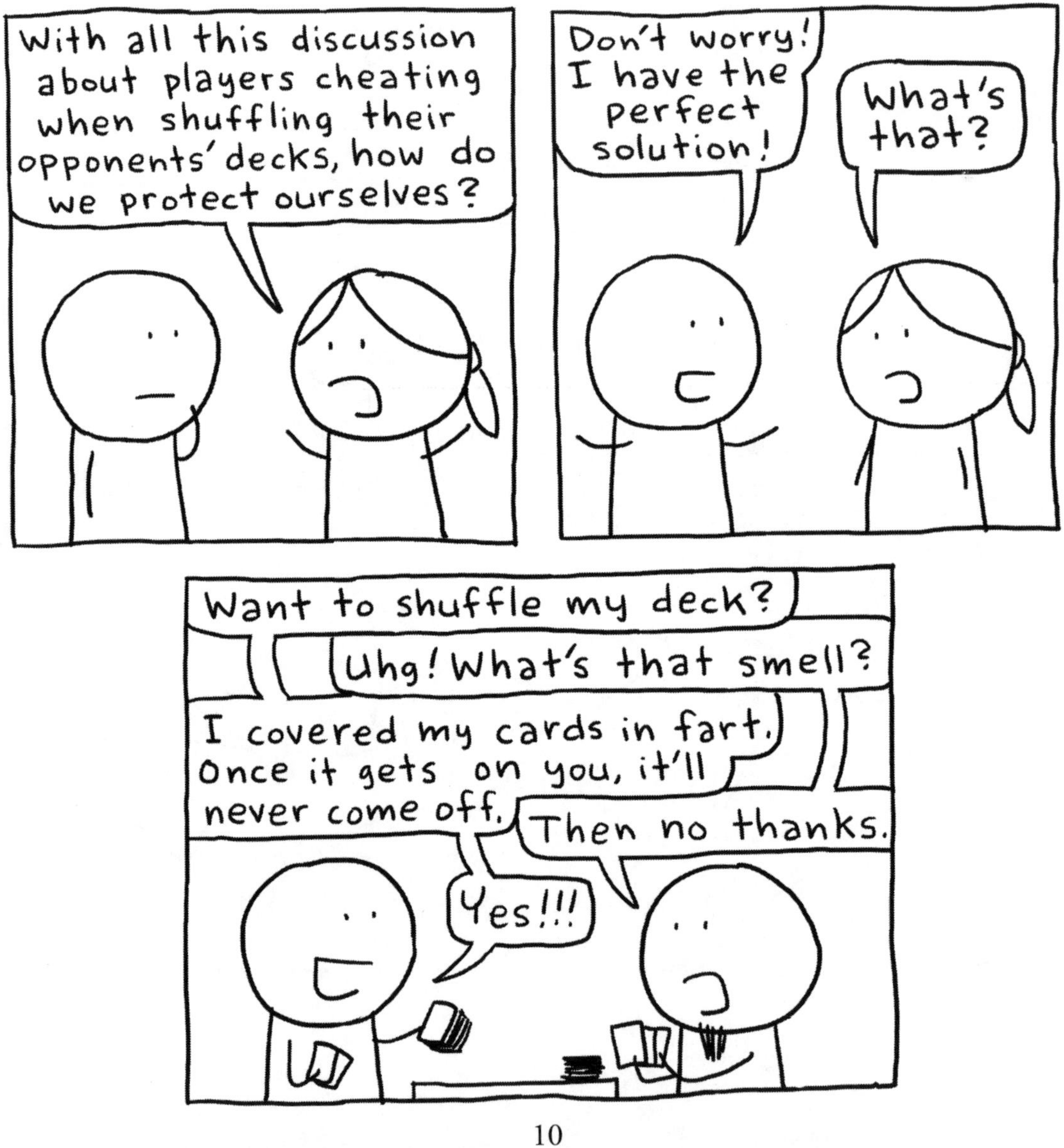
With all this discussion about players cheating when shuffling their opponents' decks, how do we protect ourselves?
Don't worry! I have the perfect solution!
What's that?
Want to shuffle my deck?
Uhg! What's that smell?
I covered my cards in fart. Once it gets on you, it'll never come off.
Then no thanks.
Yes!!!

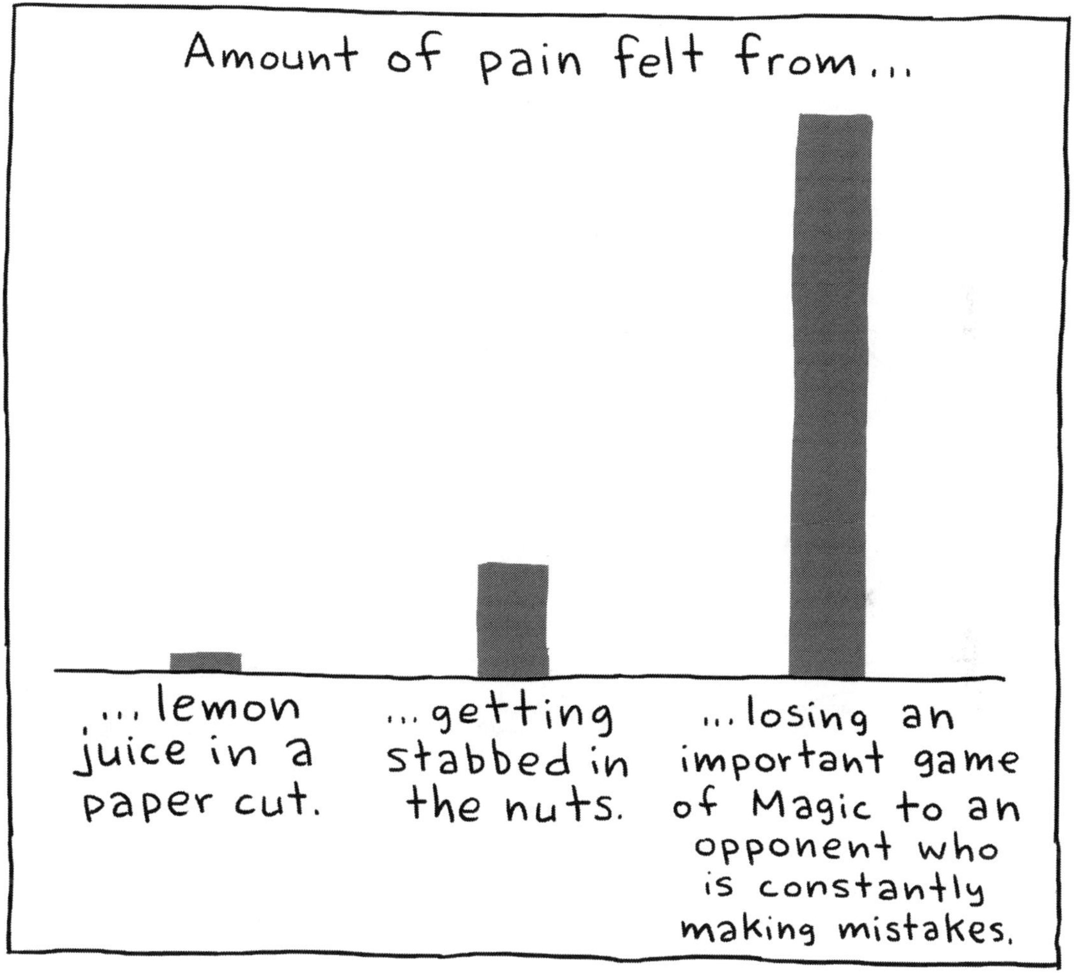
Amount of pain felt from...
...lemon juice in a paper cut.
...getting stabbed in the nuts.
...losing an important game of Magic to an opponent who is constantly making mistakes.

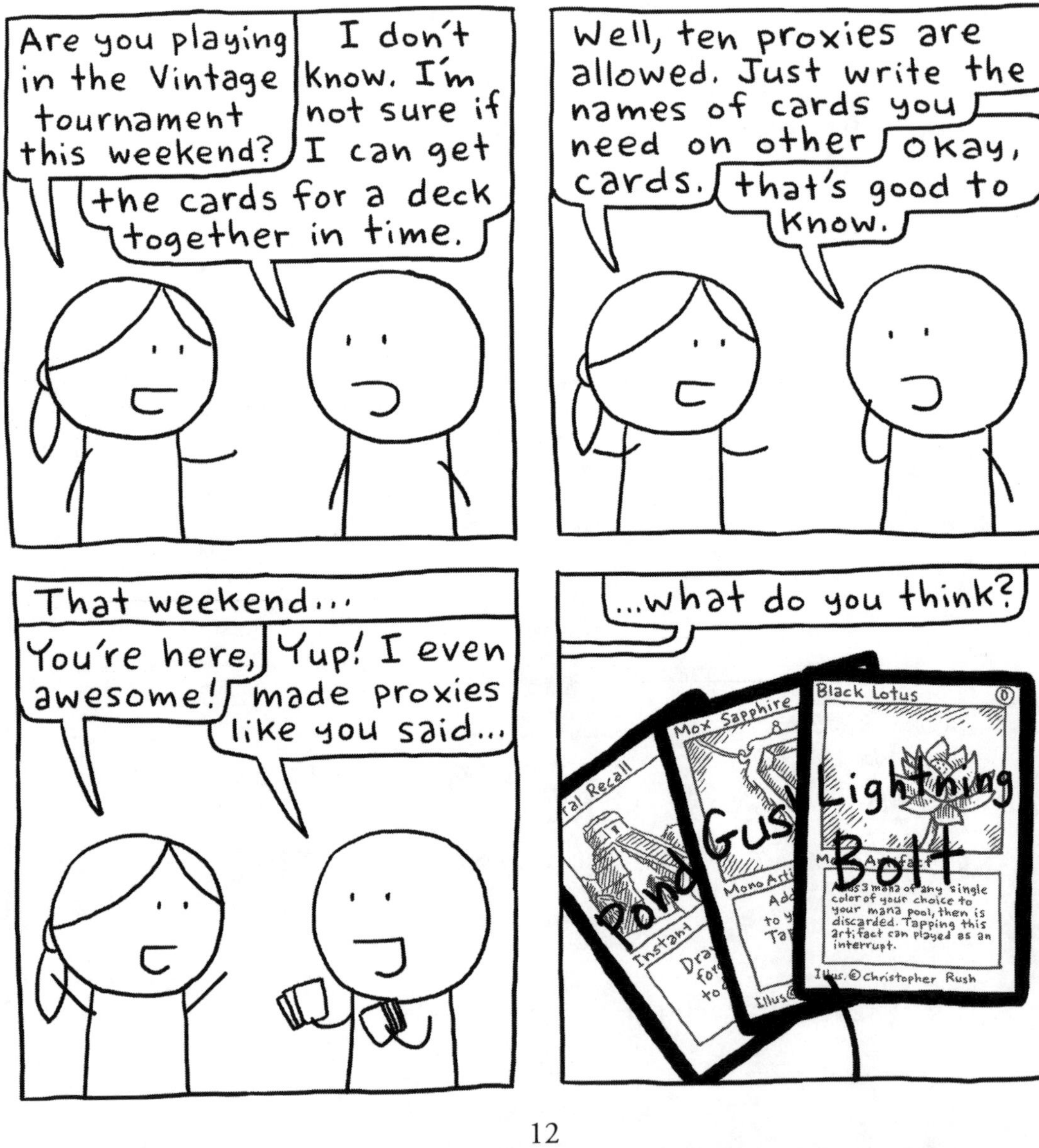
Are you playing in the Vintage tournament this weekend?
I don't know. I'm not sure if I can get the cards for a deck together in time.
Well, ten proxies are allowed. Just write the names of cards you need on other cards.
Okay, that's good to know.
That weekend...
You're here, awesome!
Yup! I even made proxies like you said...
...what do you think?
Black Lotus
Mox Sapphire
Lightning Bolt
Pond
Instant
3 mana of any single color of your choice to your mana pool, then is discarded. Tapping this artifact can played as an interrupt.
Illus. © Christopher Rush

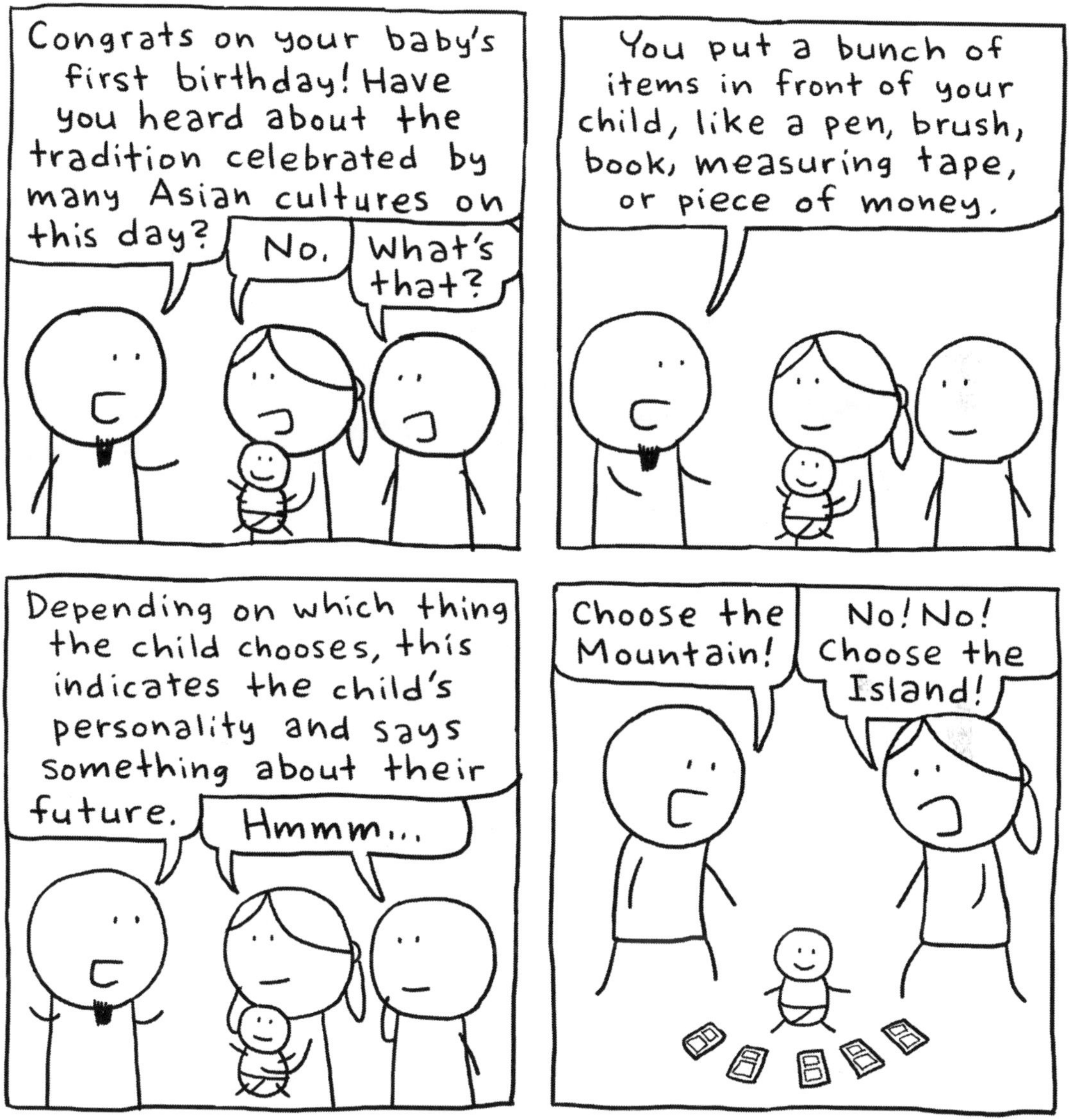
Congrats on your baby's first birthday! Have you heard about the tradition celebrated by many Asian cultures on this day?
No.
What's that?
You put a bunch of items in front of your child, like a pen, brush, book, measuring tape, or piece of money.
Depending on which thing the child chooses, this indicates the child's personality and says something about their future.
Hmmm...
Choose the Mountain!
No! No! Choose the Island!

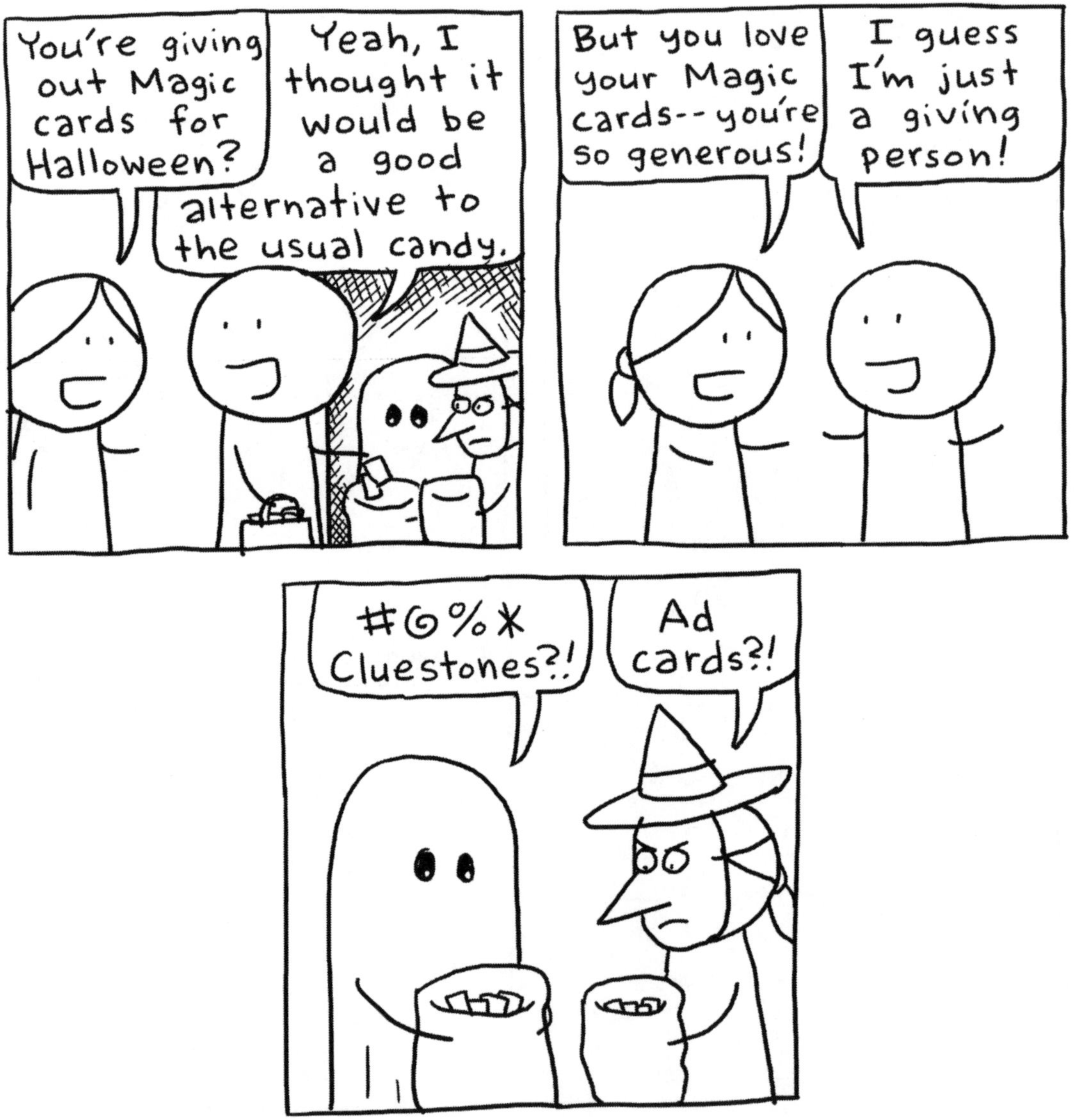
You're giving out Magic cards for Halloween?
Yeah, I thought it would be a good alternative to the usual candy.
But you love your Magic cards--you're so generous!
I guess I'm just a giving person!
#@%* Cluestones?!
Ad cards?!

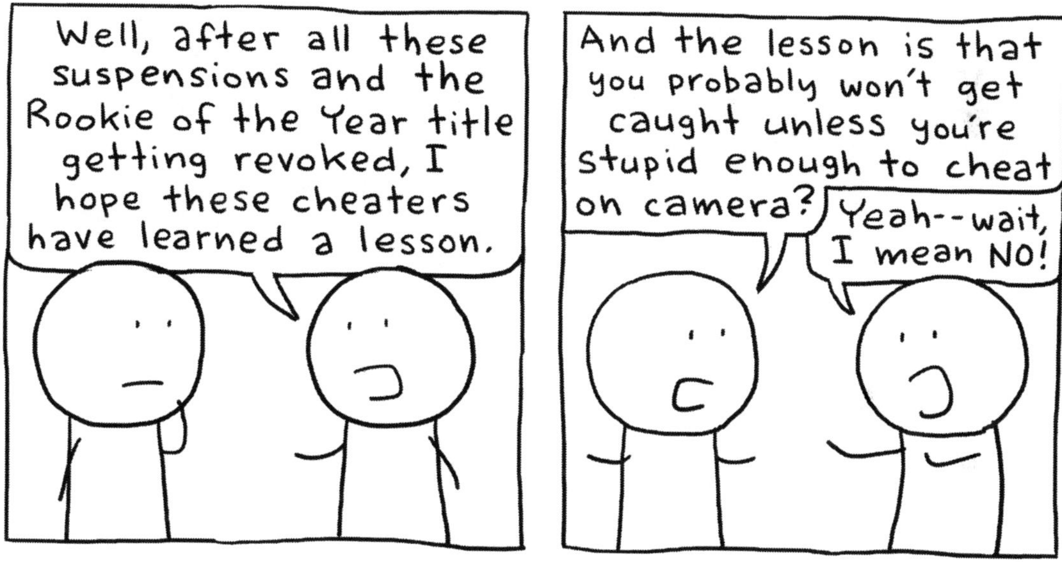
Well, after all these suspensions and the Rookie of the Year title getting revoked, I hope these cheaters have learned a lesson.
And the lesson is that you probably won't get caught unless you're stupid enough to cheat on camera?
Yeah--wait, I mean NO!

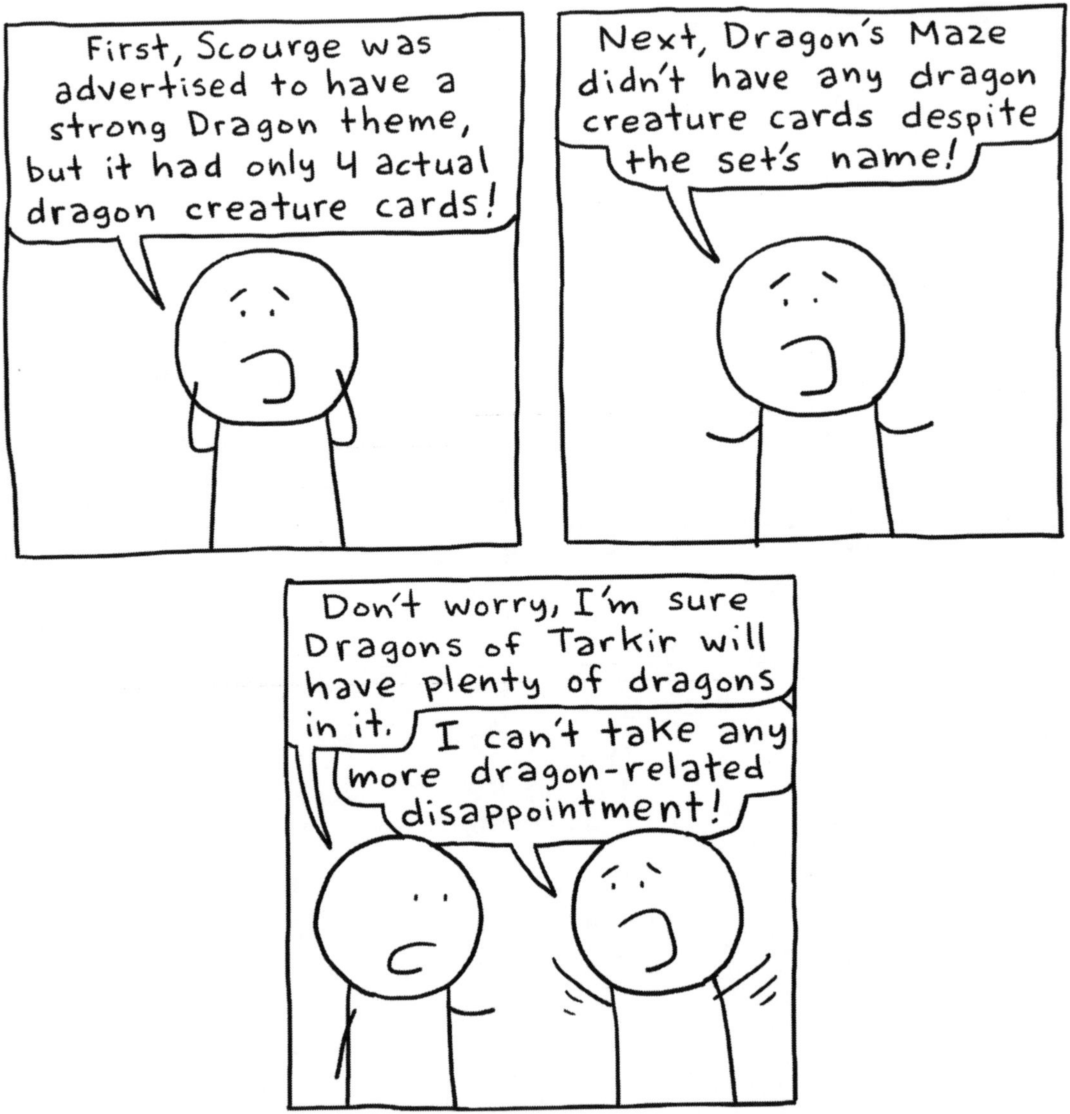
First, Scourge was advertised to have a strong Dragon theme, but it had only 4 actual dragon creature cards!
Next, Dragon's Maze didn't have any dragon creature cards despite the set's name!
Don't worry, I'm sure Dragons of Tarkir will have plenty of dragons in it.
I can't take any more dragon-related disappointment!

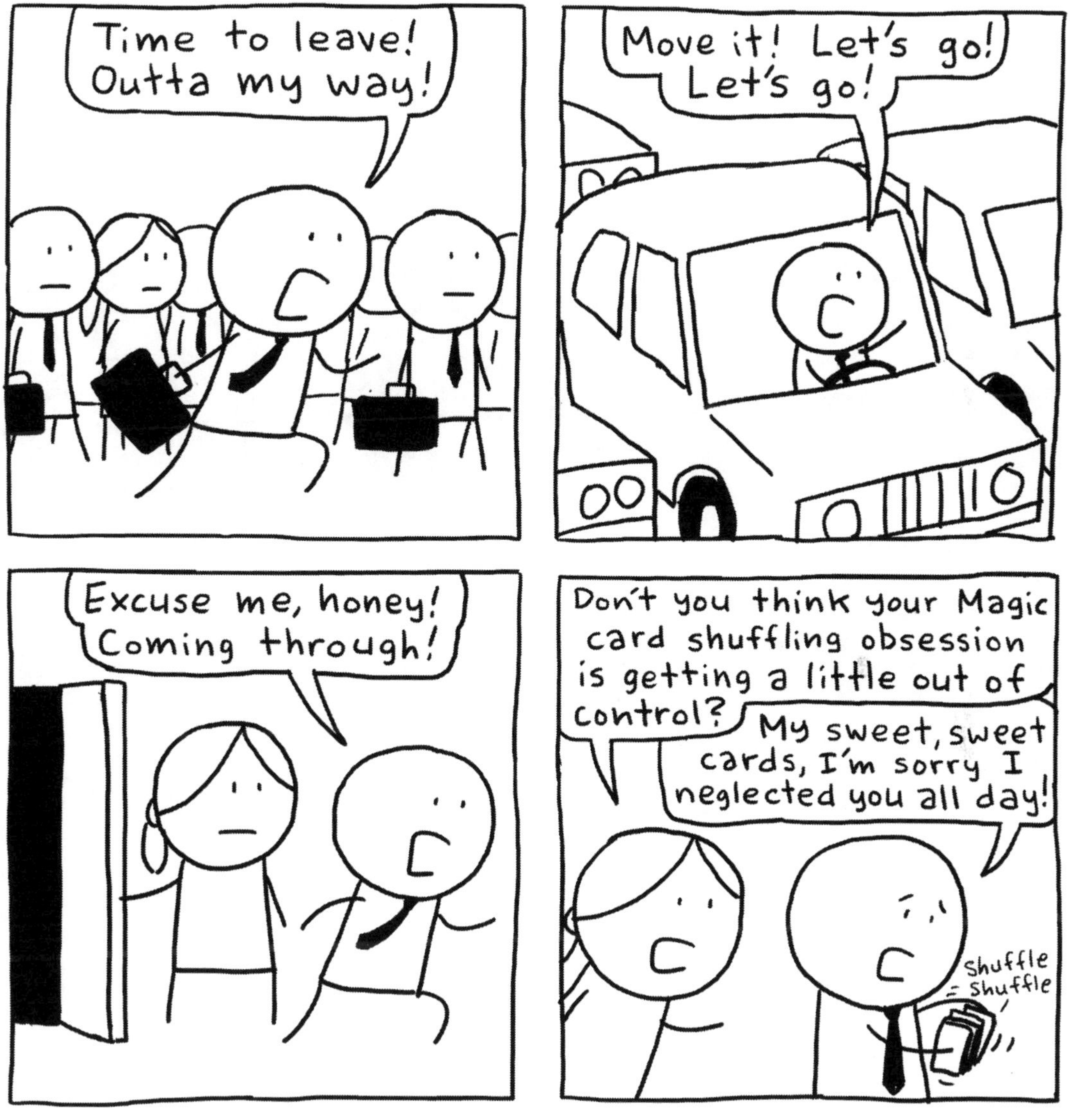
Time to leave! Outta my way!
Move it! Let's go! Let's go!
Excuse me, honey! Coming through!
Don't you think your Magic card shuffling obsession is getting a little out of control?
My sweet, sweet cards, I'm sorry I neglected you all day!
Shuffle Shuffle

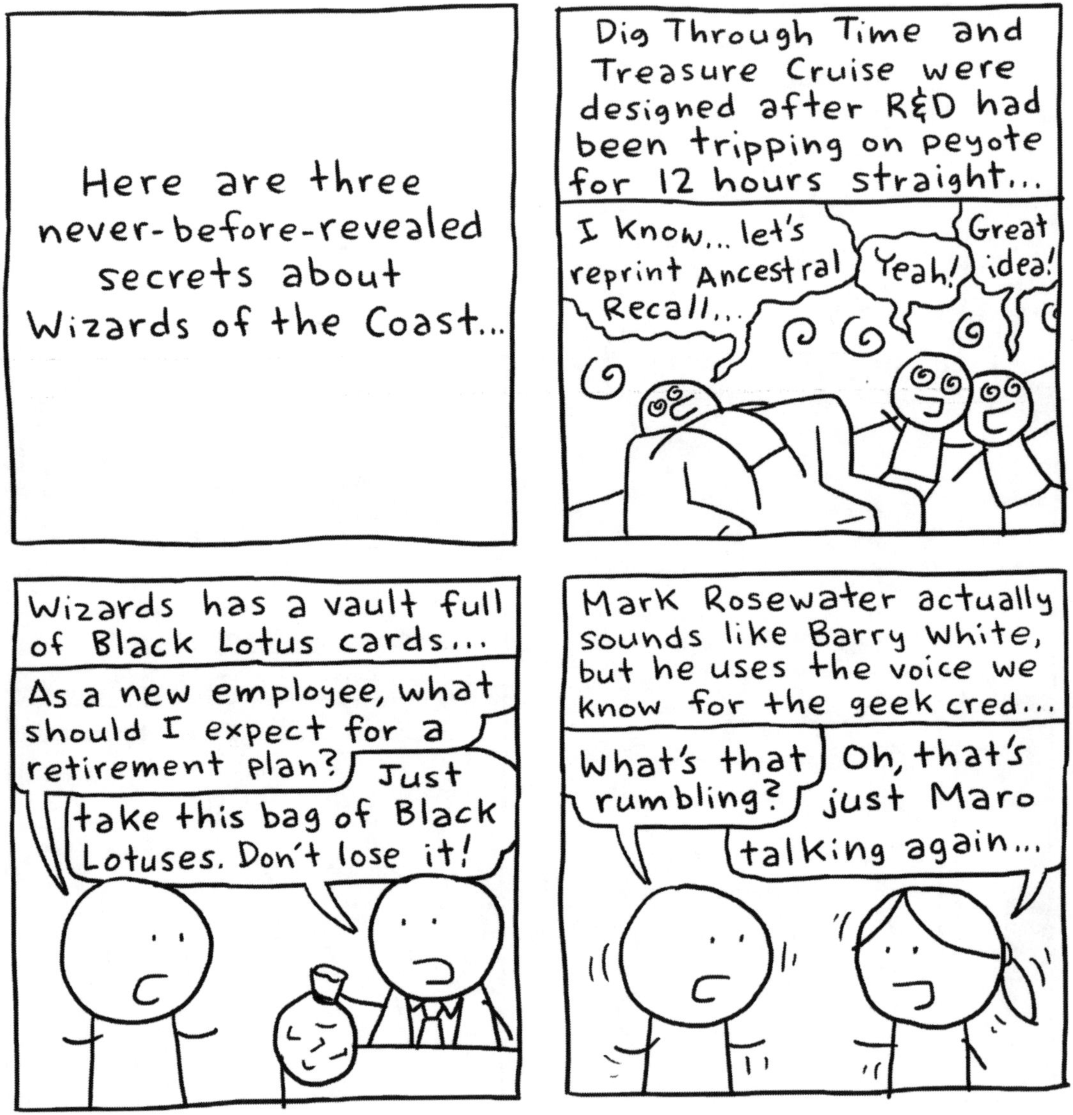
Here are three never-before-revealed secrets about Wizards of the Coast...
Dig Through Time and Treasure Cruise were designed after R&D had been tripping on peyote for 12 hours straight...
I know... let's reprint Ancestral Recall...
Yeah!
Great idea!
Wizards has a vault full of Black Lotus cards...
As a new employee, what should I expect for a retirement plan?
Just take this bag of Black Lotuses. Don't lose it!
Mark Rosewater actually sounds like Barry White, but he uses the voice we know for the geek cred...
What's that rumbling?
Oh, that's just Maro talking again...

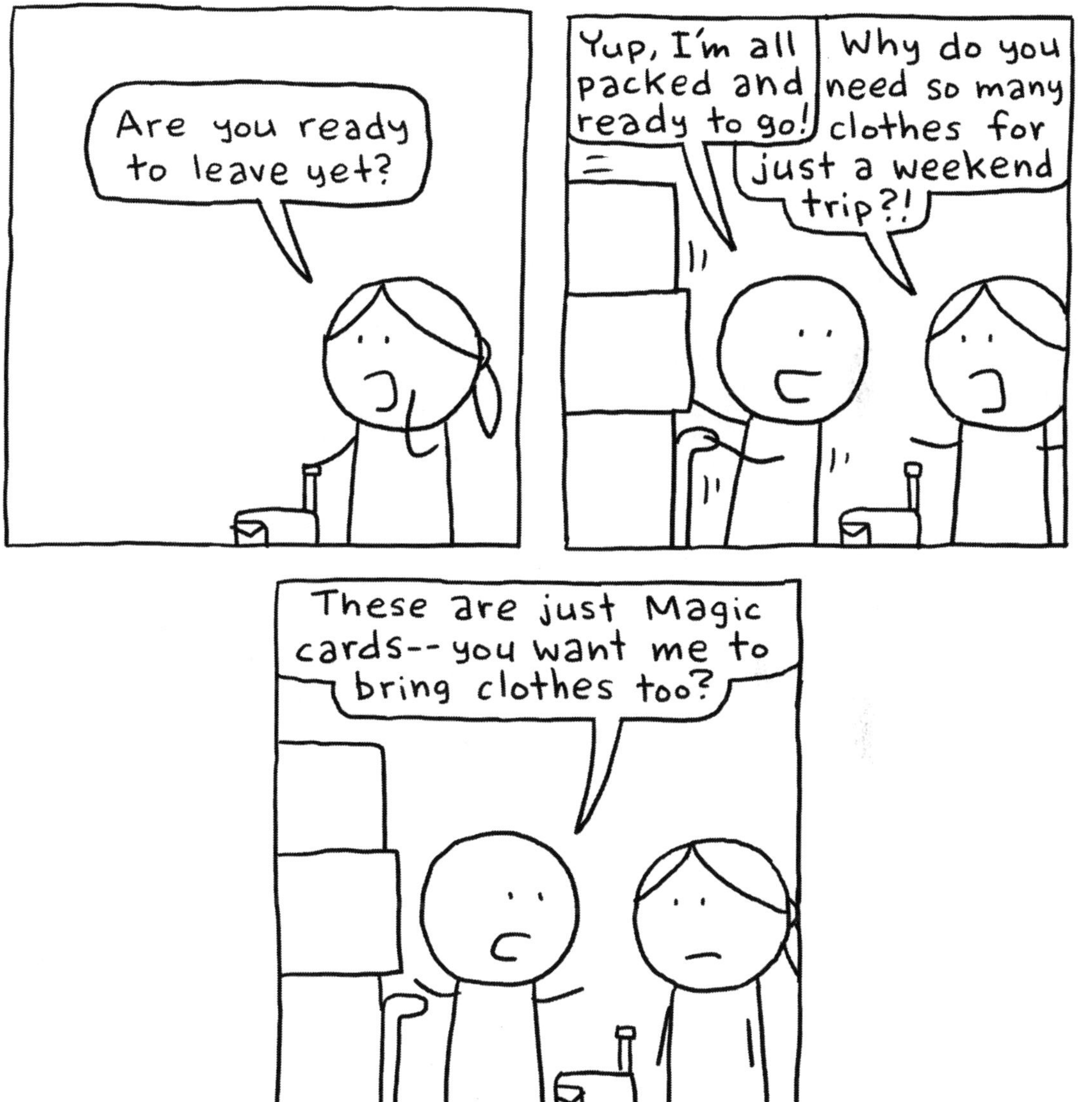
Are you ready to leave yet?
Yup, I'm all packed and ready to go!
Why do you need so many clothes for just a weekend trip?!
These are just Magic cards-- you want me to bring clothes too?

I know you don't like blue in Magic, but maybe you're taking it too far.
Jeez, why would you say that?
Earlier...
Would you like some water?
Why the #%@* would I like water?! Are you crazy?!

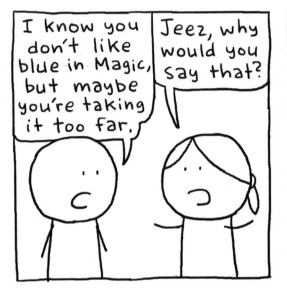

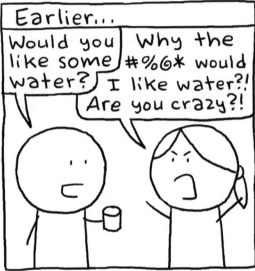

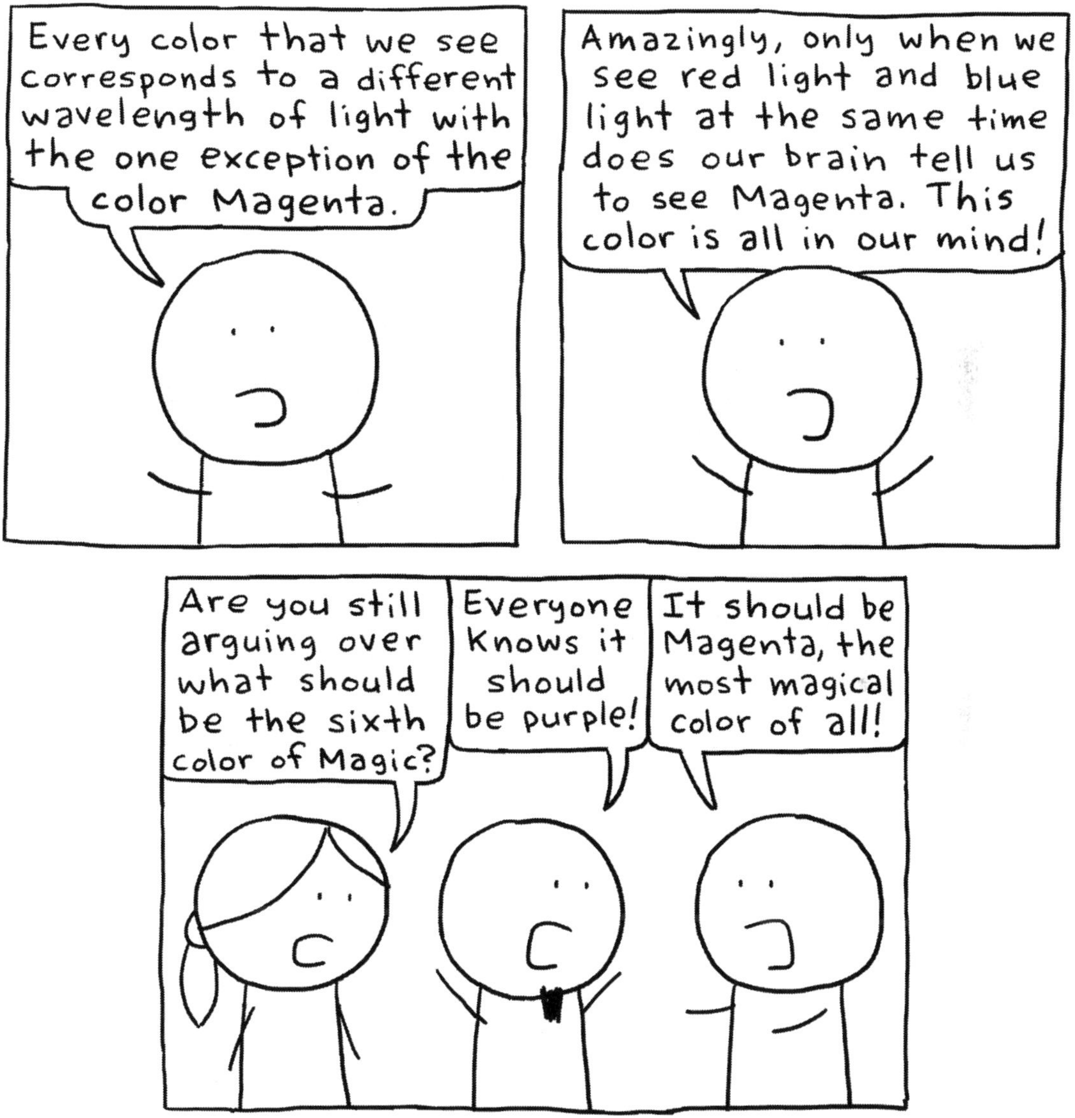

Every color that we see corresponds to a different wavelength of light with the one exception of the color Magenta.
Amazingly, only when we see red light and blue light at the same time does our brain tell us to see Magenta. This color is all in our mind!
Are you still arguing over what should be the sixth color of Magic?
Everyone Knows it should be purple!
It should be Magenta, the most magical color of all!

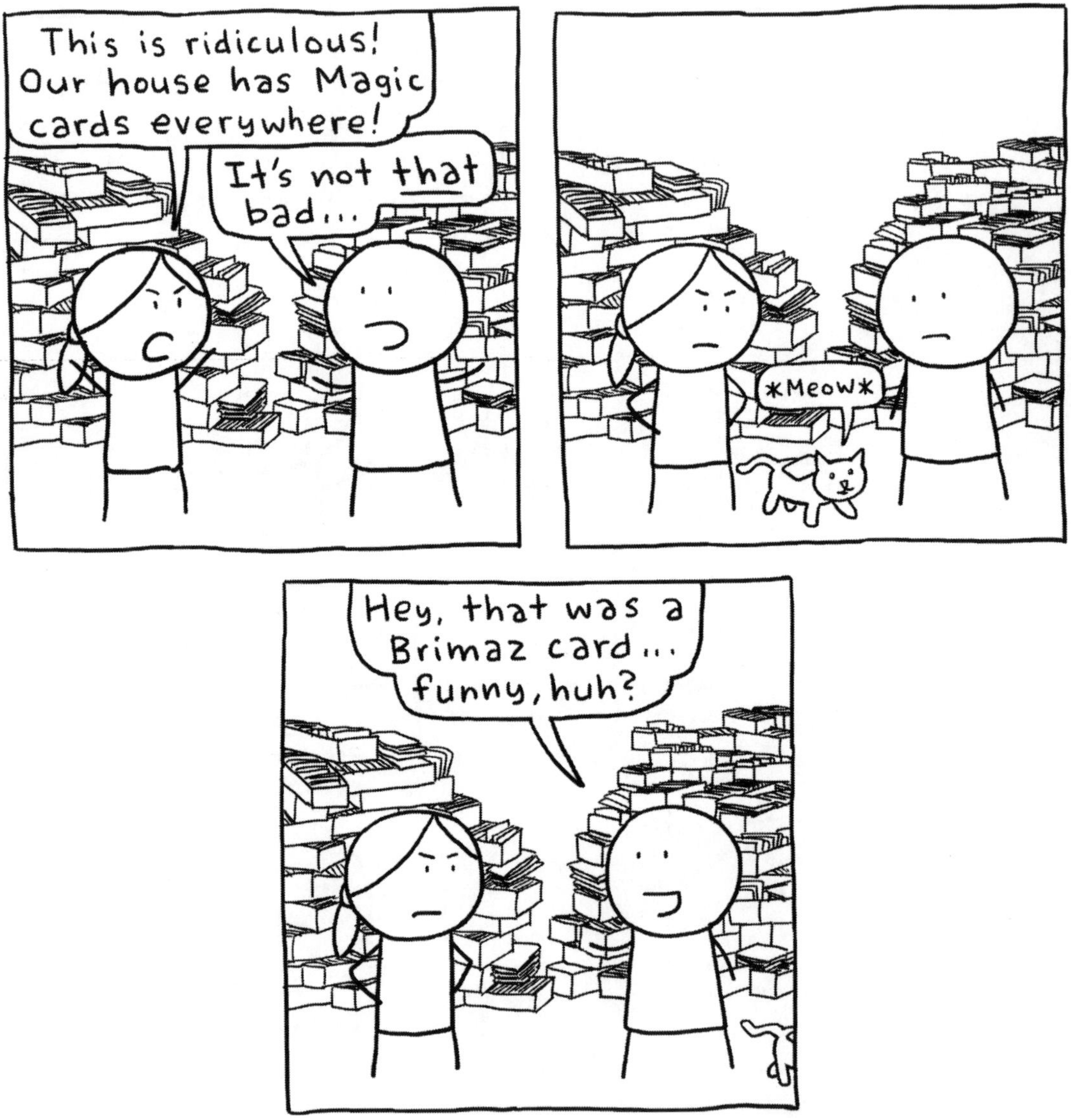
This is ridiculous! Our house has Magic cards everywhere!
It's not that bad...
Meow
Hey, that was a Brimaz card... funny, huh?

What's the matter?
I'm really worried about the Magic movie that they're working on right now.
Jeez, you worry too much! The movie will bring more attention to this great game! Plus, it will be awesome to see planes-walkers on the big screen! What's the worst that can happen?!
Consider this--a Magic set that uses movie screenshots for all the card art.

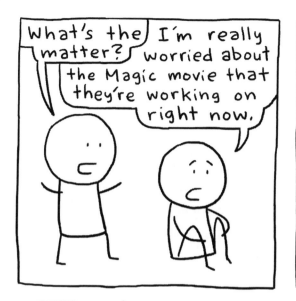

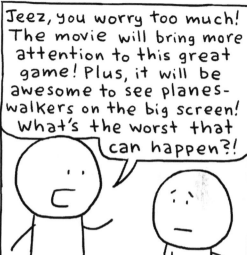

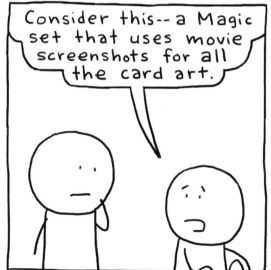

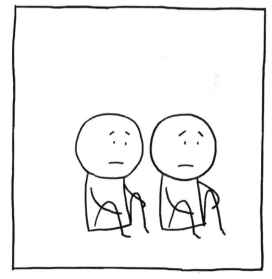

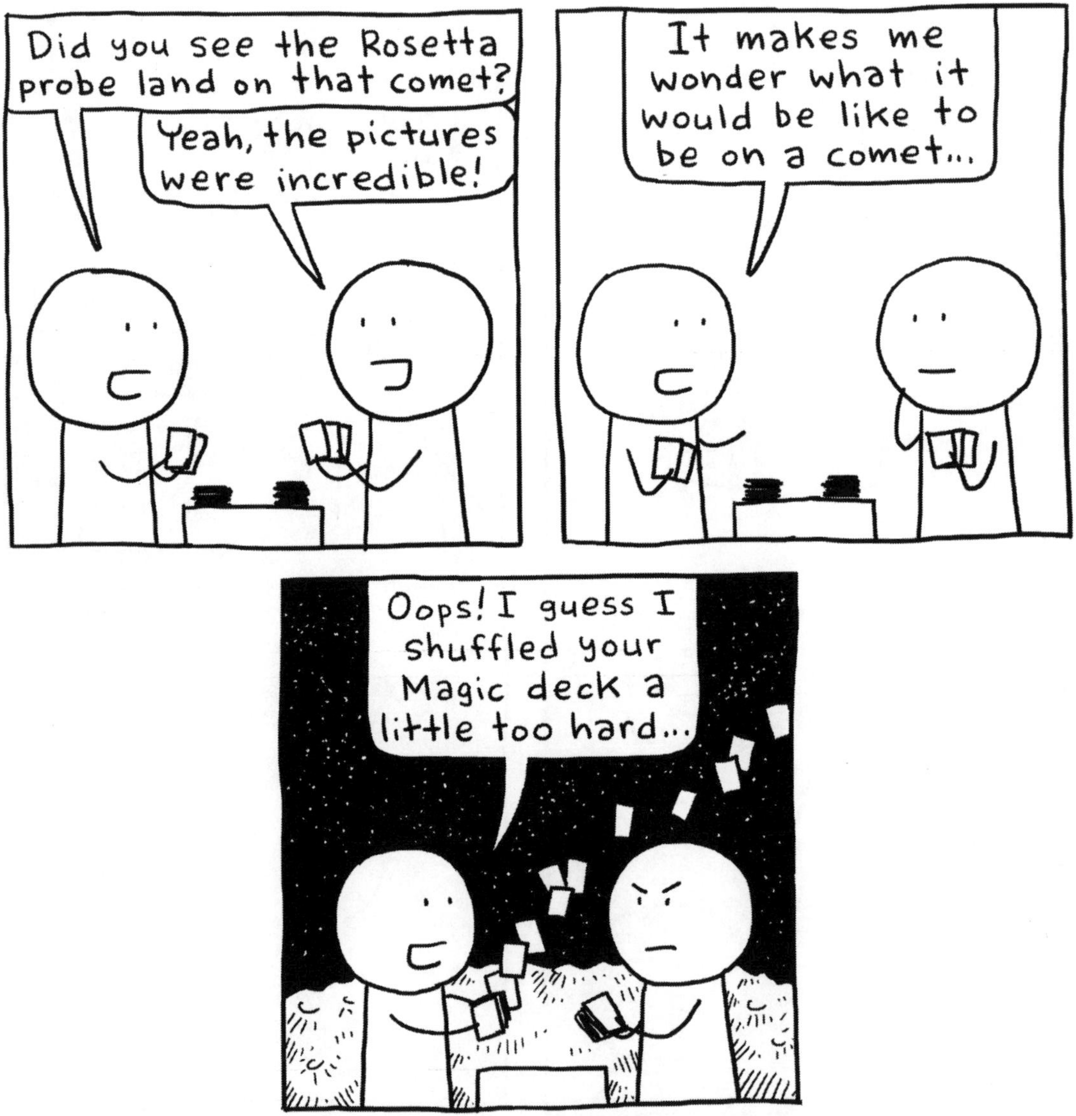
Did you see the Rosetta probe land on that comet?
Yeah, the pictures were incredible!
It makes me wonder what it would be like to be on a comet...
Oops! I guess I shuffled your Magic deck a little too hard...

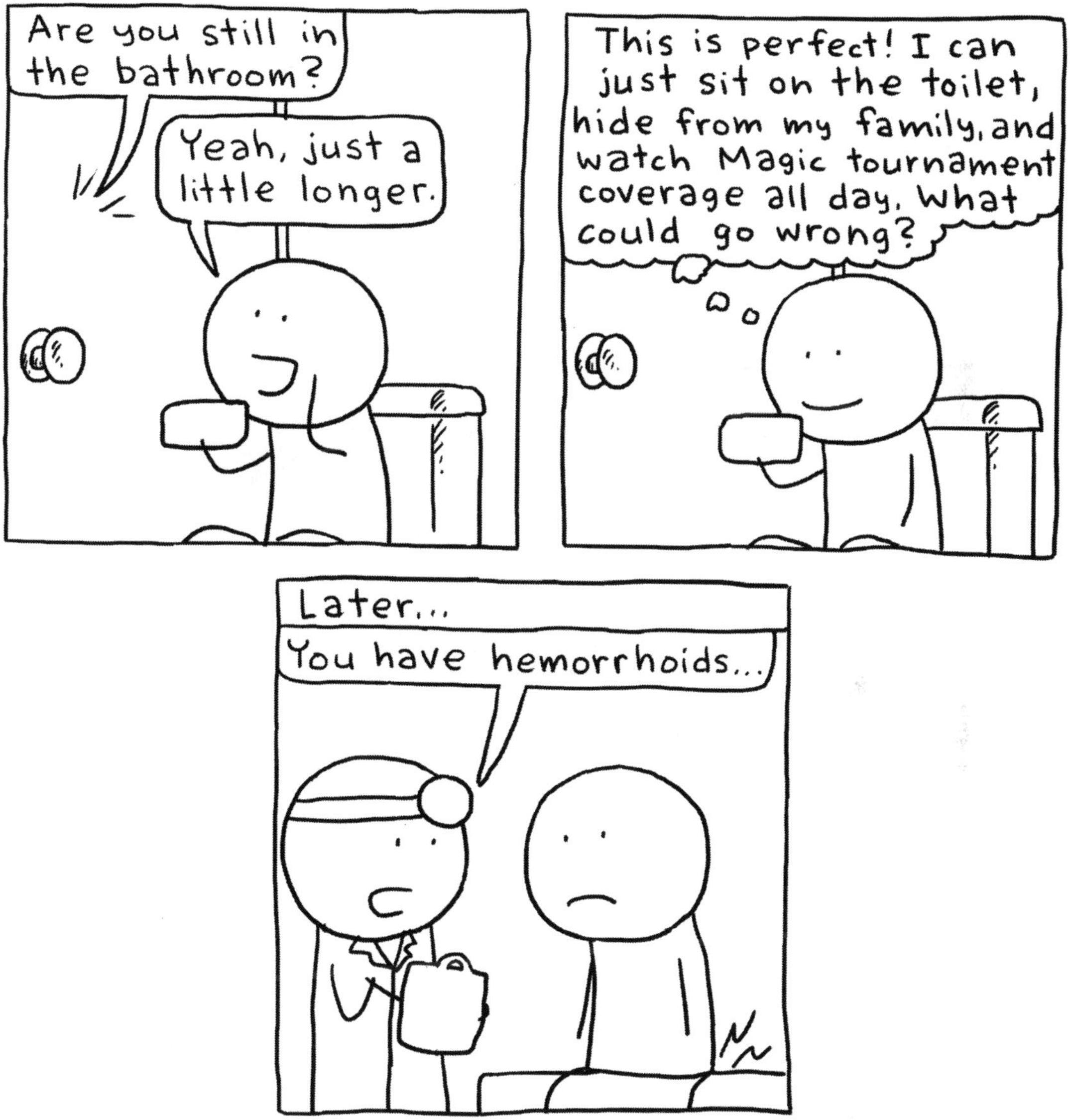
Are you still in the bathroom?
Yeah, just a little longer.
This is perfect! I can just sit on the toilet, hide from my family, and watch Magic tournament coverage all day. What could go wrong?
Later...
You have hemorrhoids...

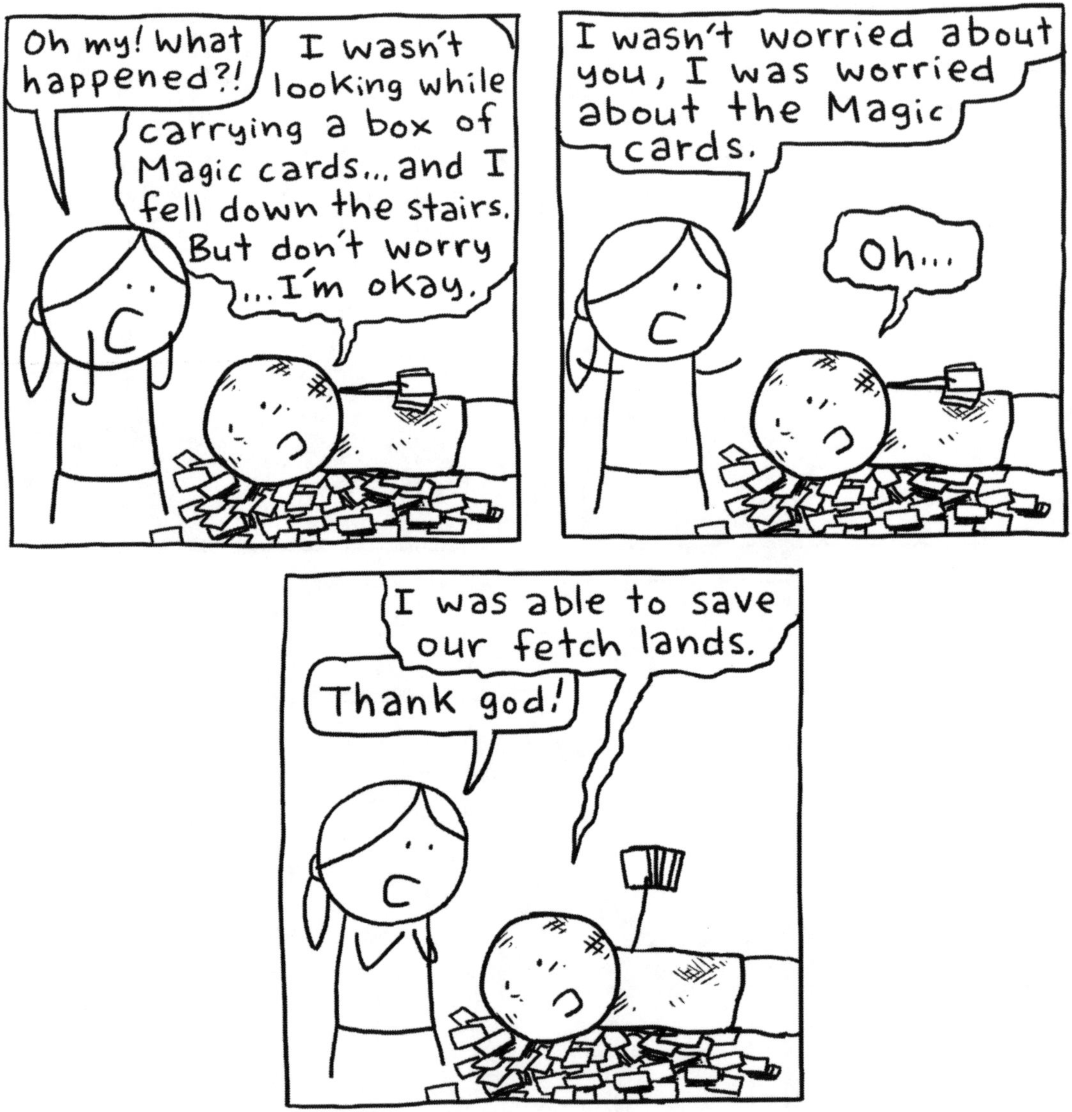
Oh my! What happened?!
I wasn't looking while carrying a box of Magic cards... and I fell down the stairs. But don't worry ...I'm okay.
I wasn't worried about you, I was worried about the Magic cards.
Oh...
I was able to save our fetch lands.
Thank god!

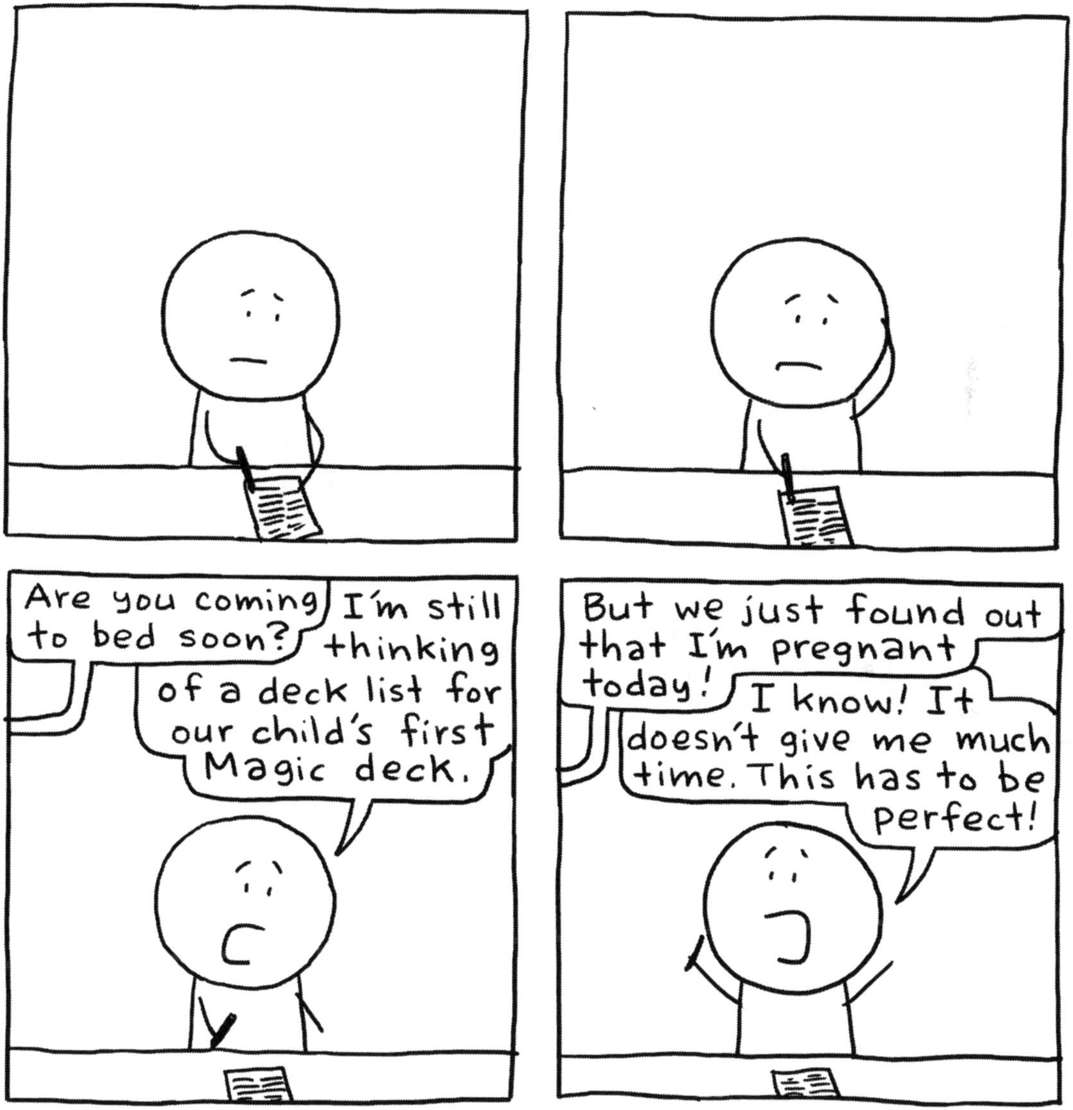
Are you coming to bed soon?
I'm still thinking of a deck list for our child's first Magic deck.
But we just found out that I'm pregnant today!
I know! It doesn't give me much time. This has to be perfect!

Back in October...
Jeskai Ascendancy is going to ruin Modern!
It kills too fast and too consistently!!
Get your Glittering Wishes before their price skyrockets more!
It might be time to consider an emergency banning!!
Now...
So what do you have to say for yourself?
What are you talking about? That's a weird question.

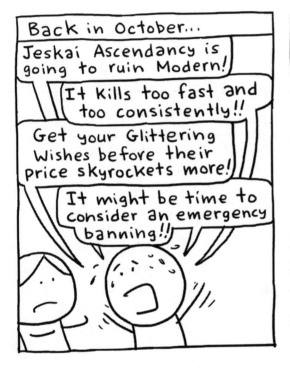

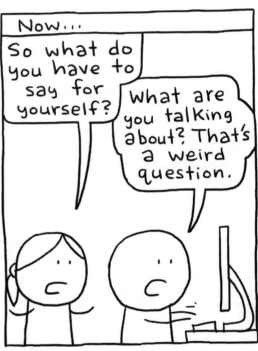

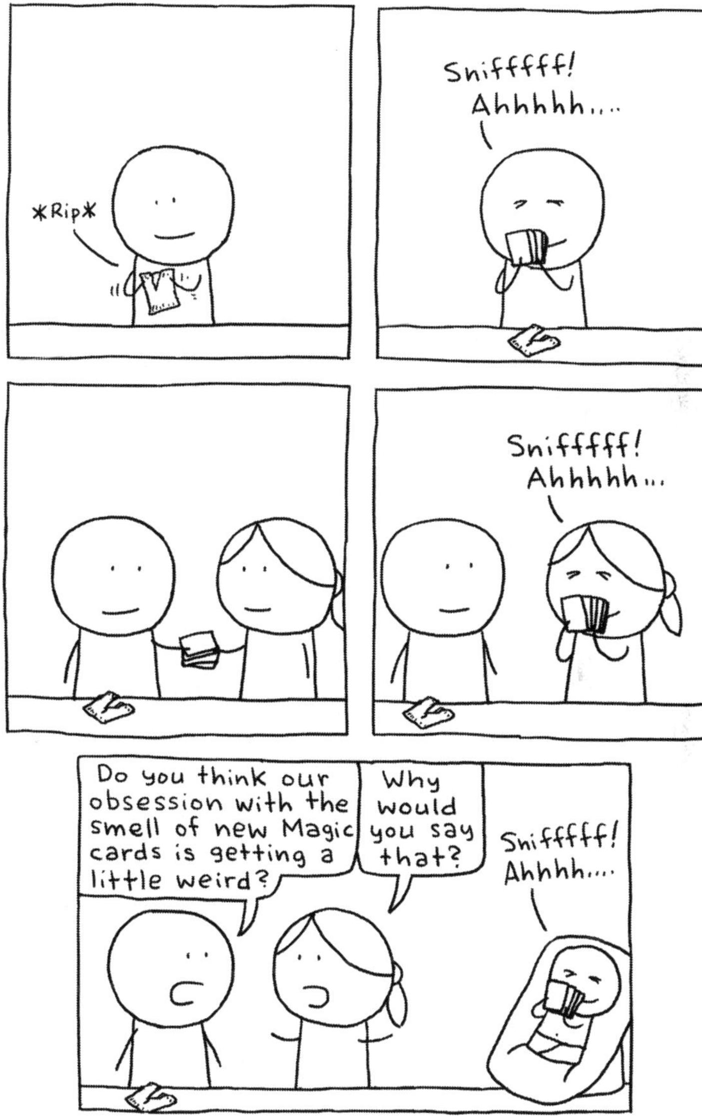
Rip
Snifffff! Ahhhhh....
Snifffff! Ahhhhh...
Do you think our obsession with the smell of new Magic cards is getting a little weird?
Why would you say that?
Snifffff! Ahhhh....

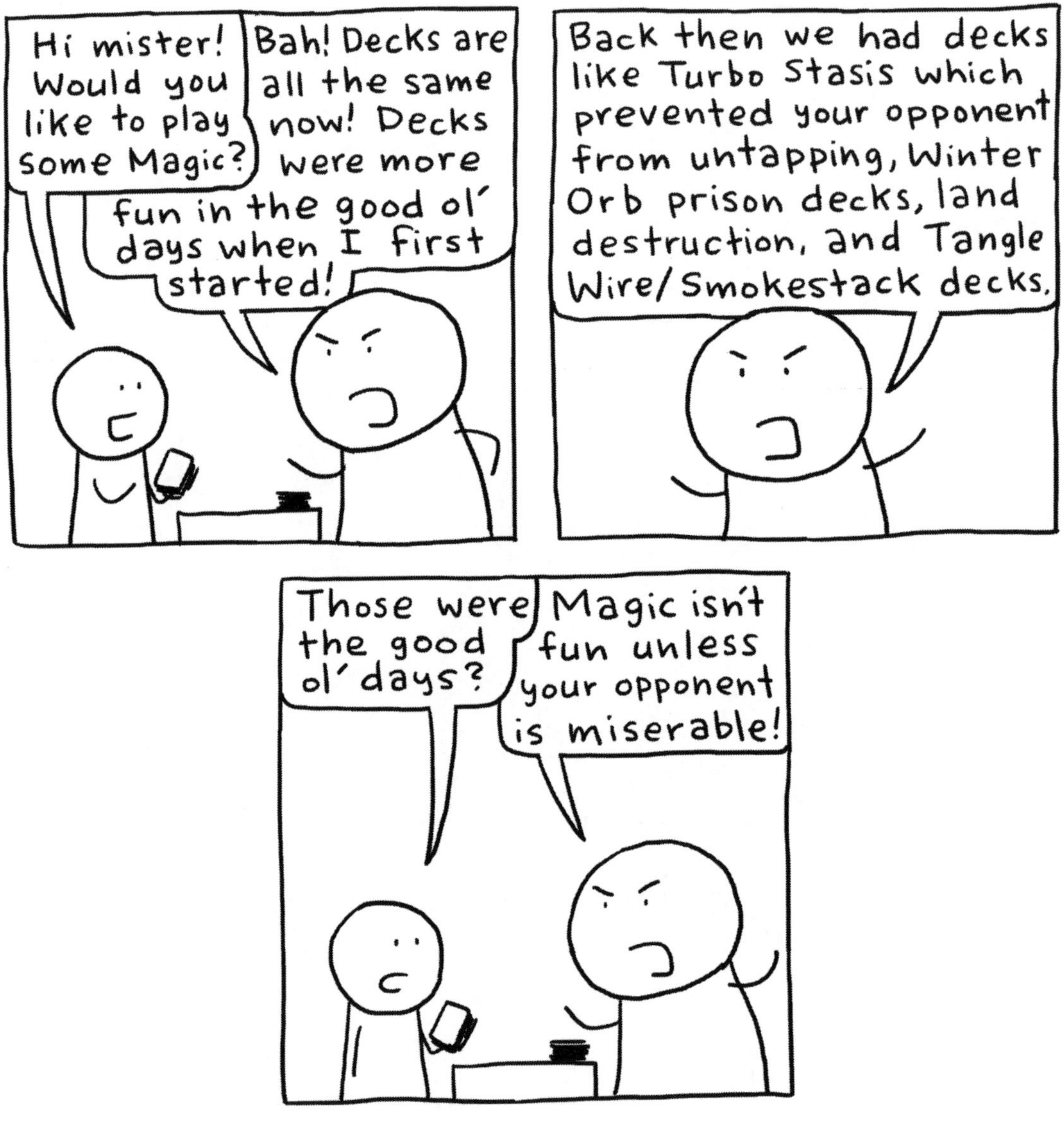
Hi mister! Would you like to play some Magic?
Bah! Decks are all the same now! Decks were more fun in the good ol' days when I first started!
Back then we had decks like Turbo Stasis which prevented your opponent from untapping, Winter Orb prison decks, land destruction, and Tangle Wire/Smokestack decks.
Those were the good ol' days?
Magic isn't fun unless your opponent is miserable!

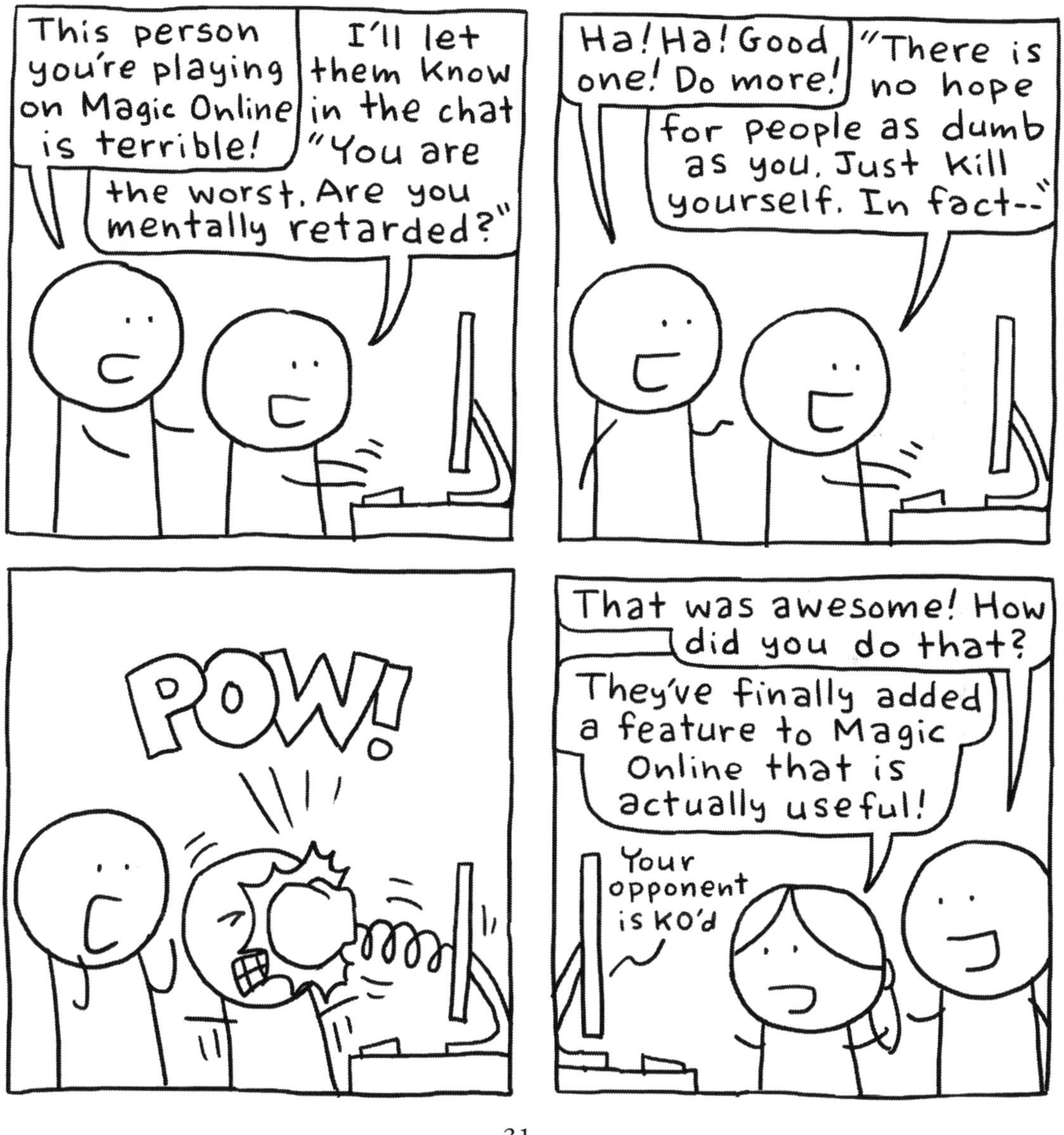
This person you're playing on Magic Online is terrible!
I'll let them know in the chat "You are the worst. Are you mentally retarded?"
Ha! Ha! Good one! Do more!
"There is no hope for people as dumb as you. Just kill yourself. In fact--"
POW!
That was awesome! How did you do that?
They've finally added a feature to Magic Online that is actually useful!
Your opponent is KO'd

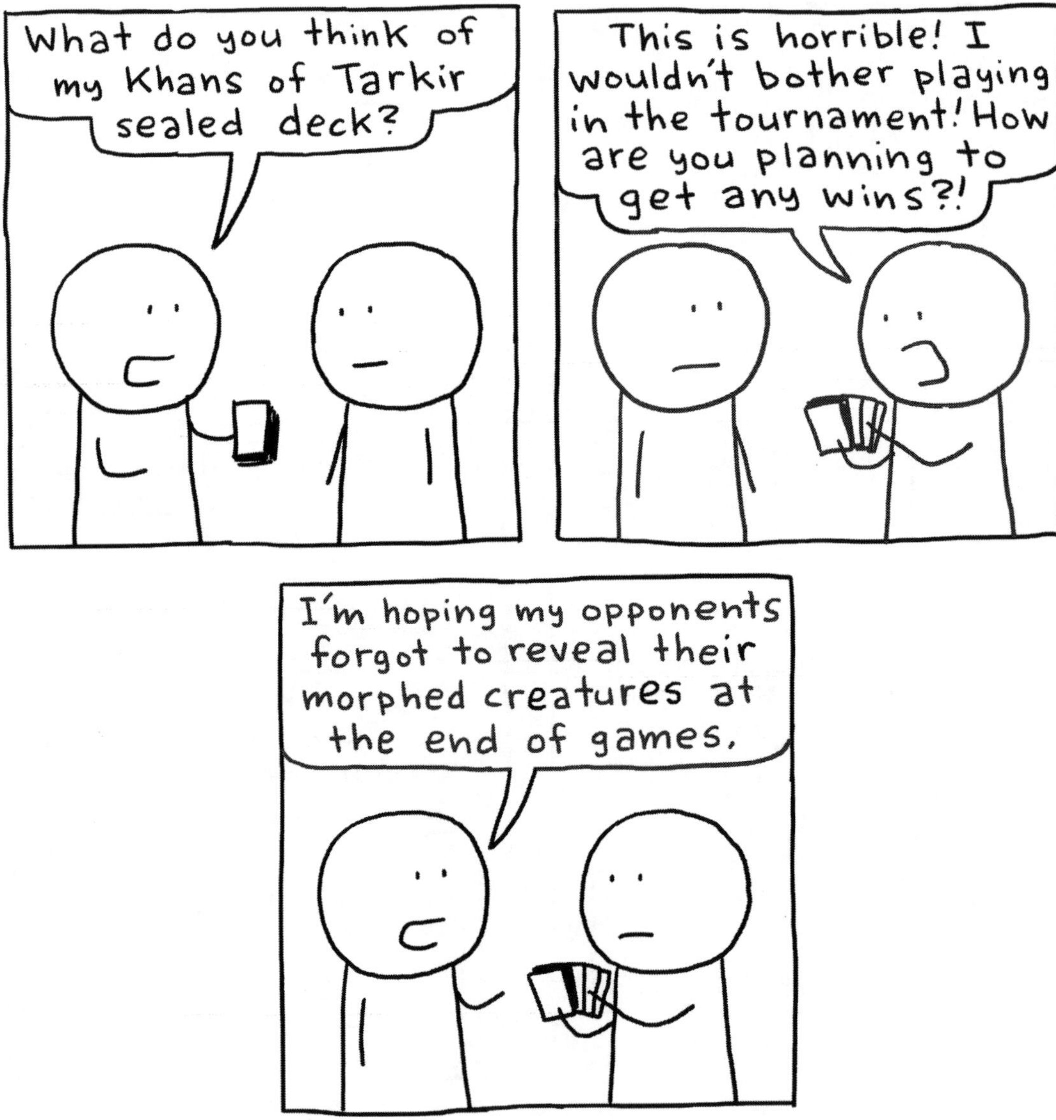
What do you think of my Khans of Tarkir sealed deck?
This is horrible! I wouldn't bother playing in the tournament! How are you planning to get any wins?!
I'm hoping my opponents forgot to reveal their morphed creatures at the end of games.

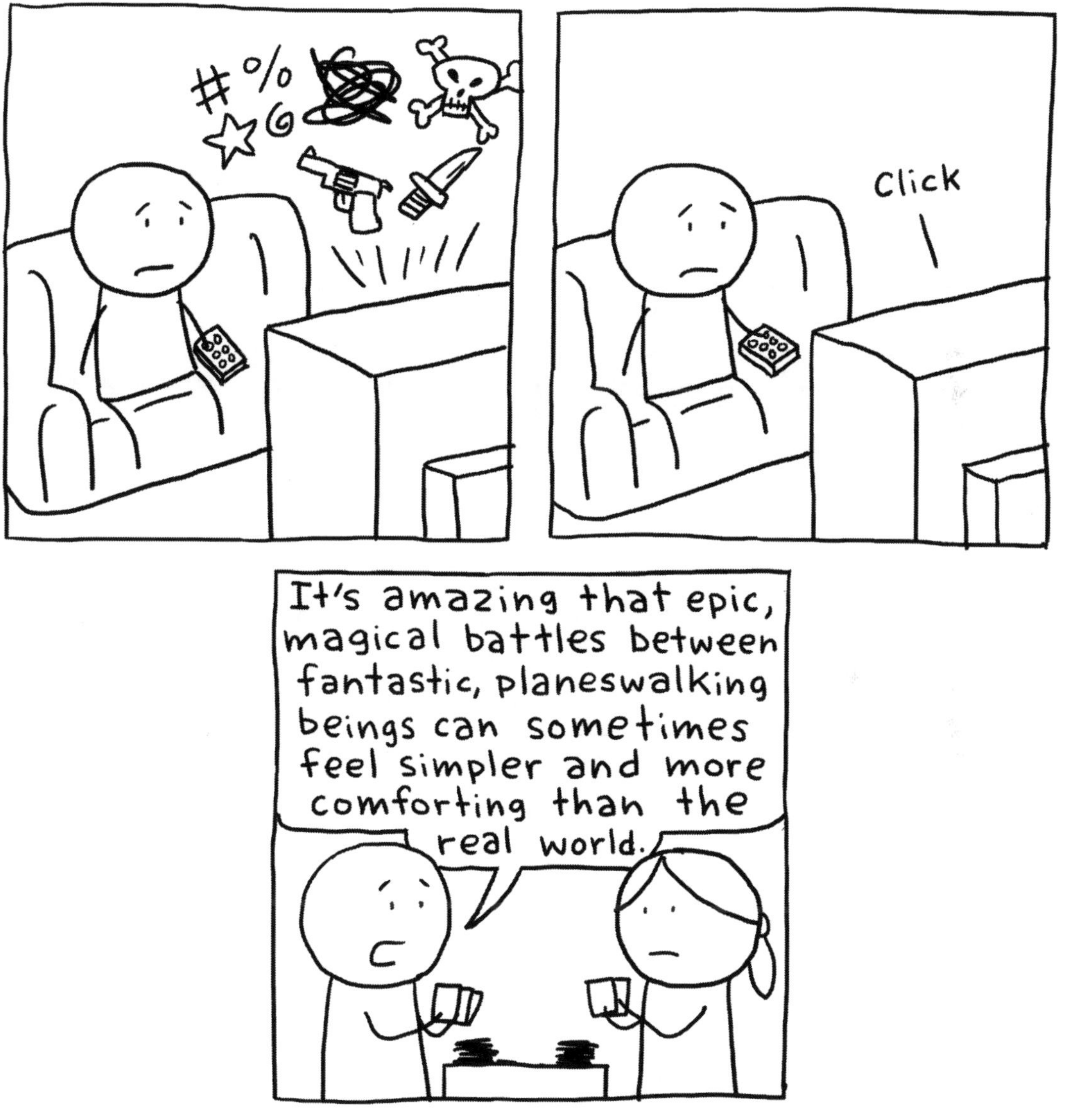
Click
It's amazing that epic, magical battles between fantastic, planeswalking beings can sometimes feel simpler and more comforting than the real world.

The years 1901 to 1904 are often referred to as Picasso's "Blue Period."
Is that because he mainly painted in blue during that time?
No, it was because he was a controlling prick.

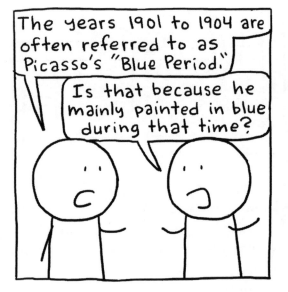

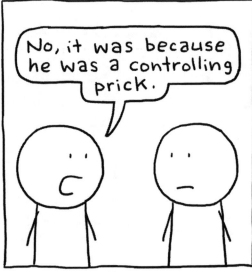

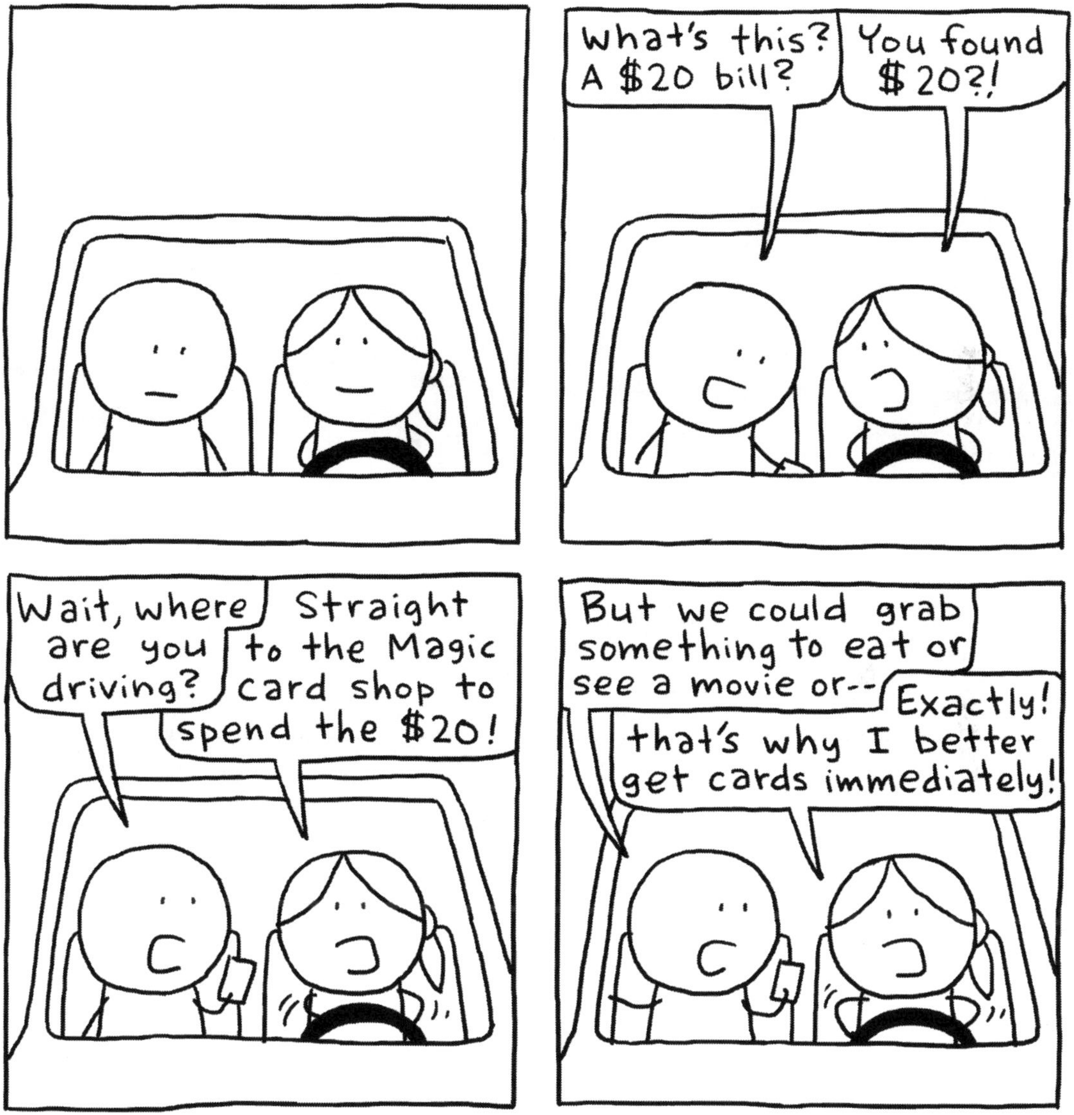
What's this? A $20 bill?
You found $20?!
Wait, where are you driving?
Straight to the Magic card shop to spend the $20!
But we could grab something to eat or see a movie or--
Exactly! that's why I better get cards immediately!

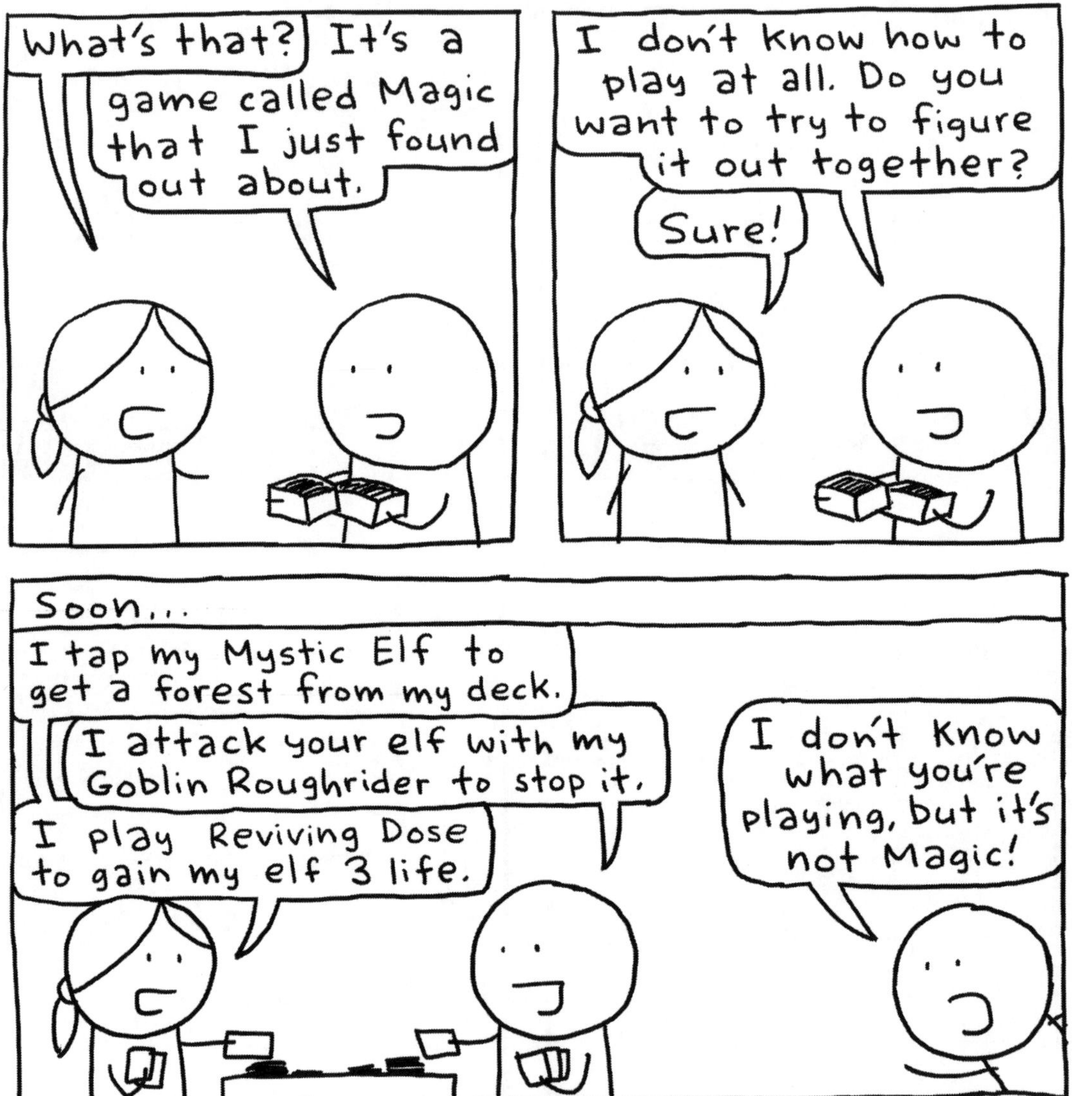
What's that?
It's a game called Magic that I just found out about.
I don't know how to play at all. Do you want to try to figure it out together?
Sure!
Soon...
I tap my Mystic Elf to get a forest from my deck.
I attack your elf with my Goblin Roughrider to stop it.
I play Reviving Dose to gain my elf 3 life.
I don't know what you're playing, but it's not Magic!

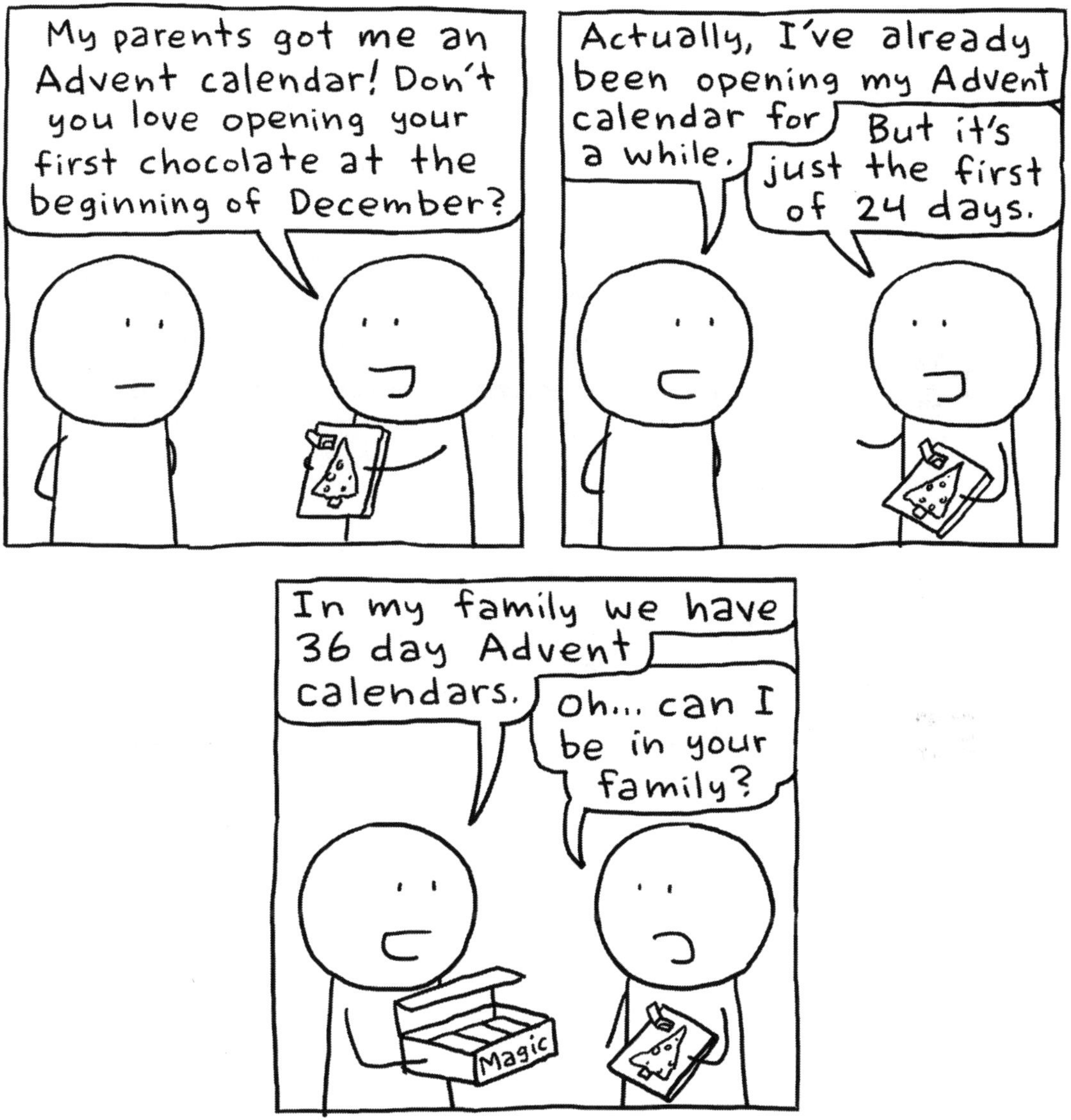
My parents got me an Advent calendar! Don't you love opening your first chocolate at the beginning of December?
Actually, I've already been opening my Advent calendar for a while.
But it's just the first of 24 days.
In my family we have 36 day Advent calendars.
Oh... can I be in your family?
Magic

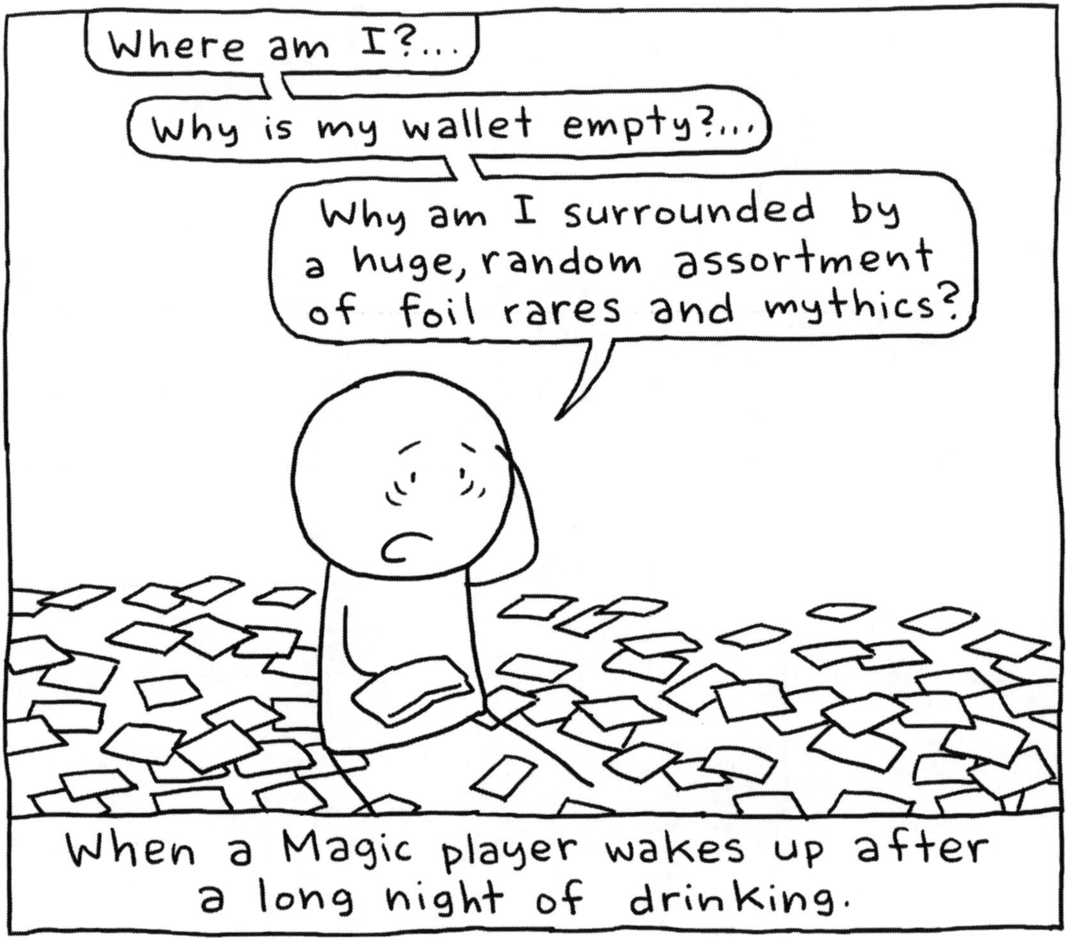
Where am I?...
Why is my wallet empty?...
Why am I surrounded by a huge, random assortment of foil rares and mythics?

When a Magic player wakes up after a long night of drinking.

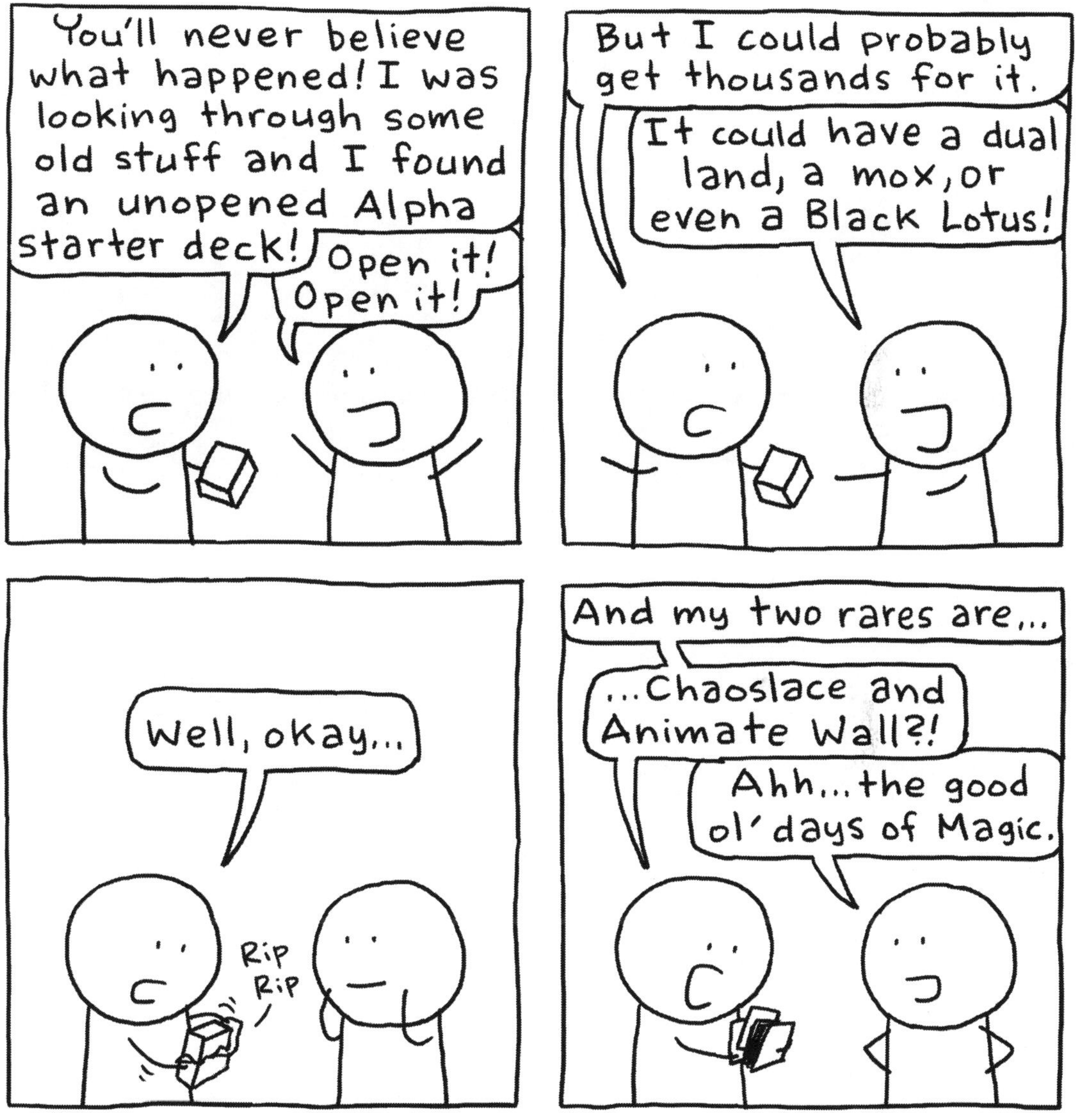
You'll never believe what happened! I was looking through some old stuff and I found an unopened Alpha starter deck!
Open it! Open it!
But I could probably get thousands for it.
It could have a dual land, a mox, or even a Black Lotus!
Well, okay...
Rip Rip
And my two rares are...
...Chaoslace and Animate Wall?!
Ahh... the good ol' days of Magic.

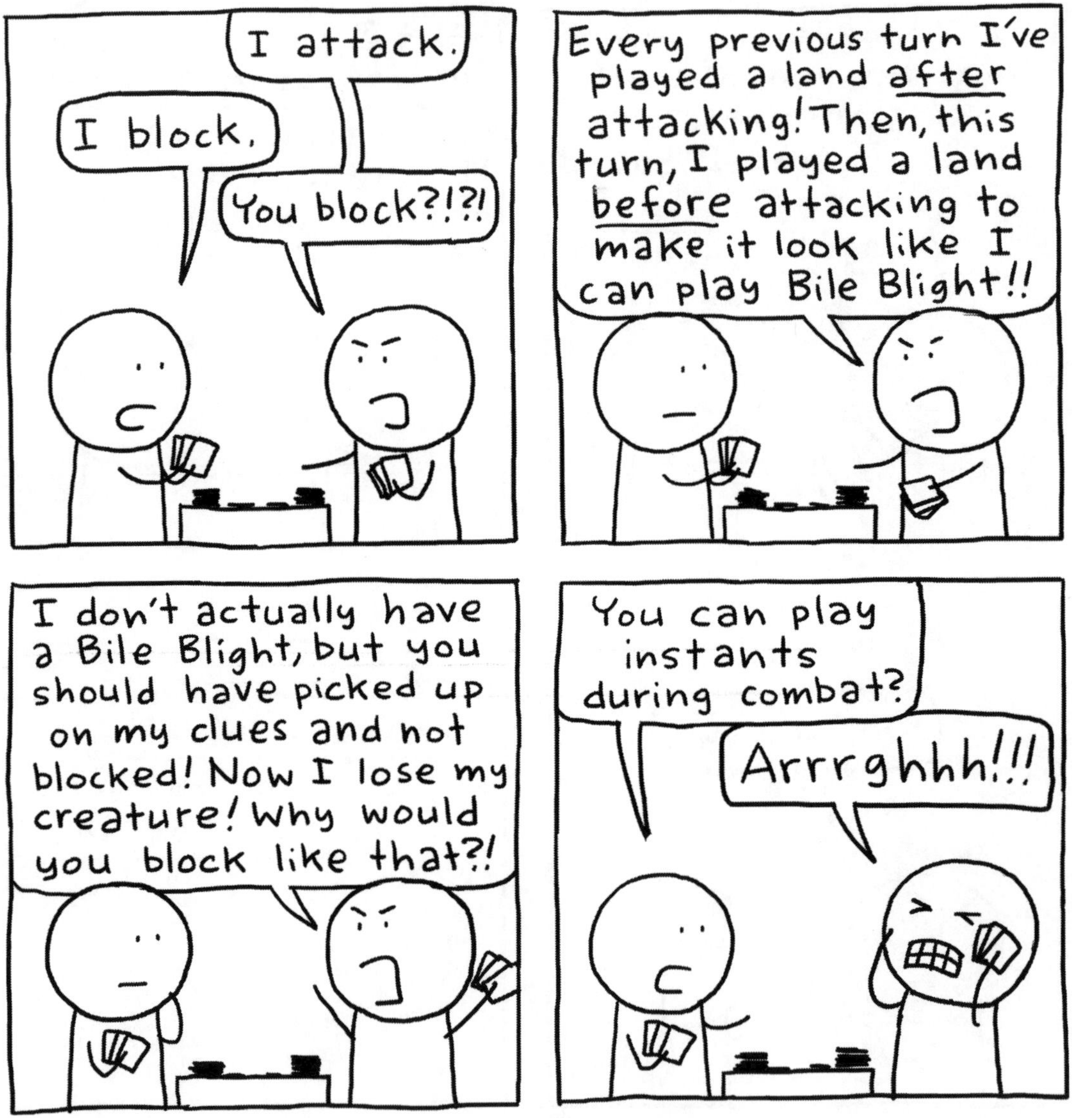
I attack.
I block.
You block?!?!
Every previous turn I've played a land after attacking! Then, this turn, I played a land before attacking to make it look like I can play Bile Blight!!
I don't actually have a Bile Blight, but you should have picked up on my clues and not blocked! Now I lose my creature! Why would you block like that?!
You can play instants during combat?
Arrrghhh!!!

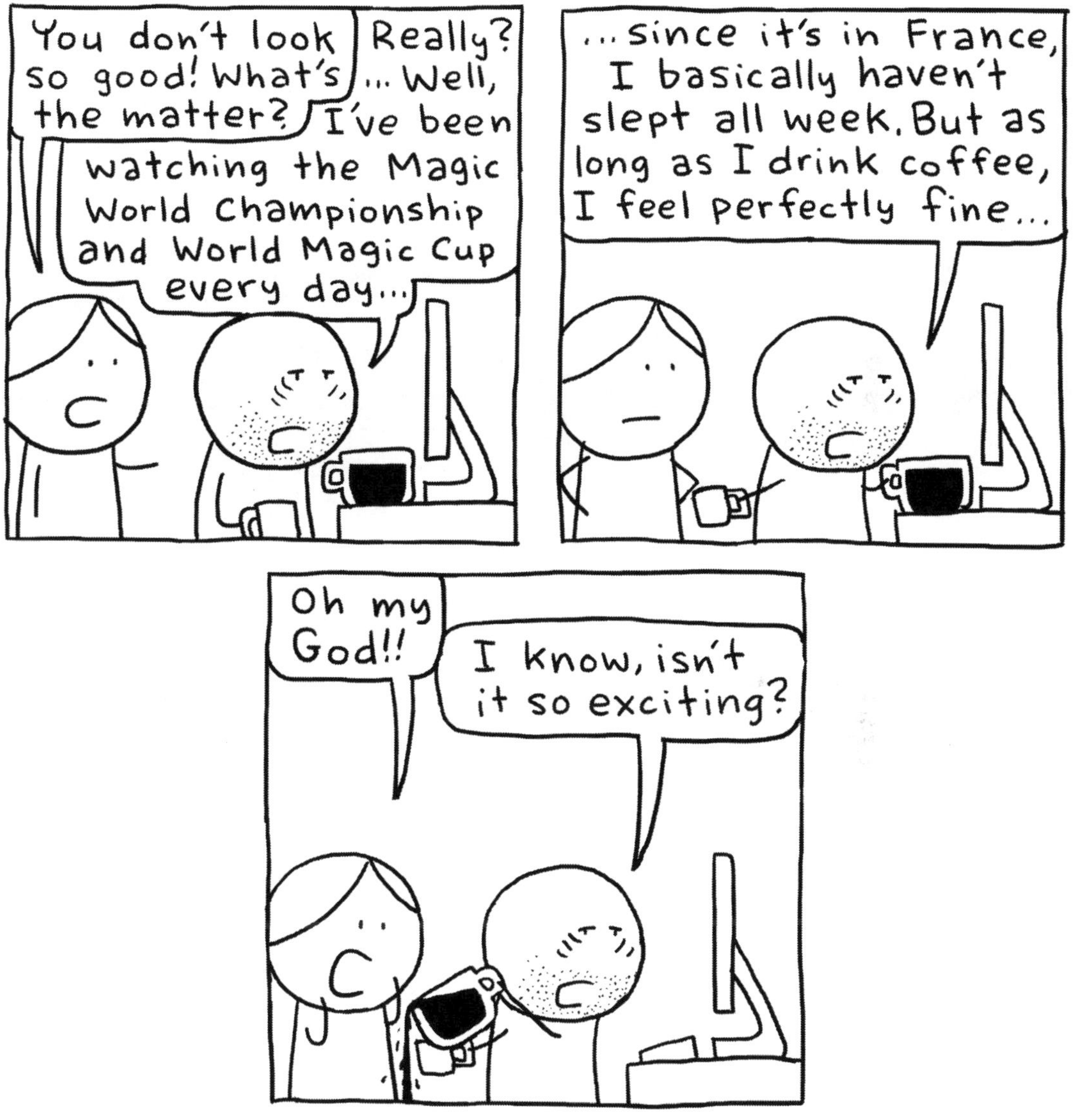
You don't look so good! What's the matter?
Really? ...Well, I've been watching the Magic World Championship and World Magic Cup every day...
...since it's in France, I basically haven't slept all week. But as long as I drink coffee, I feel perfectly fine...
Oh my God!!
I know, isn't it so exciting?

Before...
People may sometimes do or say bad things, but deep down inside, everyone's good.
After watching the Twitch chat during Magic coverage...
The human race is doomed.

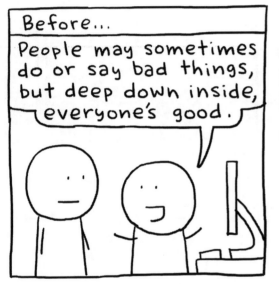

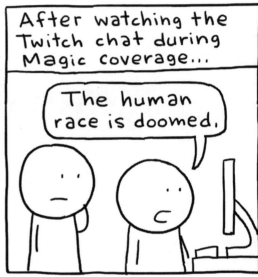

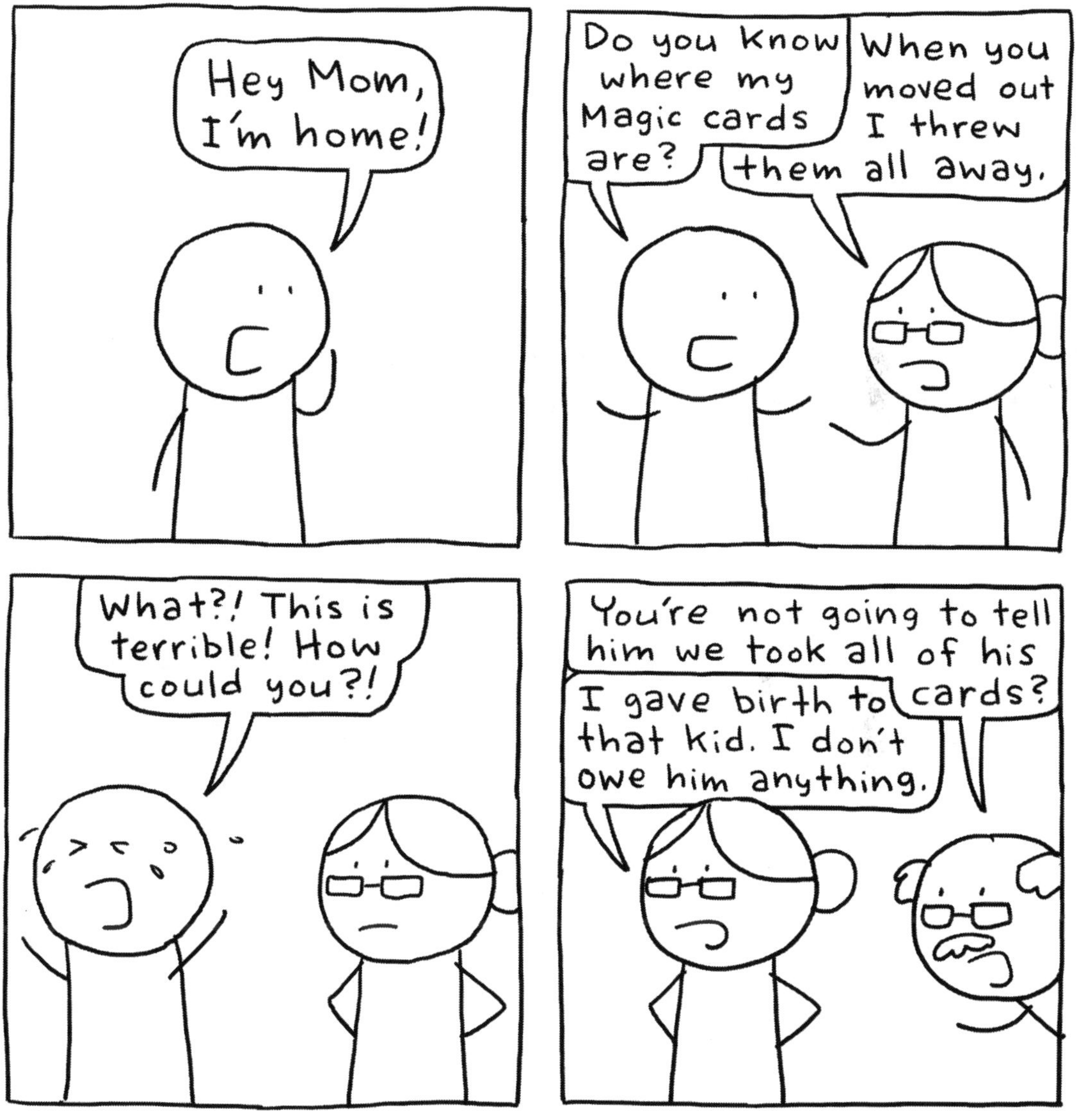
Hey Mom, I'm home!
Do you know where my Magic cards are?
When you moved out I threw them all away.
What?! This is terrible! How could you?!
You're not going to tell him we took all of his cards?
I gave birth to that kid. I don't owe him anything.

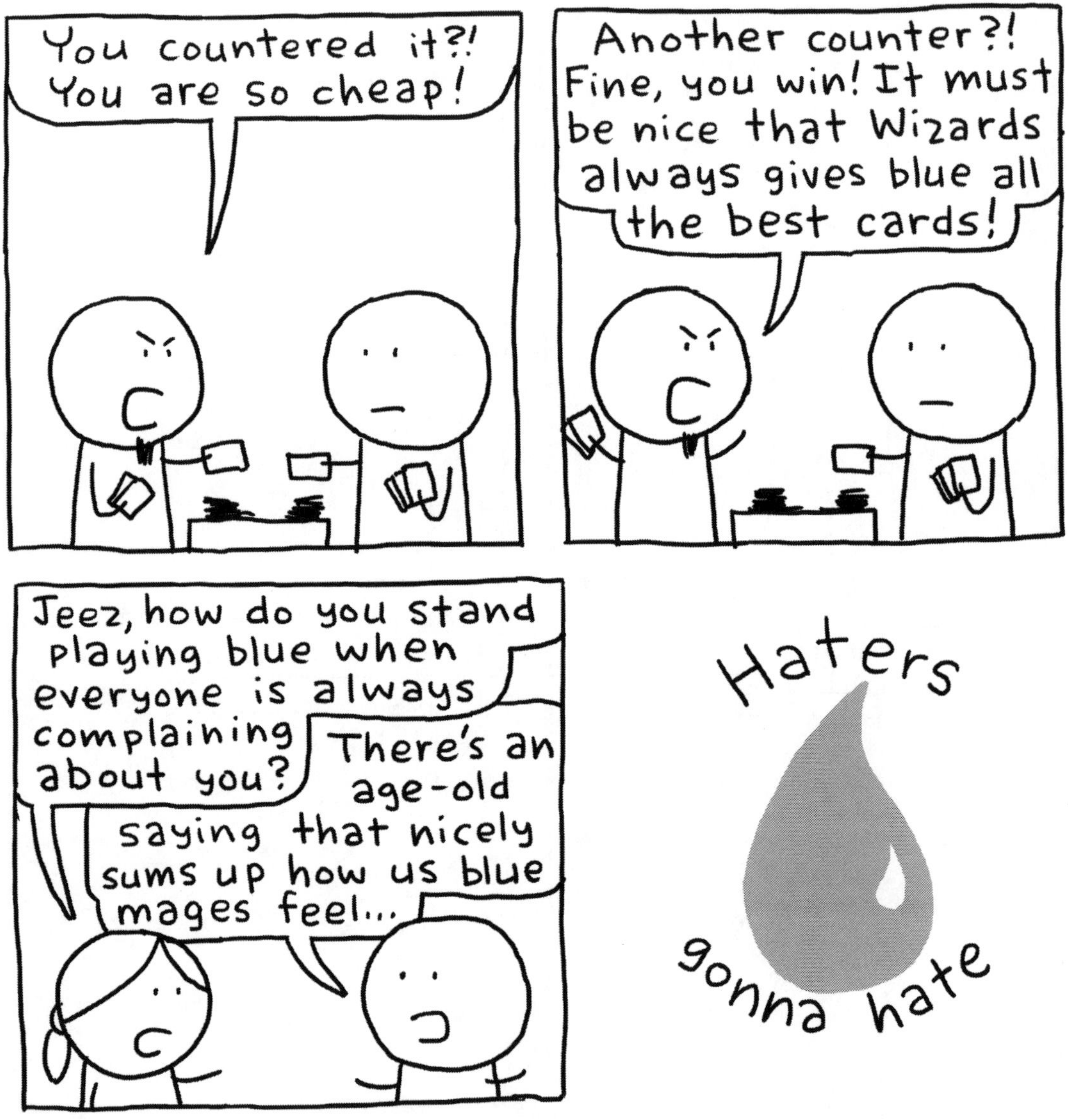
You countered it?! You are so cheap!
Another counter?! Fine, you win! It must be nice that Wizards always gives blue all the best cards!
Jeez, how do you stand playing blue when everyone is always complaining about you?
There's an age-old saying that nicely sums up how us blue mages feel...
Haters gonna hate

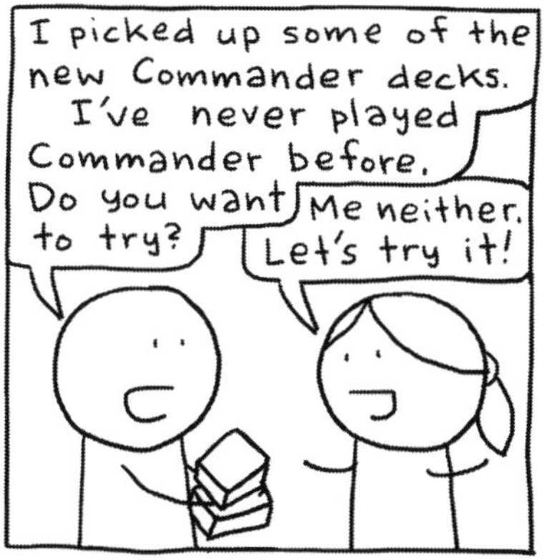
I picked up some of the new Commander decks. I've never played Commander before. Do you want to try?
Me neither. Let's try it!

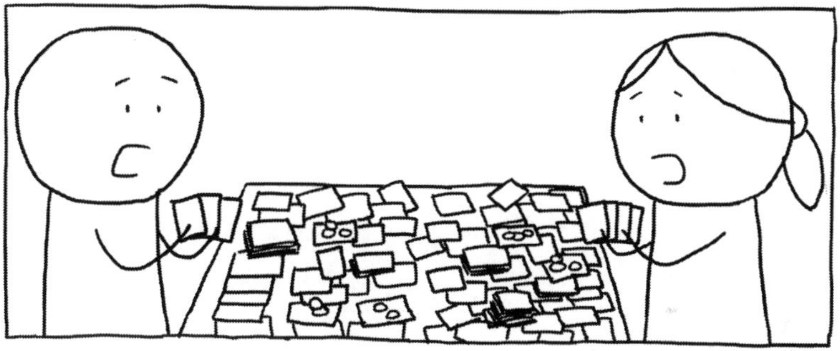

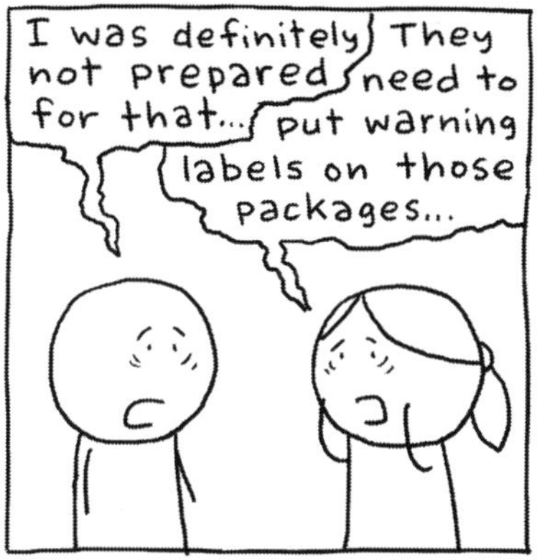
I was definitely not prepared for that...
They need to put warning labels on those packages...

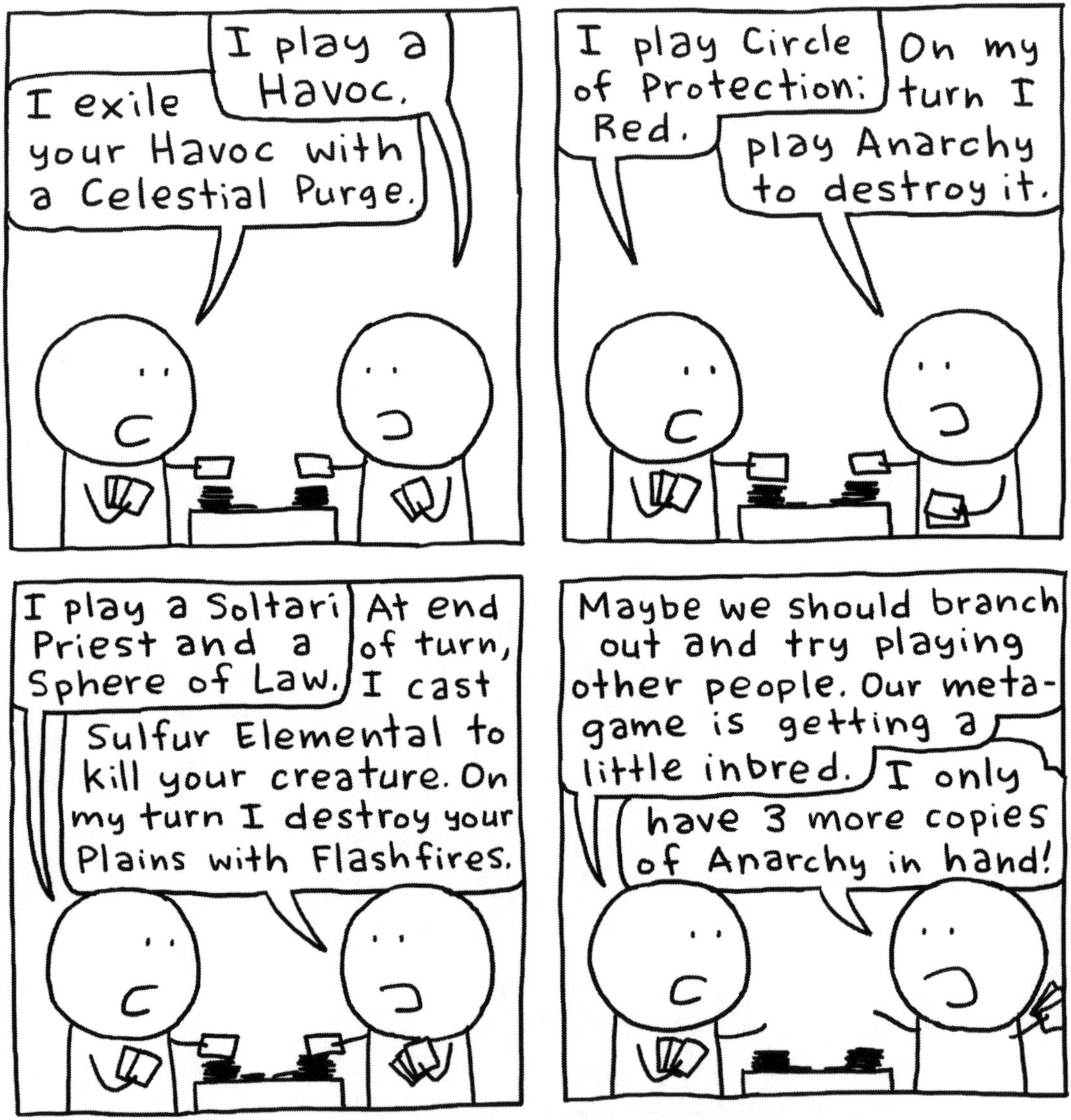
I play a Havoc.
I exile your Havoc with a Celestial Purge.
I play Circle of Protection: Red.
On my turn I play Anarchy to destroy it.
I play a Soltari Priest and a Sphere of Law.
At end of turn, I cast Sulfur Elemental to kill your creature. On my turn I destroy your Plains with Flashfires.
Maybe we should branch out and try playing other people. Our meta-game is getting a little inbred.
I only have 3 more copies of Anarchy in hand!

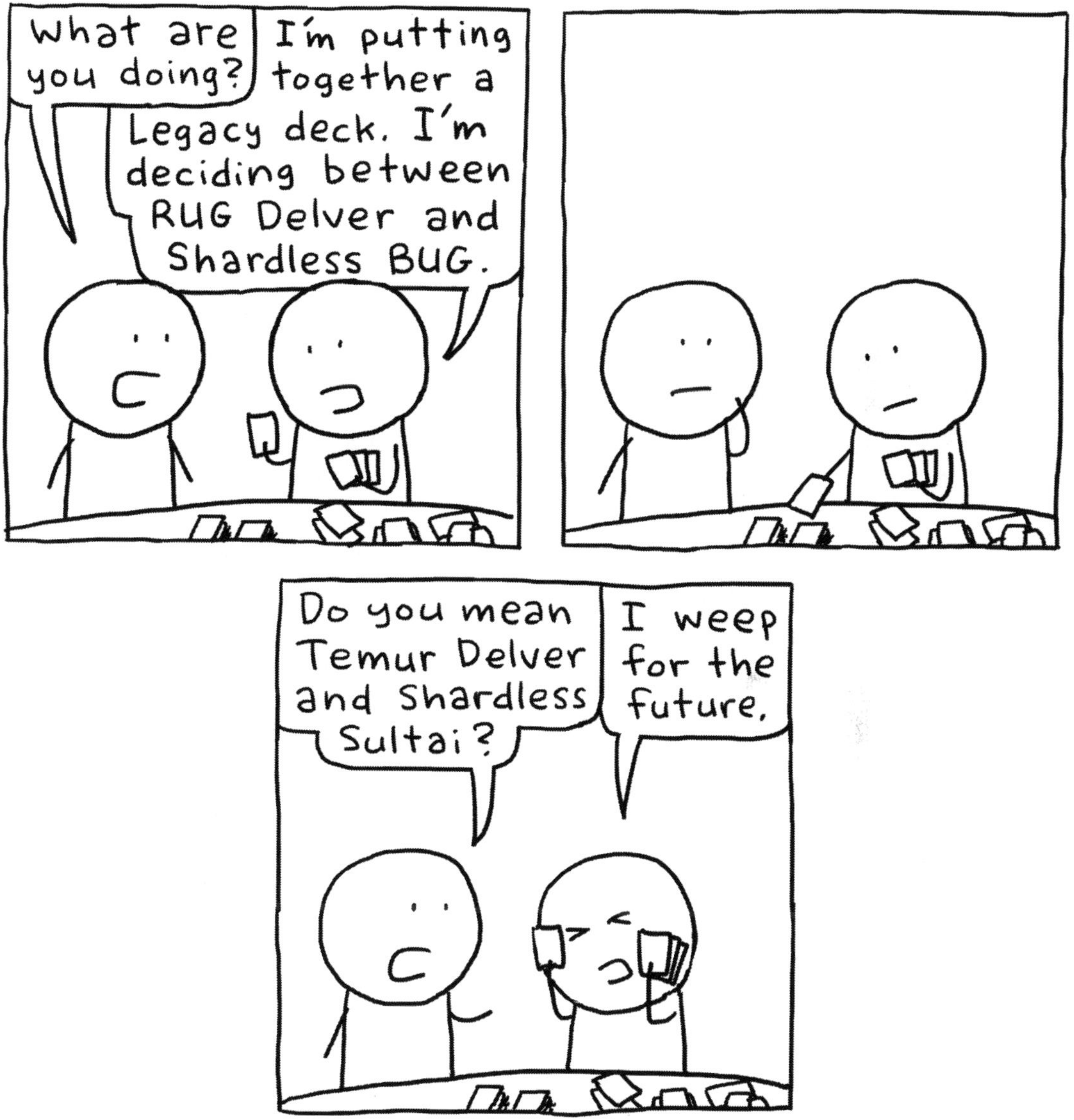
What are you doing?
I'm putting together a Legacy deck. I'm deciding between RUG Delver and Shardless BUG.
Do you mean Temur Delver and Shardless Sultai?
I weep for the future.

I can't stand it when people netdeck! They should show some originality instead of stealing from online!
Wait, where's the recipe I was going to use for dinner?
You're using someone else's recipe? Jeez, show some originality!

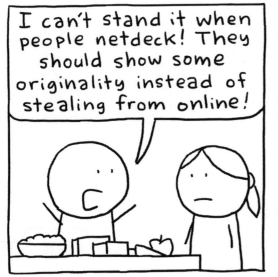

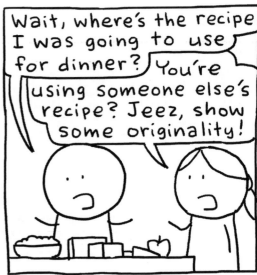

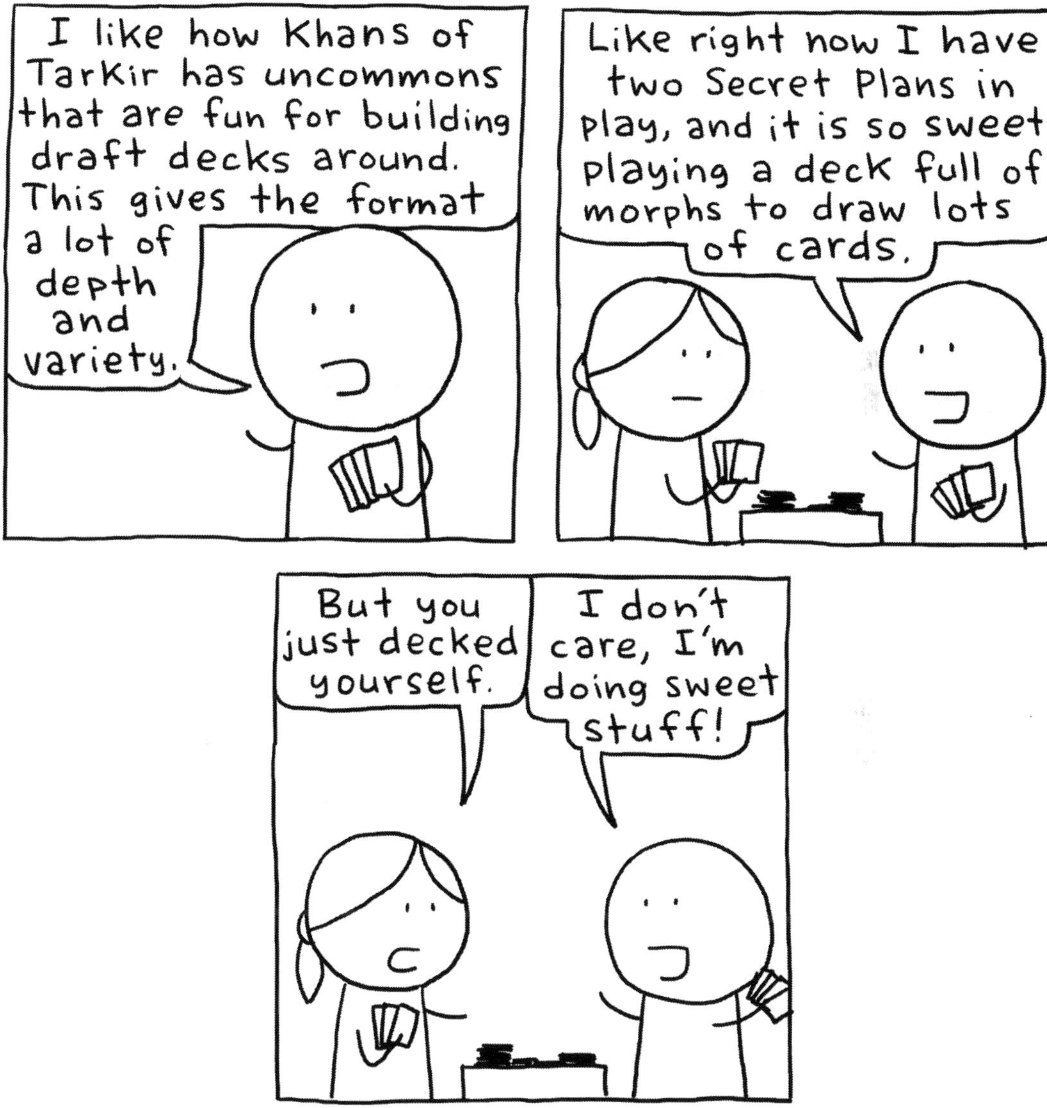
I like how Khans of TarKir has uncommons that are fun for building draft decks around. This gives the format a lot of depth and variety.
Like right now I have two Secret Plans in play, and it is so sweet playing a deck full of morphs to draw lots of cards.
But you just decked yourself.
I don't care, I'm doing sweet stuff!

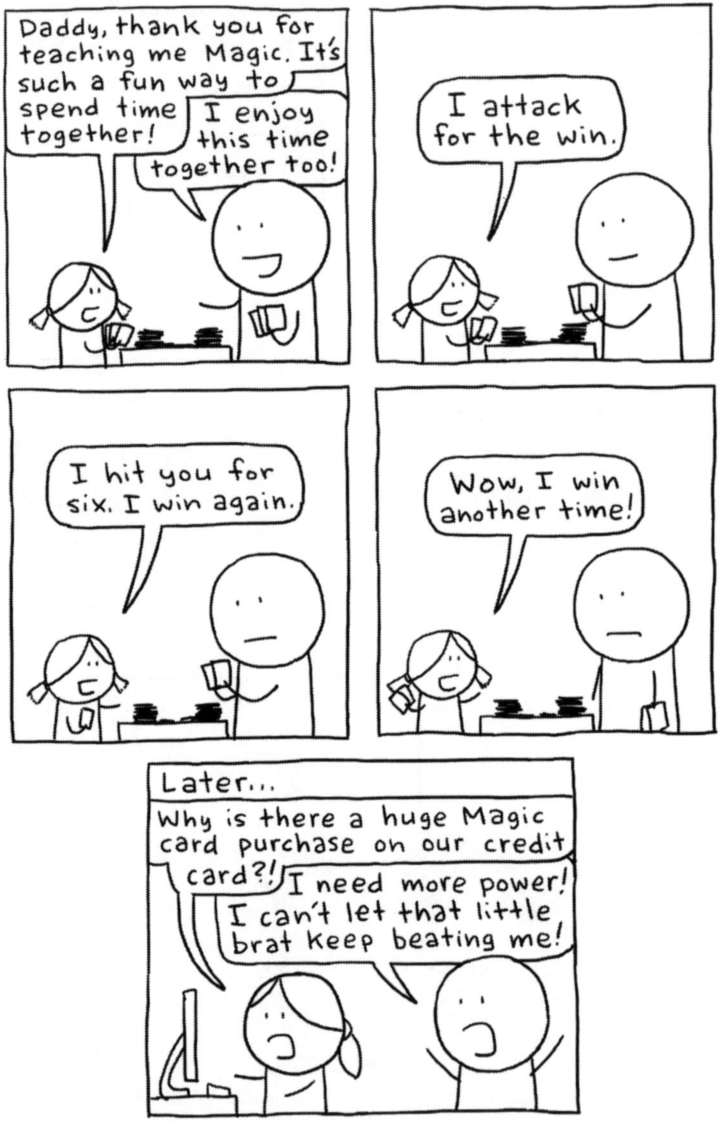
Daddy, thank you for teaching me Magic. It's such a fun way to spend time together!
I enjoy this time together too!
I attack for the win.
I hit you for six. I win again.
Wow, I win another time!
Later...
Why is there a huge Magic card purchase on our credit card?!
I need more power! I can't let that little brat keep beating me!

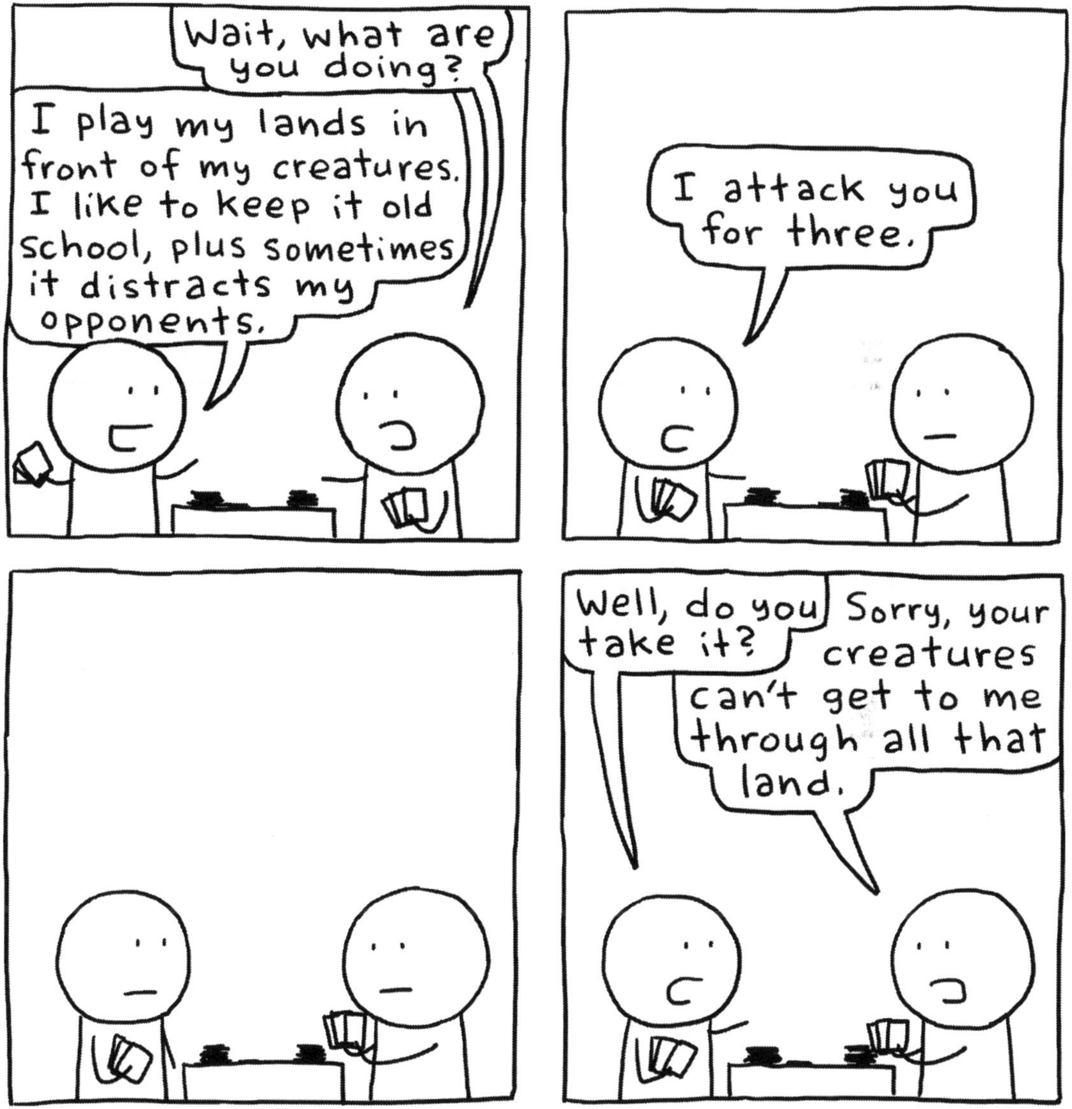
Wait, what are you doing?
I play my lands in front of my creatures. I like to keep it old school, plus sometimes it distracts my opponents.
I attack you for three.
Well, do you take it?
Sorry, your creatures can't get to me through all that land.

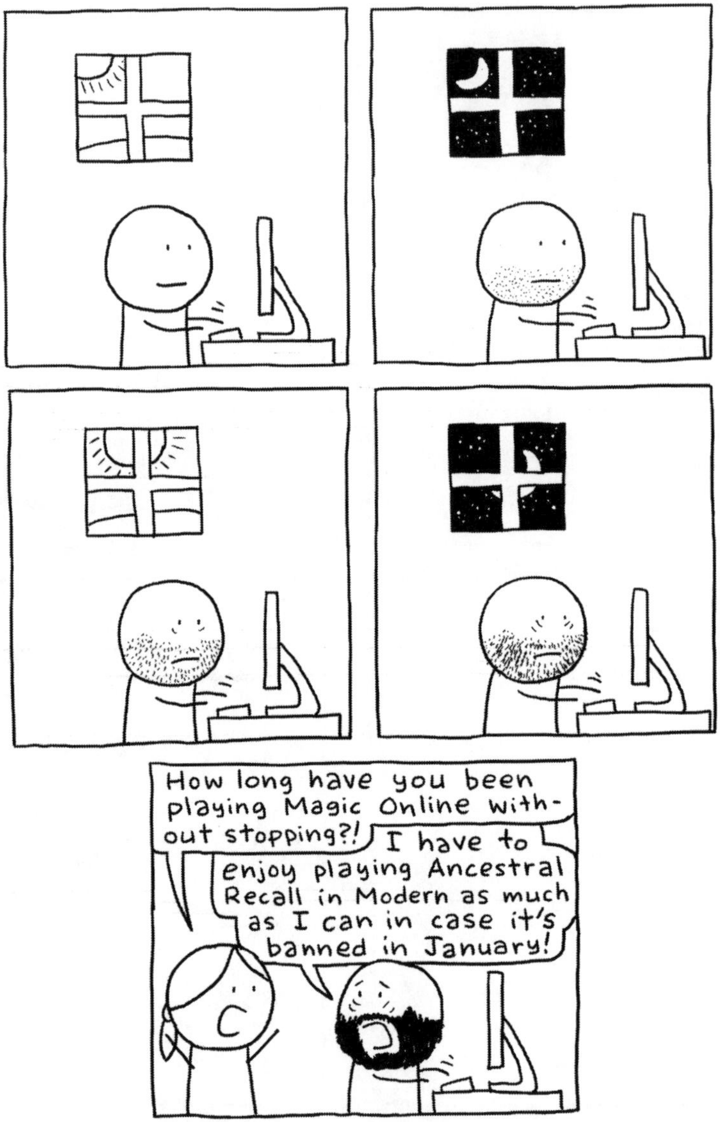
How long have you been playing Magic Online without stopping?!
I have to enjoy playing Ancestral Recall in Modern as much as I can in case it's banned in January!

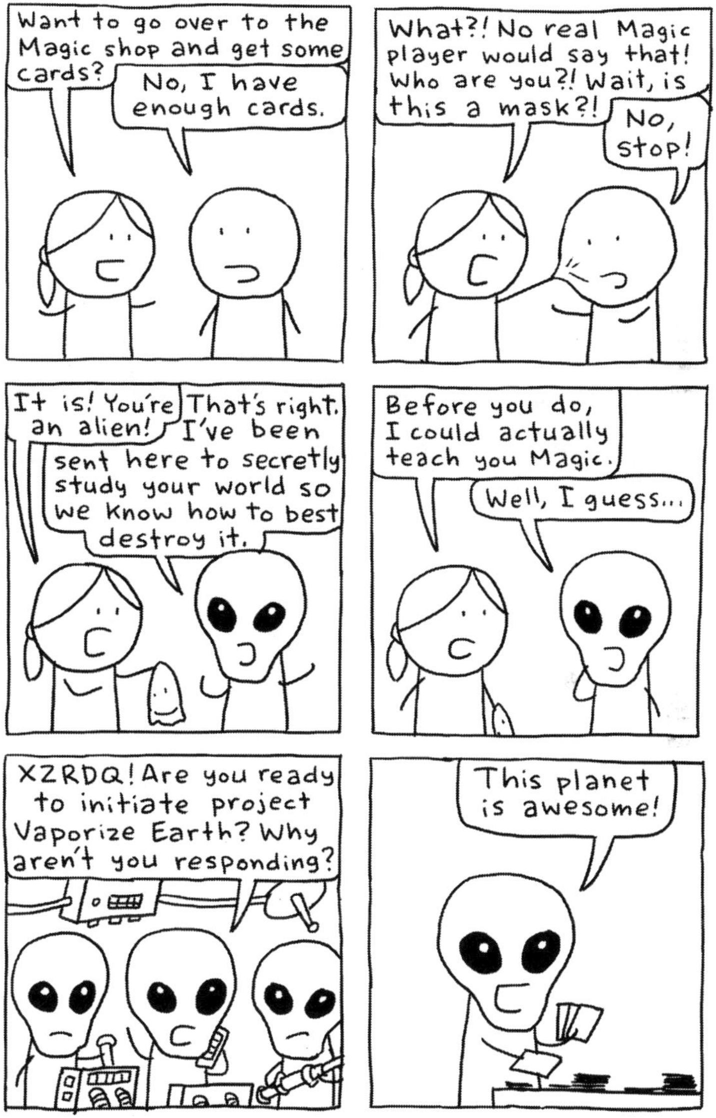

Want to go over to the Magic shop and get some cards?
No, I have enough cards.
What?! No real Magic player would say that! Who are you?! Wait, is this a mask?!
No, stop!
It is! You're an alien!
That's right. I've been sent here to secretly study your world so we know how to best destroy it.
Before you do, I could actually teach you Magic.
Well, I guess...
XZRDQ! Are you ready to initiate project Vaporize Earth? Why aren't you responding?
This planet is awesome!

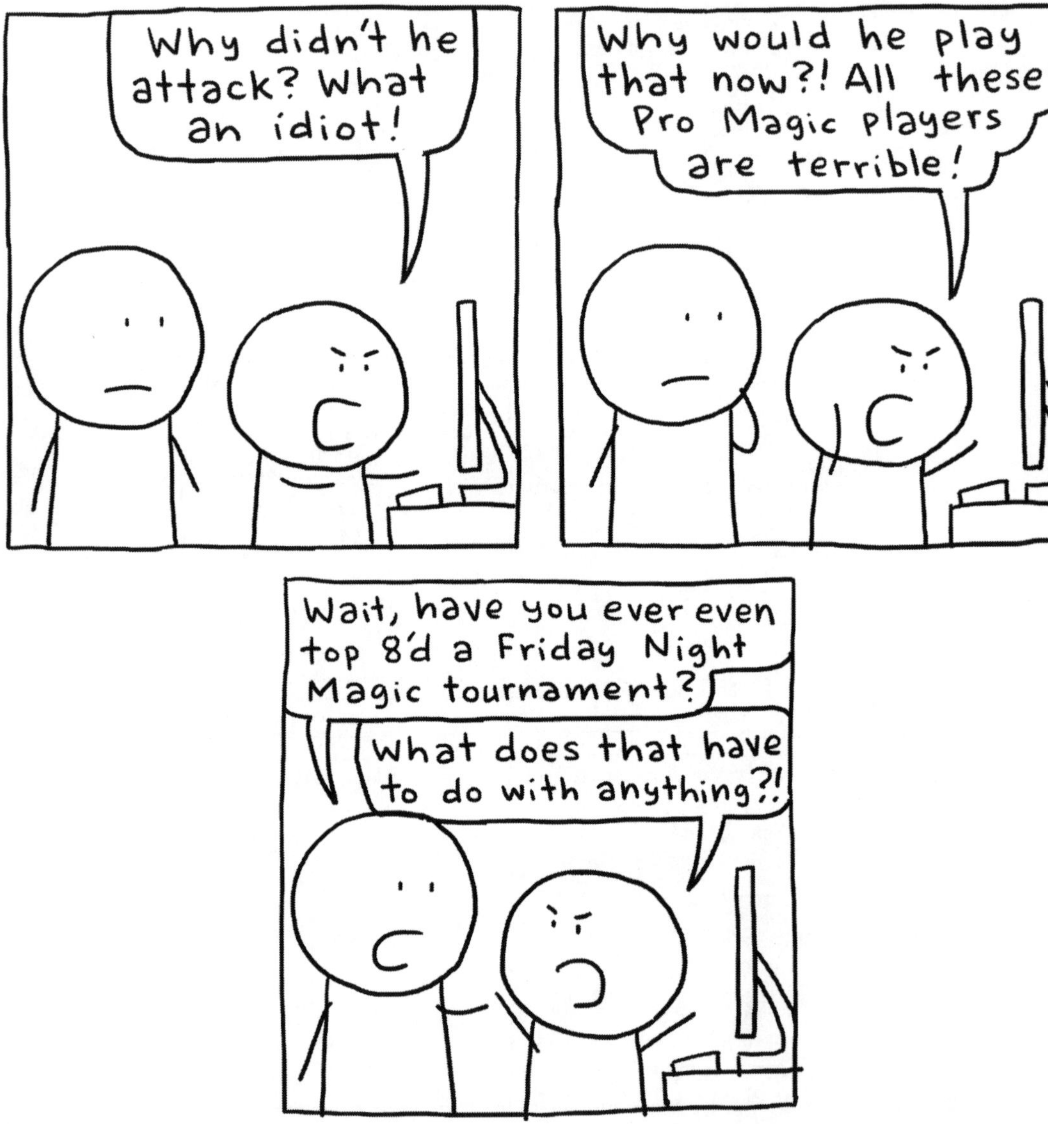
Why didn't he attack? What an idiot!
Why would he play that now?! All these Pro Magic players are terrible!
Wait, have you ever even top 8'd a Friday Night Magic tournament?
What does that have to do with anything?!

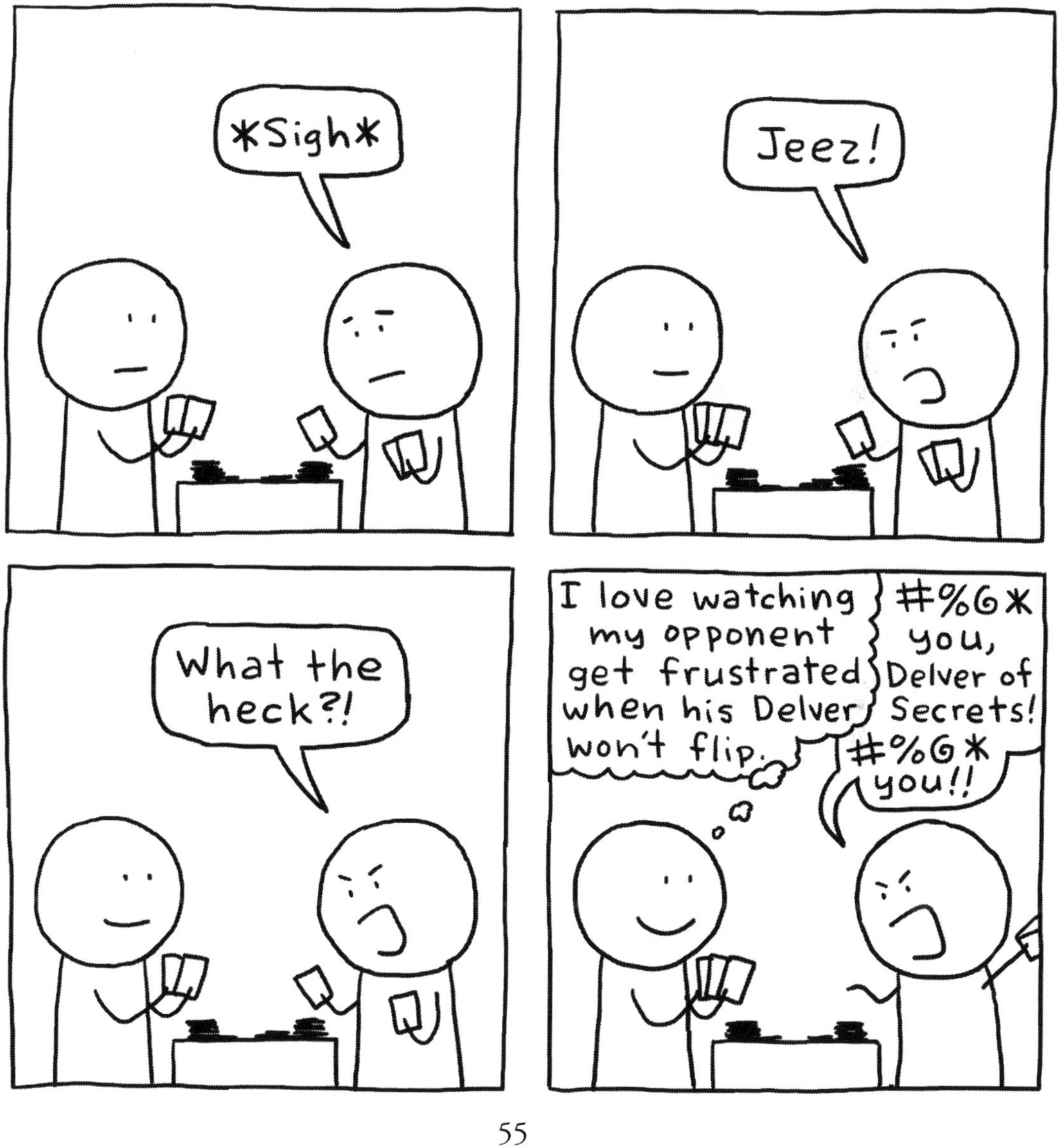
Sigh
Jeez!
What the heck?!
I love watching my opponent get frustrated when his Delver won't flip.
#%G* you, Delver of Secrets! #%G* you!!

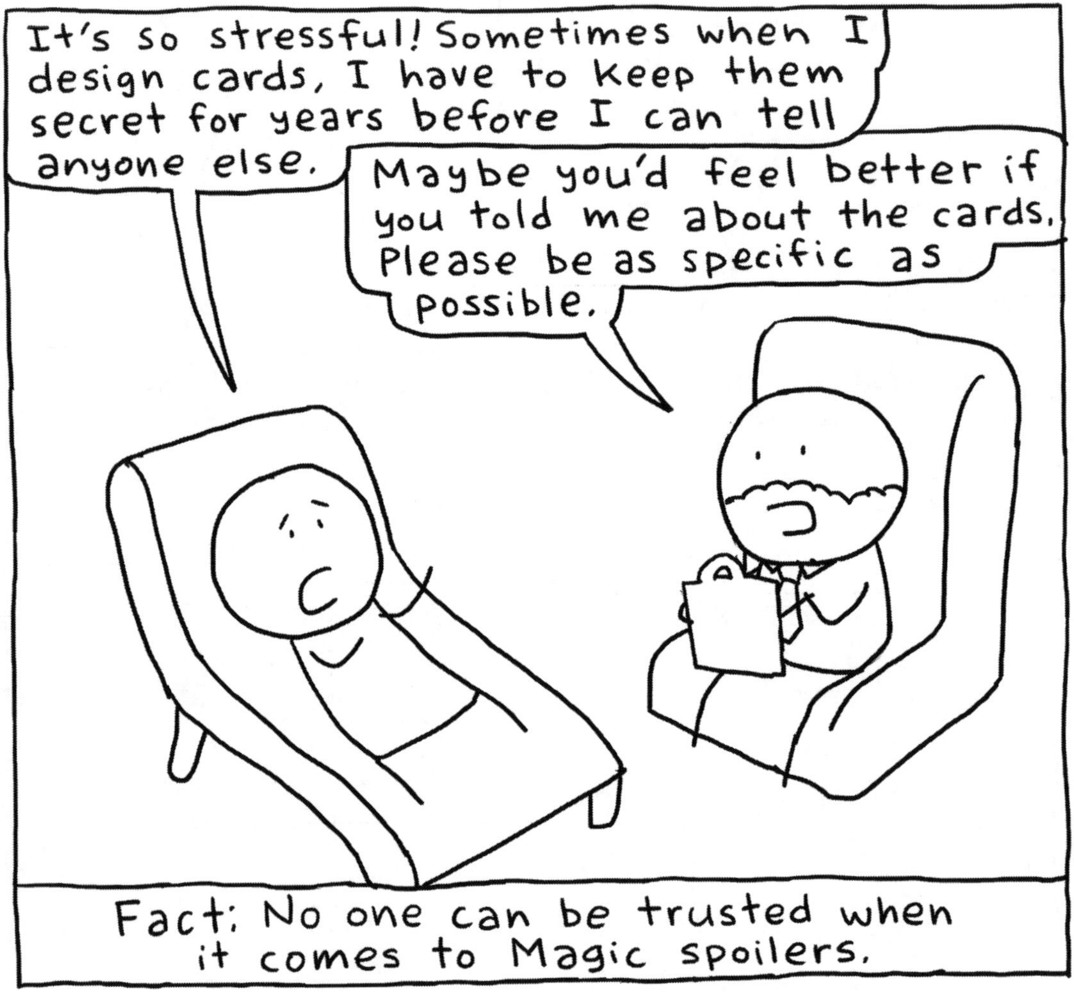
It's so stressful! Sometimes when I design cards, I have to keep them secret for years before I can tell anyone else.
Maybe you'd feel better if you told me about the cards. Please be as specific as possible.
Fact: No one can be trusted when it comes to Magic spoilers.

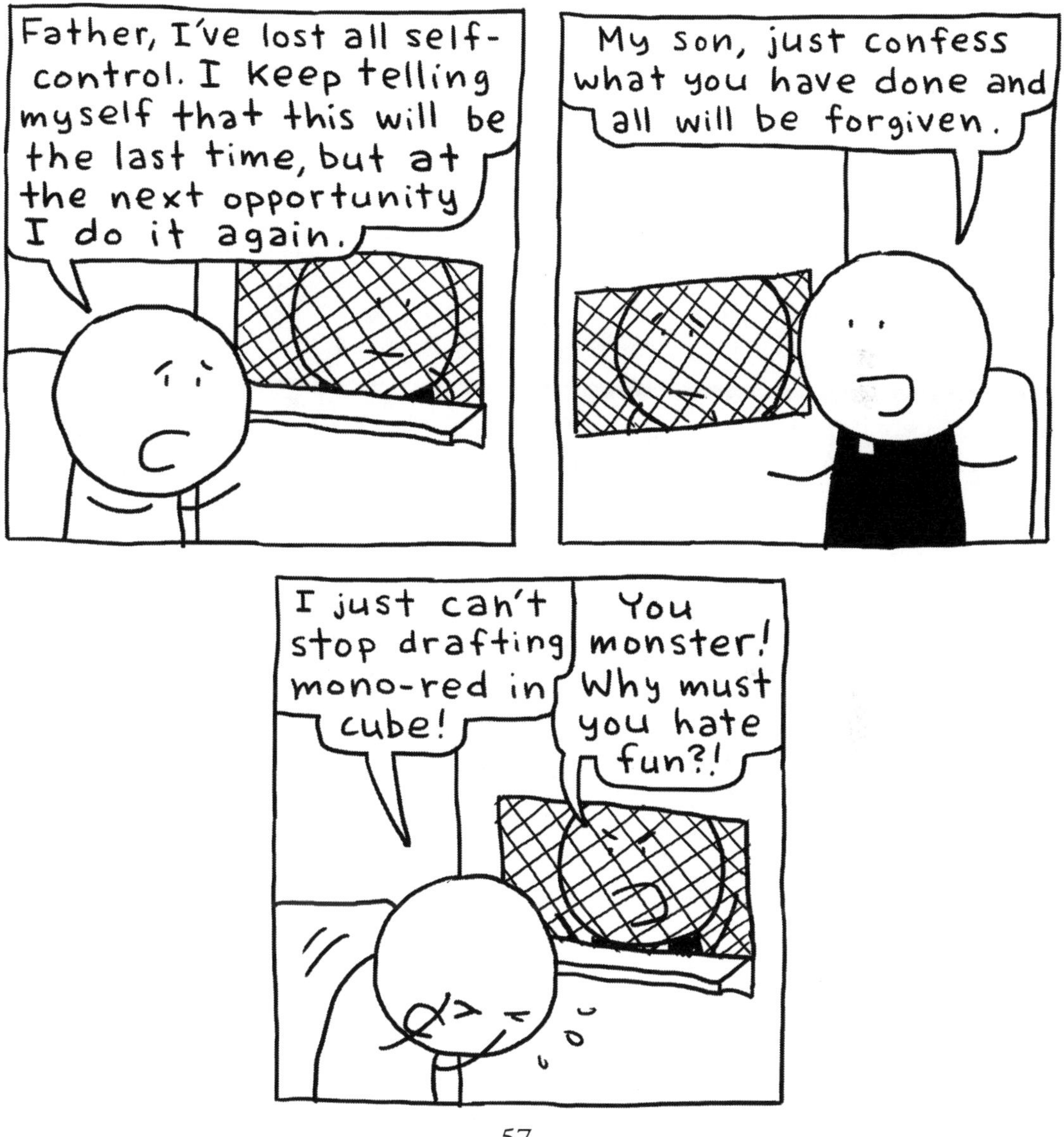
Father, I've lost all self-control. I keep telling myself that this will be the last time, but at the next opportunity I do it again.
My son, just confess what you have done and all will be forgiven.
I just can't stop drafting mono-red in cube!
You monster! Why must you hate fun?!

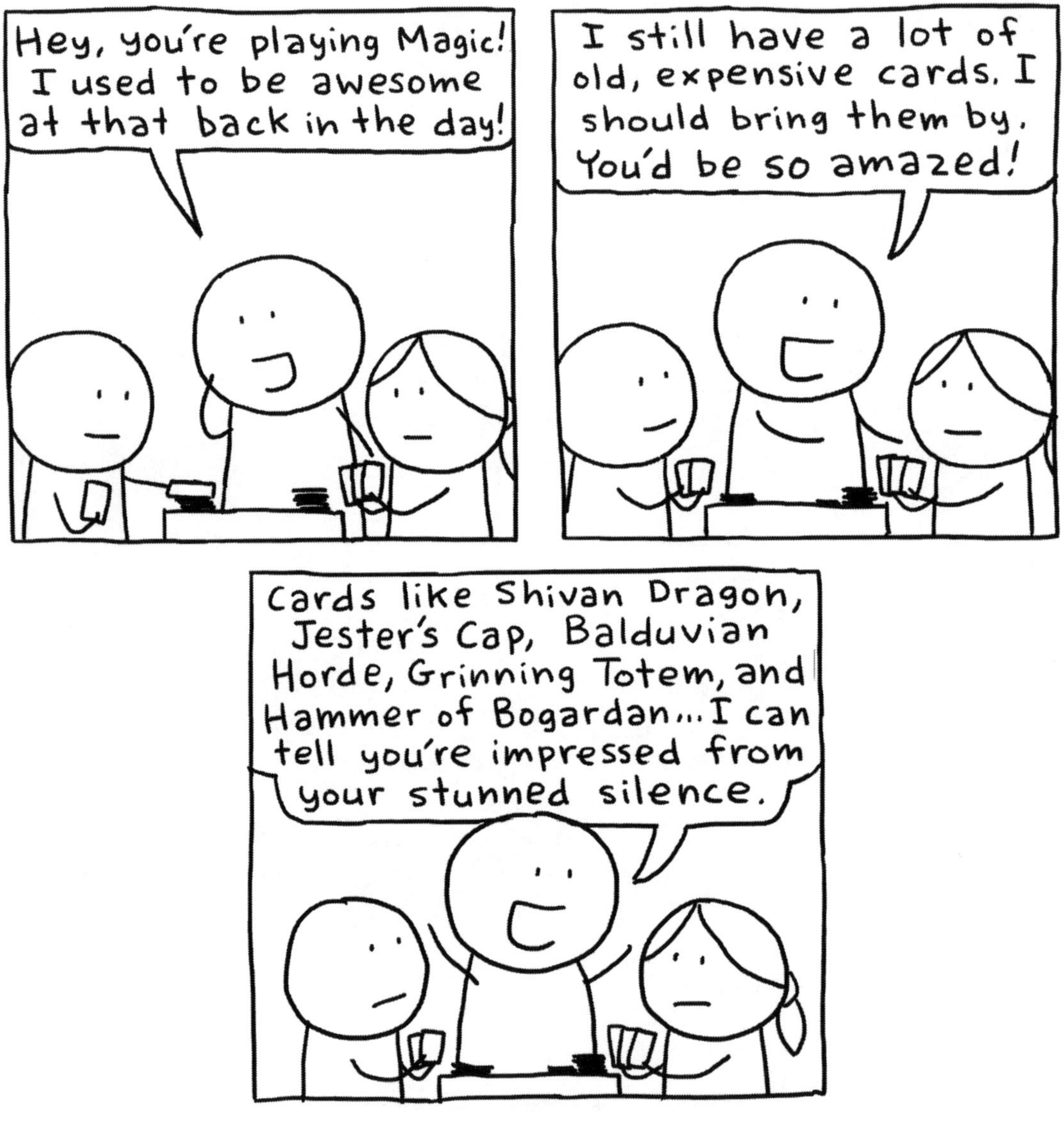
Hey, you're playing Magic! I used to be awesome at that back in the day!
I still have a lot of old, expensive cards. I should bring them by. You'd be so amazed!
Cards like Shivan Dragon, Jester's Cap, Balduvian Horde, Grinning Totem, and Hammer of Bogardan... I can tell you're impressed from your stunned silence.

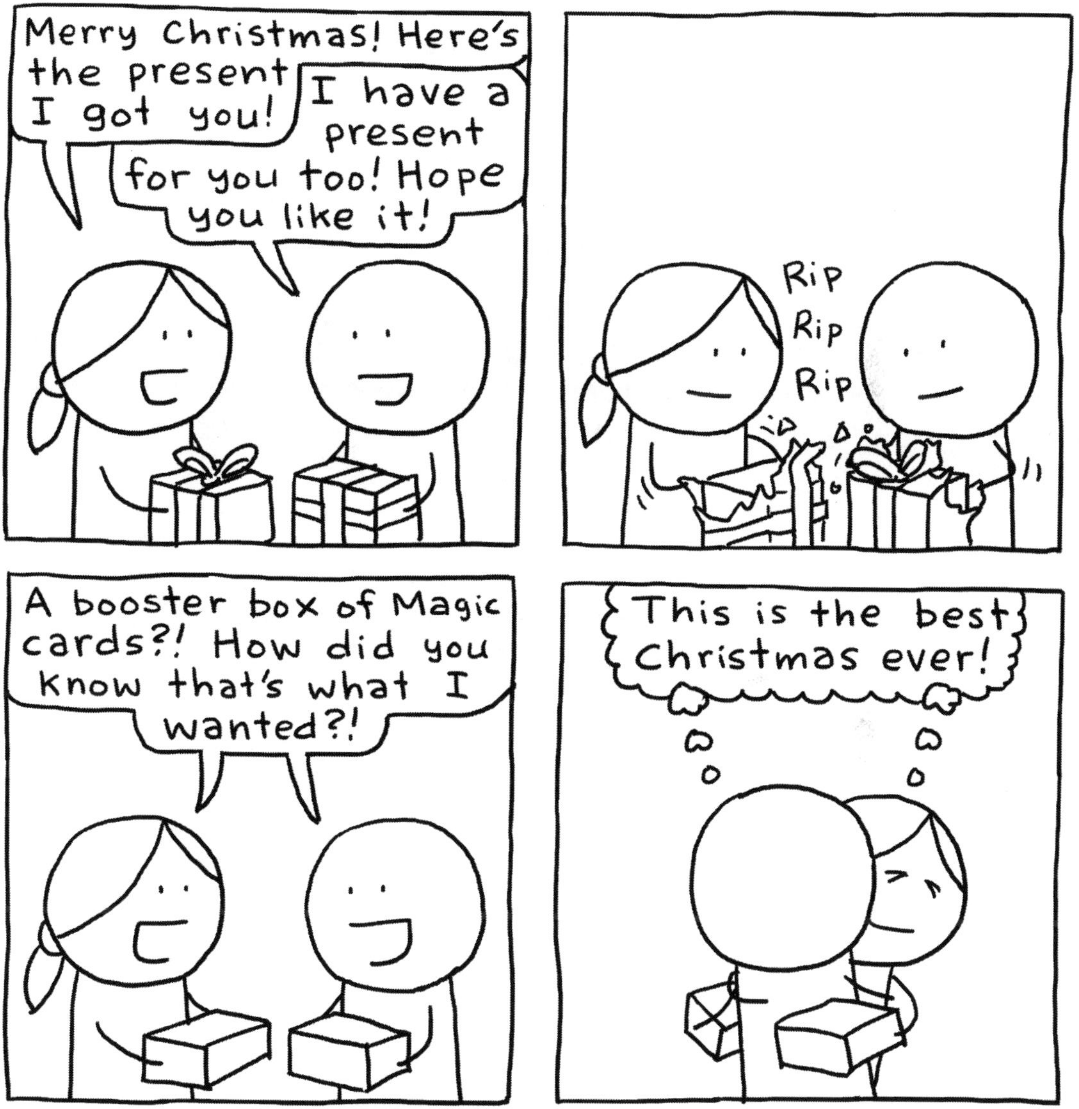
Merry Christmas! Here's the present I got you!
I have a present for you too! Hope you like it!
Rip
Rip
Rip
A booster box of Magic cards?! How did you know that's what I wanted?!
This is the best Christmas ever!

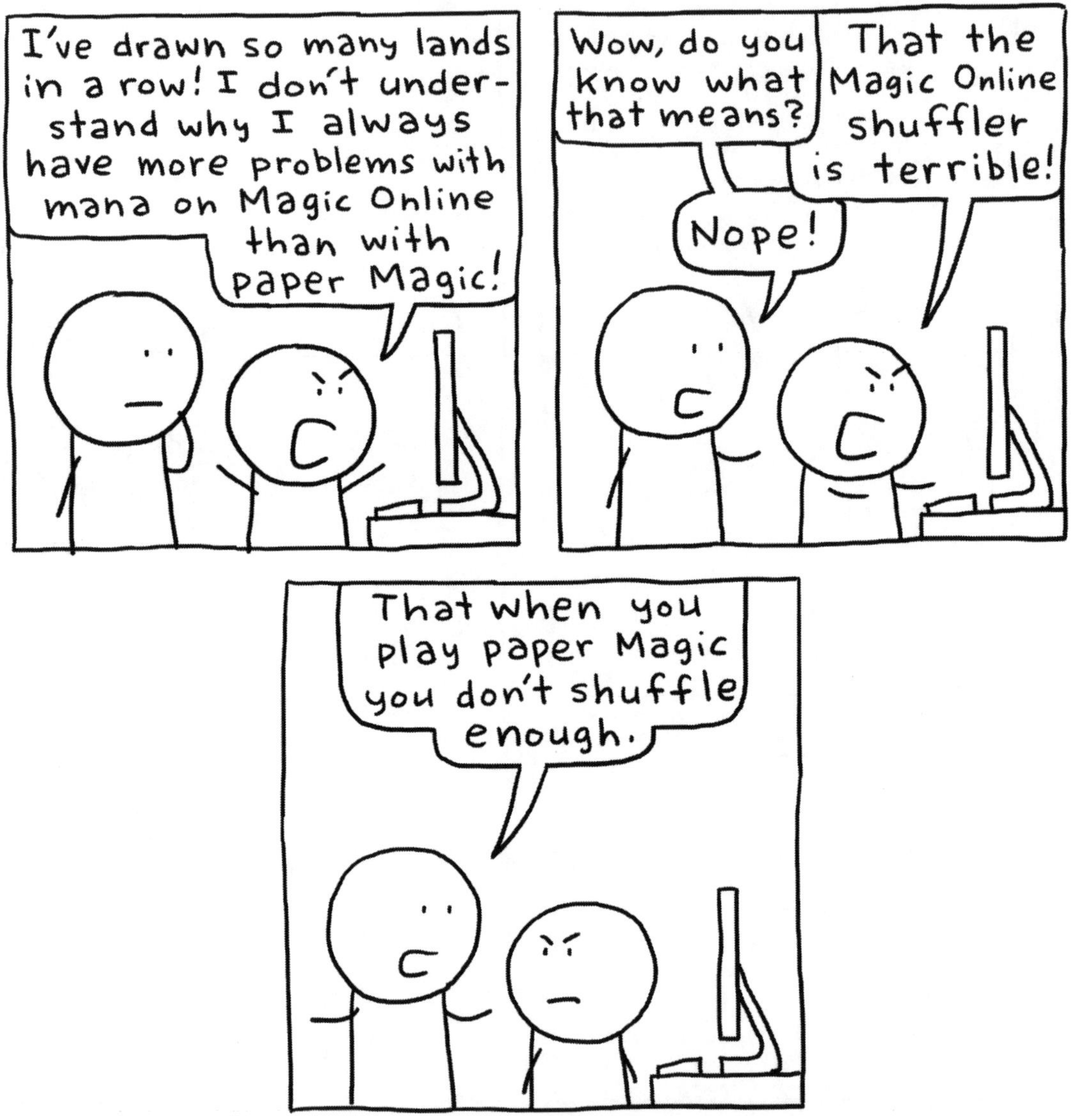
I've drawn so many lands in a row! I don't understand why I always have more problems with mana on Magic Online than with paper Magic!
Wow, do you know what that means?
Nope!
That the Magic Online shuffler is terrible!
That when you play paper Magic you don't shuffle enough.

I know your deck is full of expensive and rare foils, but this is ridiculous!
My bling is so bright that I have to wear shades!

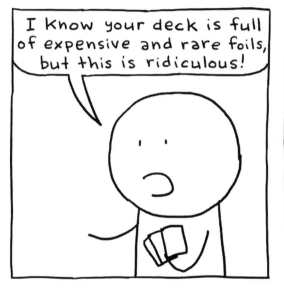

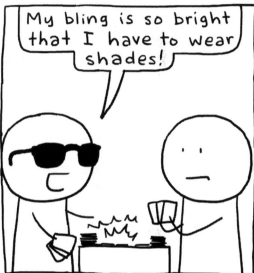

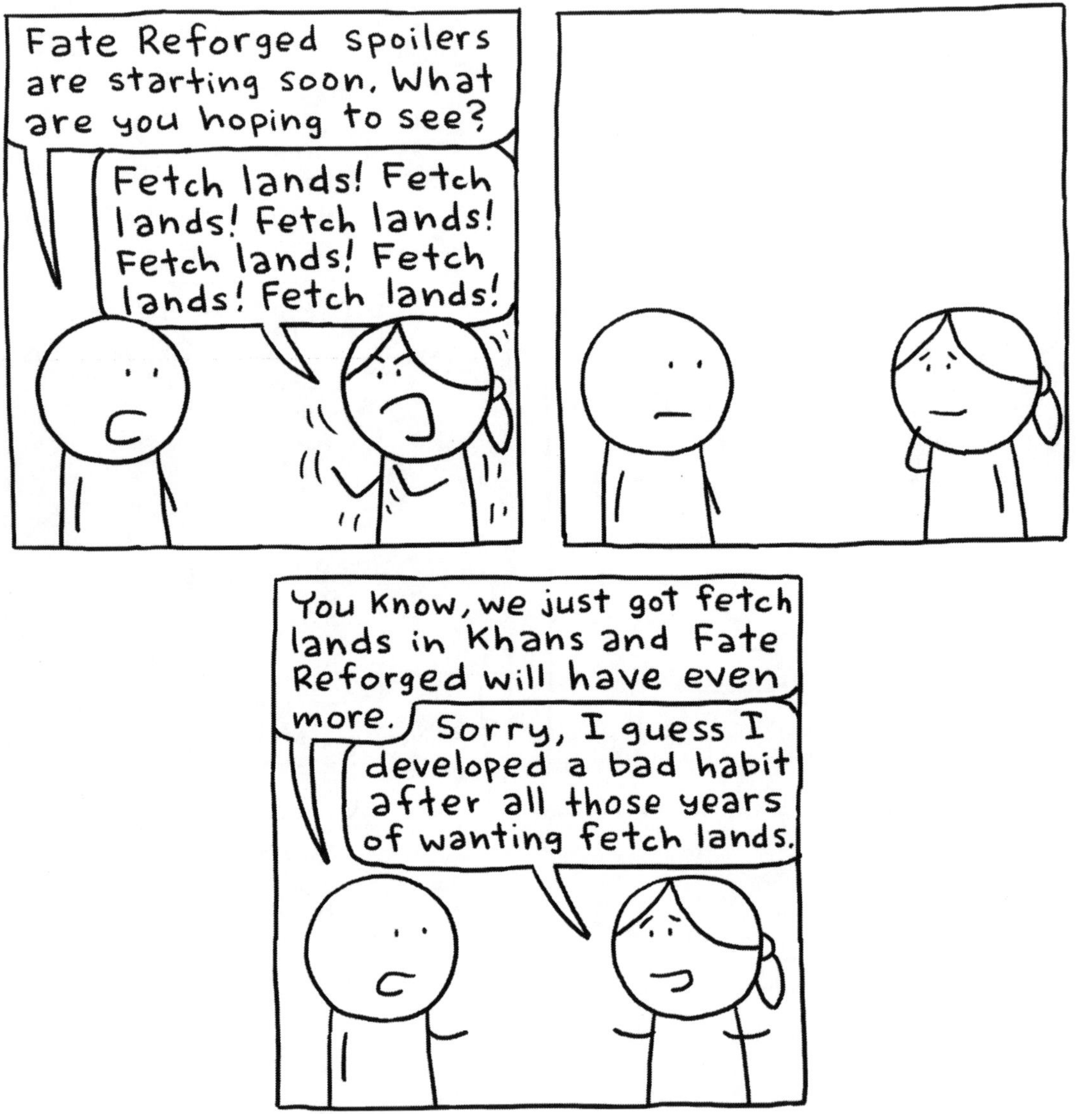
Fate Reforged spoilers are starting soon. What are you hoping to see?
Fetch lands! Fetch lands! Fetch lands! Fetch lands! Fetch lands! Fetch lands!
You know, we just got fetch lands in Khans and Fate Reforged will have even more.
Sorry, I guess I developed a bad habit after all those years of wanting fetch lands.

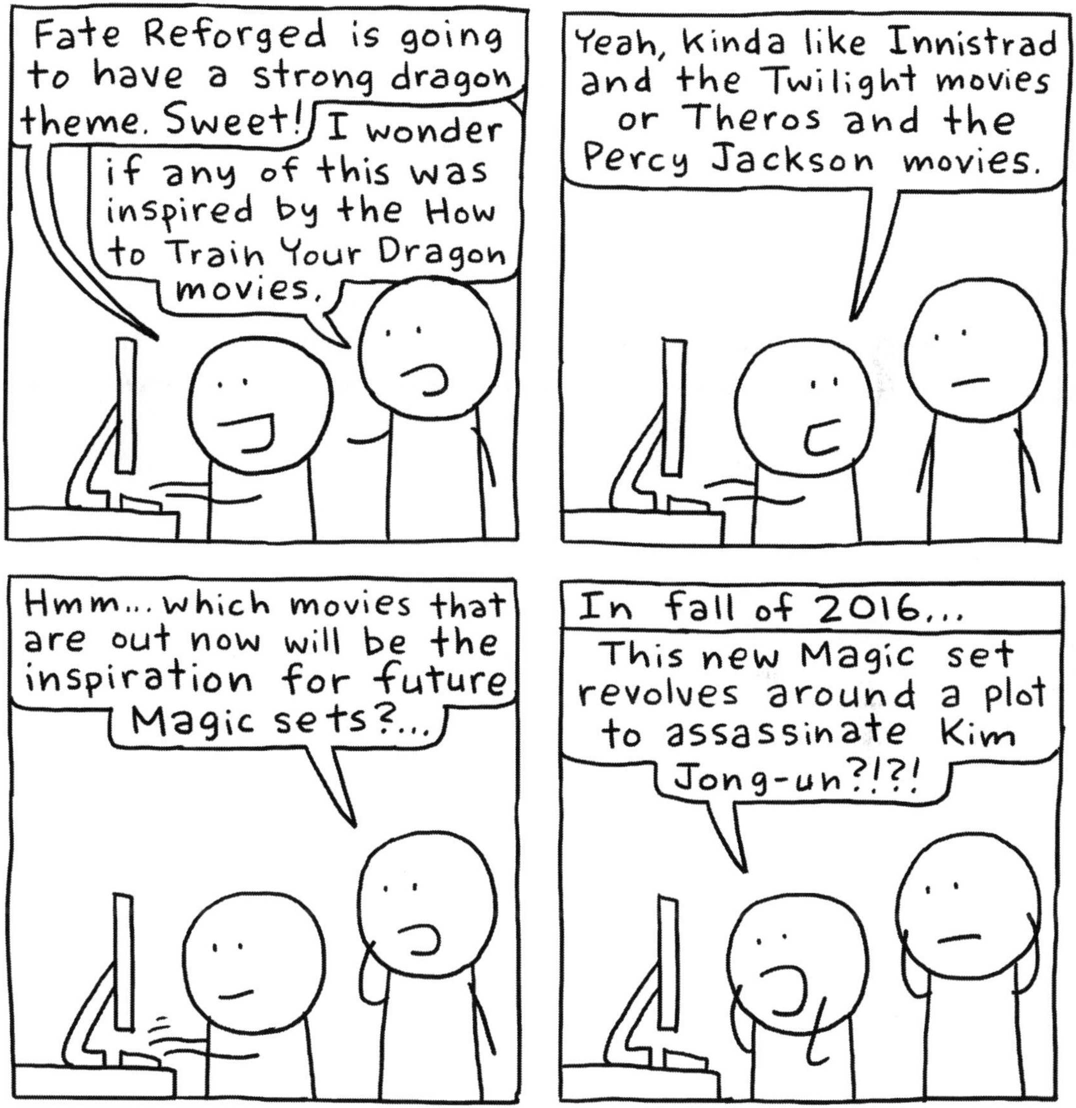
Fate Reforged is going to have a strong dragon theme. Sweet!
I wonder if any of this was inspired by the How to Train Your Dragon movies.
Yeah, kinda like Innistrad and the Twilight movies or Theros and the Percy Jackson movies.
Hmm... which movies that are out now will be the inspiration for future Magic sets?...
In fall of 2016...
This new Magic set revolves around a plot to assassinate Kim Jong-un?!?!

Did you see the recently spoiled card Temporal Trespass? It's ridiculous!
Yeah, a delve card that lets you take another turn seems pretty good.
No, I was referring to the artwork featuring a woman with unneces-sarily large breasts and completely impractical breast armor!
That must be where she hides her time-walking magic.

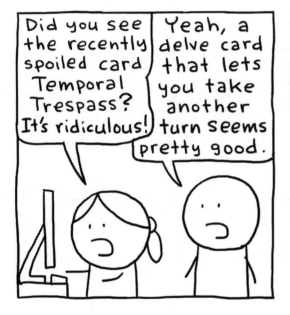

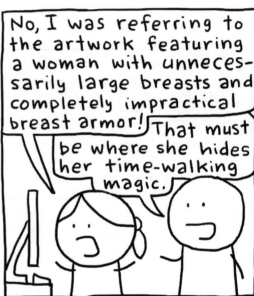

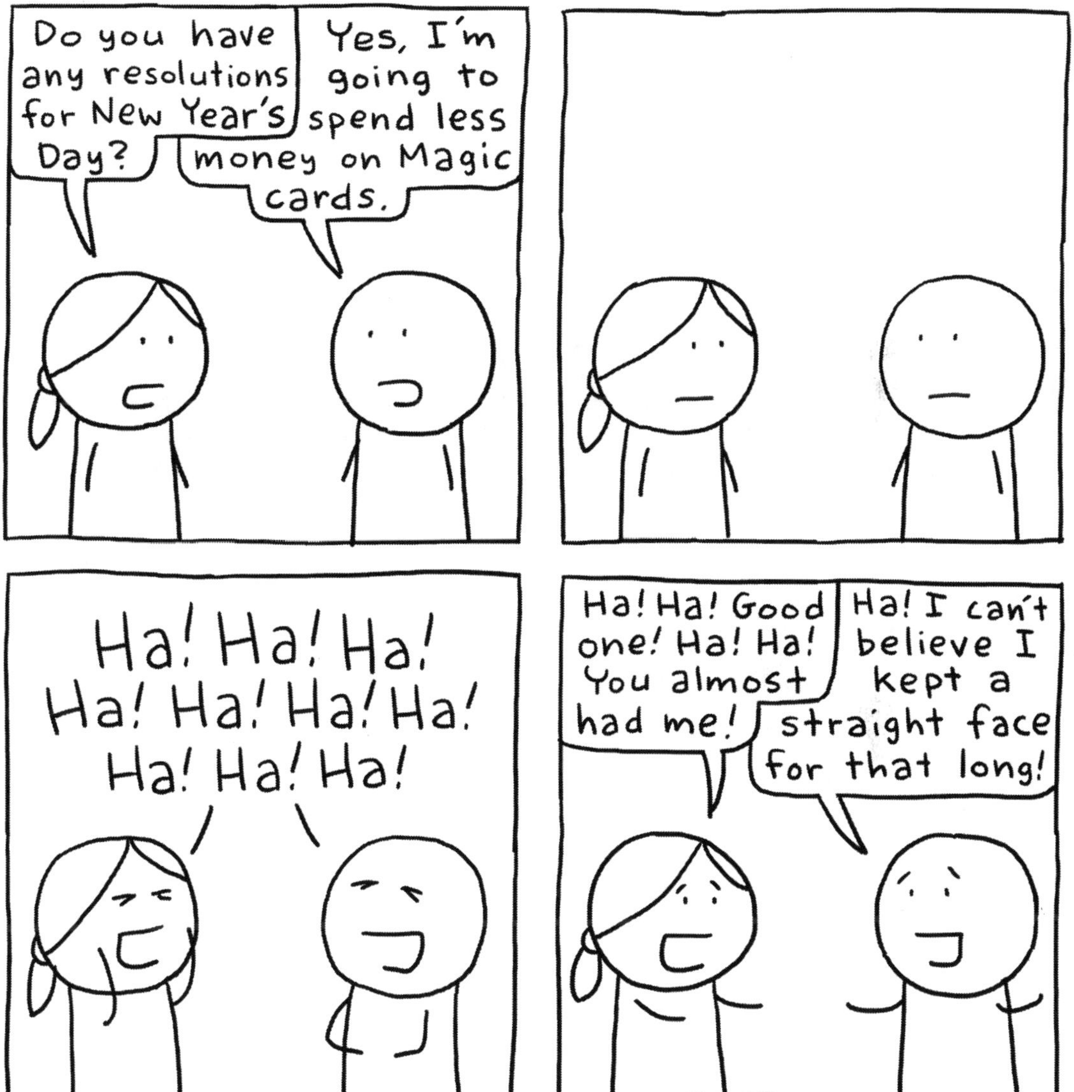
Do you have any resolutions for New Year's Day?
Yes, I'm going to spend less money on Magic cards.
Ha! Ha! Ha! Ha! Ha! Ha! Ha! Ha! Ha! Ha!
Ha! Ha! Good one! Ha! Ha! You almost had me!
Ha! I can't believe I kept a straight face for that long!

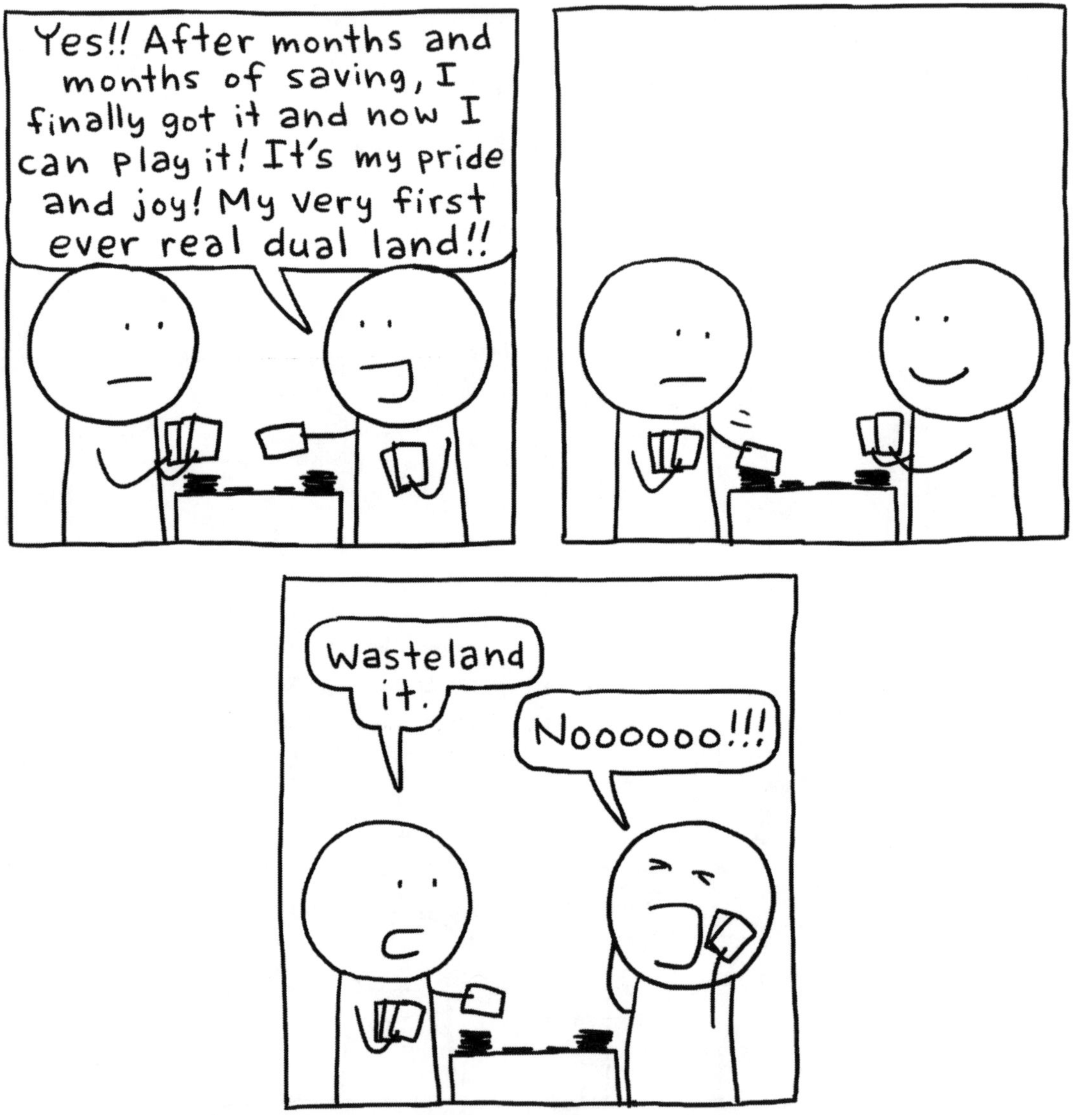
Yes!! After months and months of saving, I finally got it and now I can play it! It's my pride and joy! My very first ever real dual land!!
Wasteland it.
Noooooo!!!

Did you see the new Fate Reforged mechanic, bolster?
Yeah, that's the one that makes the smallest thing you have get bigger.
So it's like what happens to you when you're around a cute girl.
Yeah -- I mean, no!

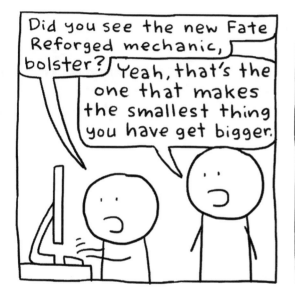

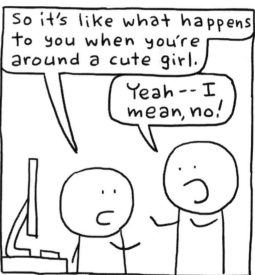

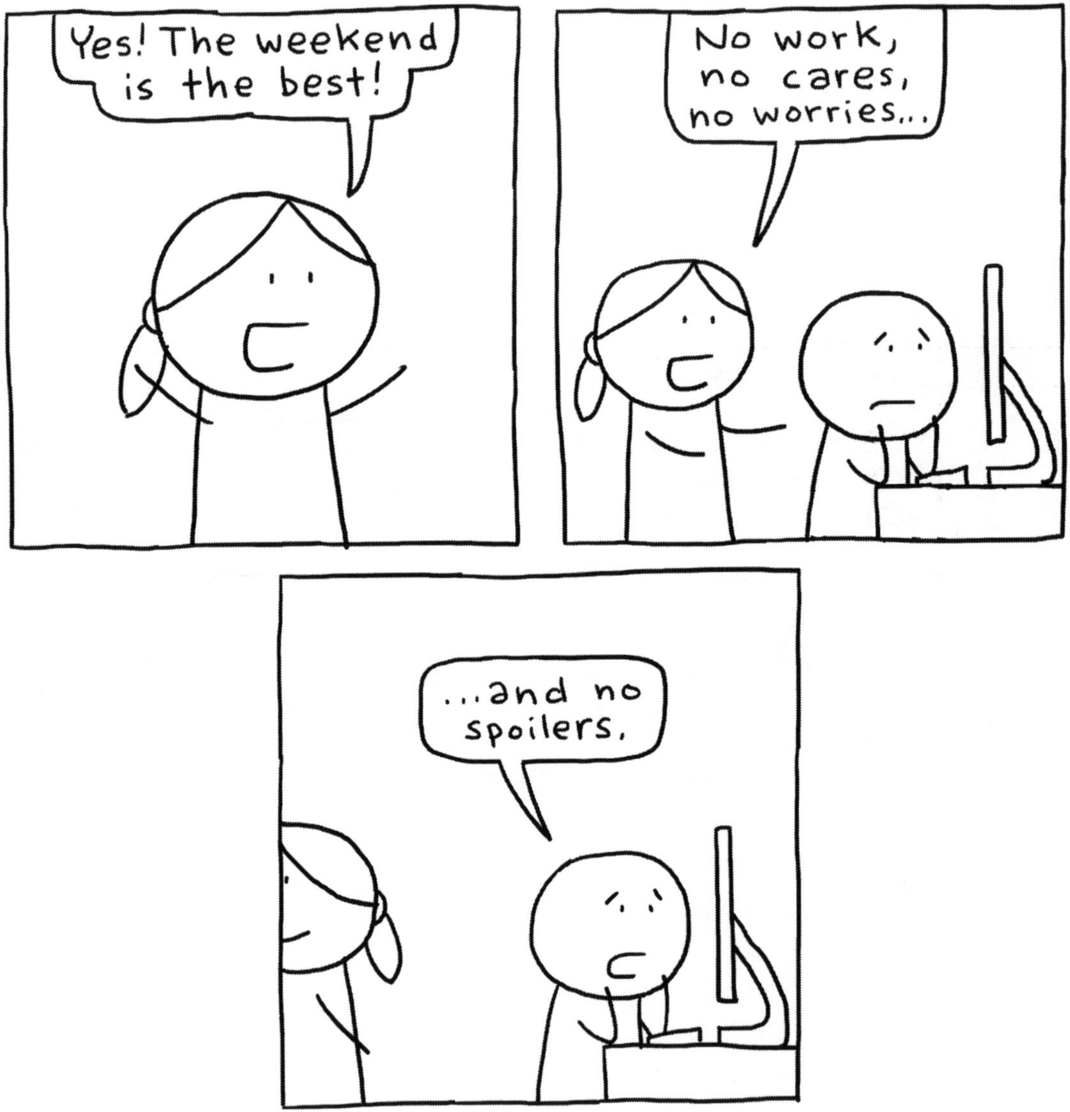
Yes! The weekend is the best!
No work, no cares, no worries...
...and no spoilers.

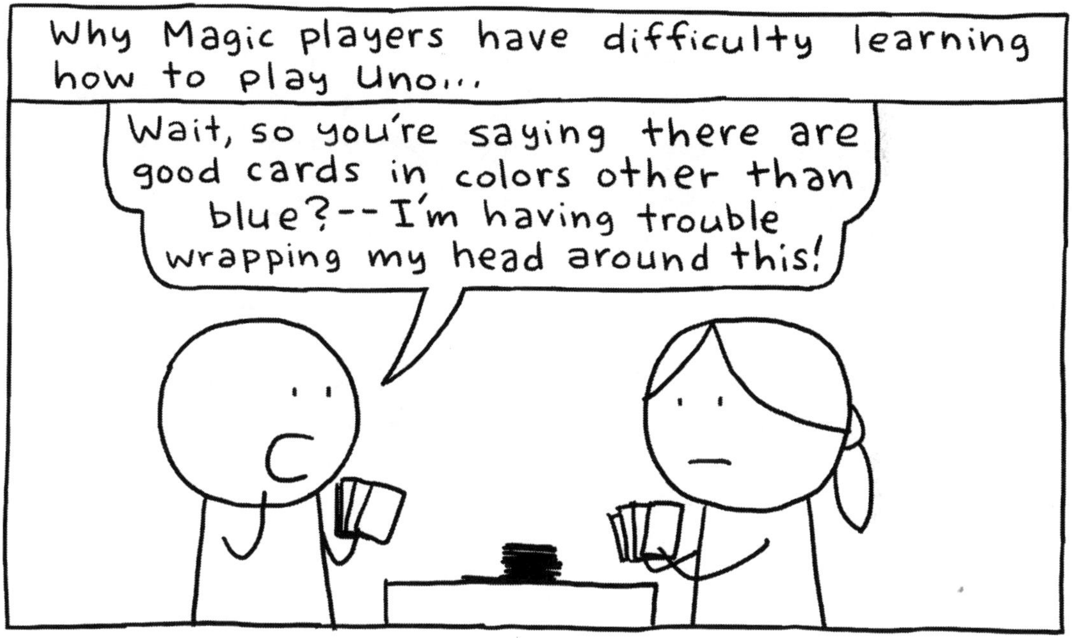
Why Magic players have difficulty learning how to play Uno...
Wait, so you're saying there are good cards in colors other than blue?--I'm having trouble wrapping my head around this!

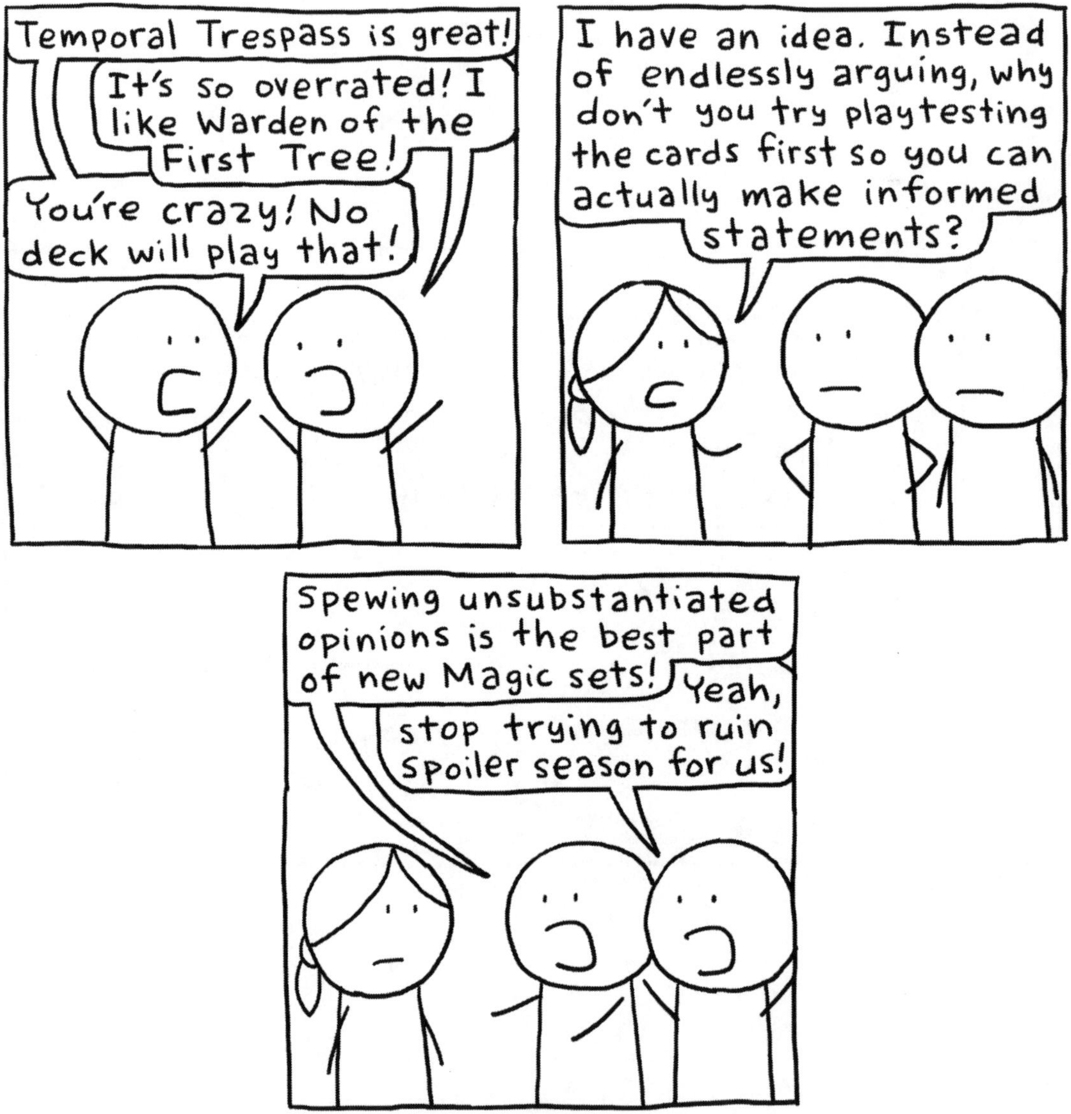
Temporal Trespass is great!
It's so overrated! I like Warden of the First Tree!
You're crazy! No deck will play that!
I have an idea. Instead of endlessly arguing, why don't you try playtesting the cards first so you can actually make informed statements?
Spewing unsubstantiated opinions is the best part of new Magic sets!
Yeah, stop trying to ruin spoiler season for us!

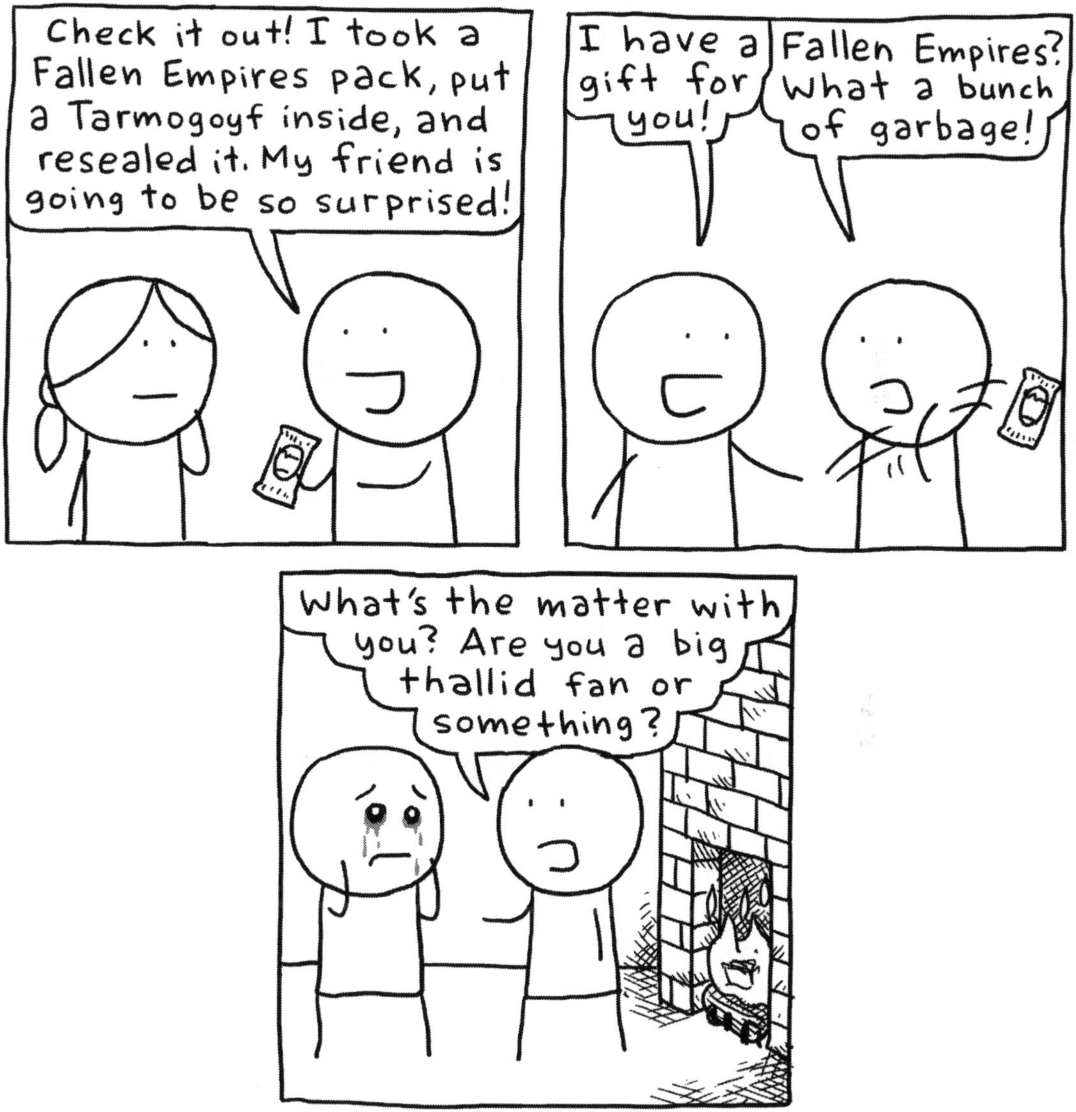
Check it out! I took a Fallen Empires pack, put a Tarmogoyf inside, and resealed it. My friend is going to be so surprised!
I have a gift for you!
Fallen Empires? What a bunch of garbage!
What's the matter with you? Are you a big thallid fan or something?

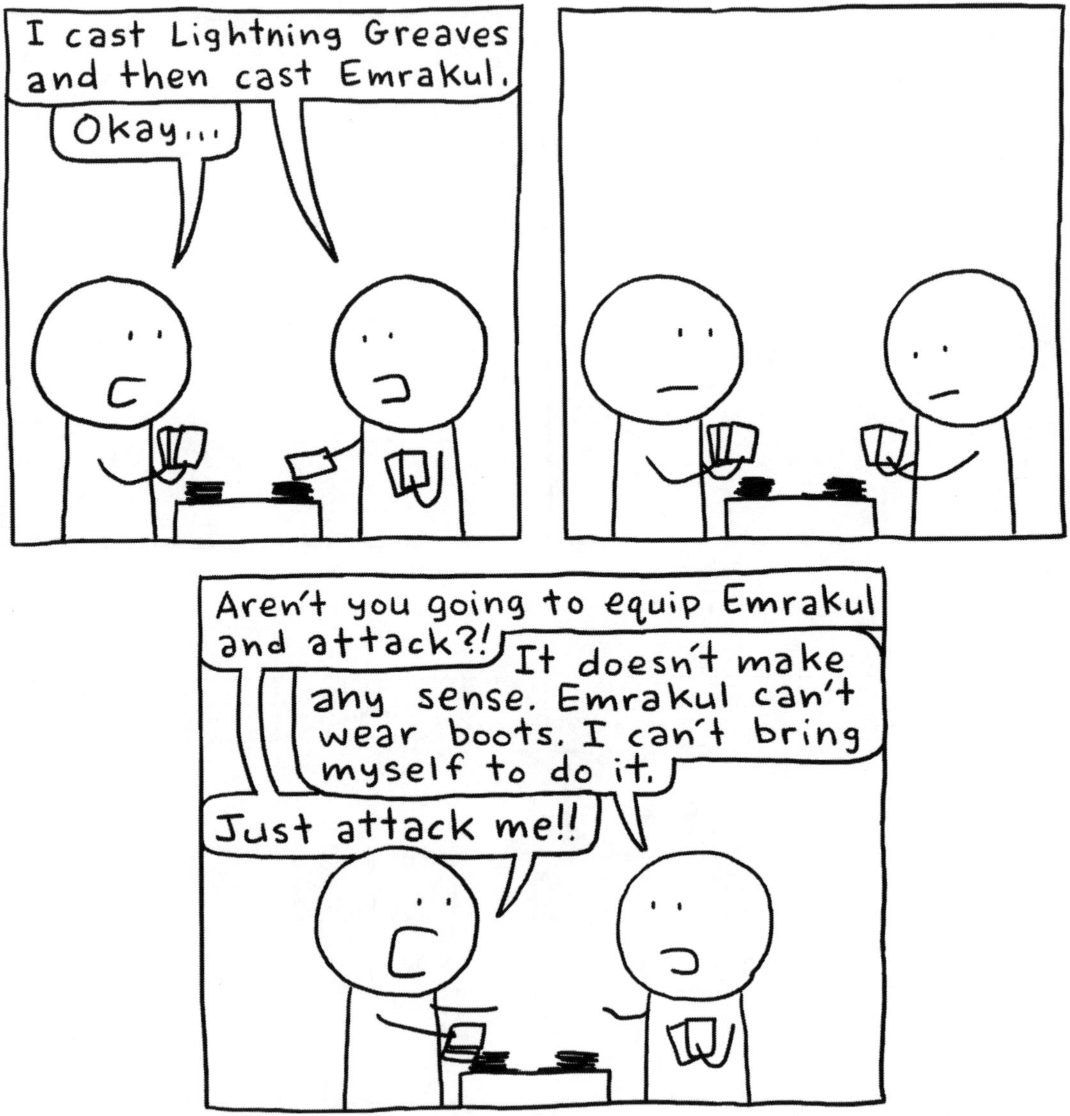
I cast Lightning Greaves and then cast Emrakul.
Okay...
Aren't you going to equip Emrakul and attack?!
It doesn't make any sense. Emrakul can't wear boots. I can't bring myself to do it.
Just attack me!!

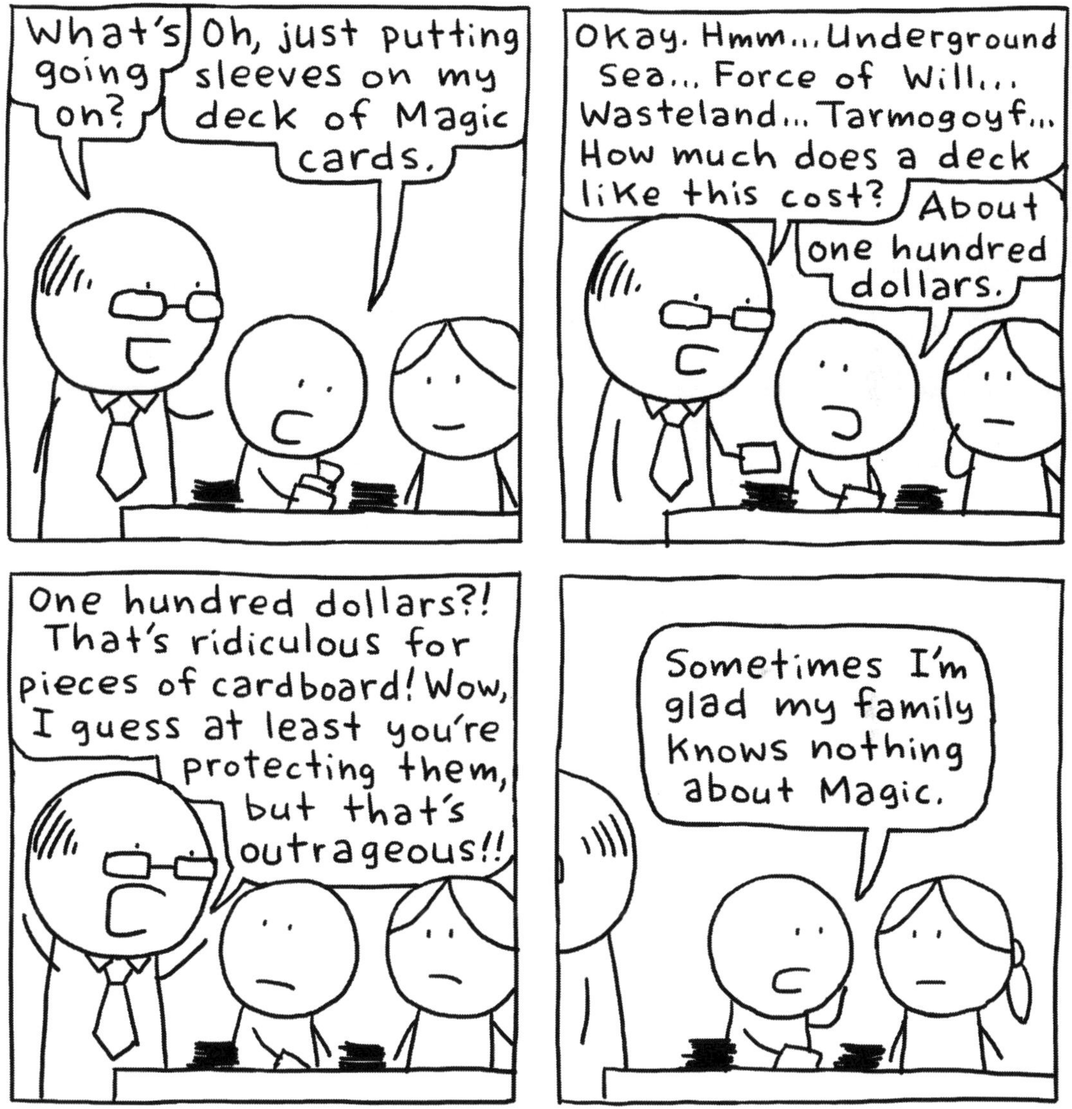
What's going on?
Oh, just putting sleeves on my deck of Magic cards.
Okay. Hmm... Underground Sea... Force of Will... Wasteland... Tarmogoyf... How much does a deck like this cost?
About one hundred dollars.
One hundred dollars?! That's ridiculous for pieces of cardboard! Wow, I guess at least you're protecting them, but that's outrageous!!
Sometimes I'm glad my family knows nothing about Magic.

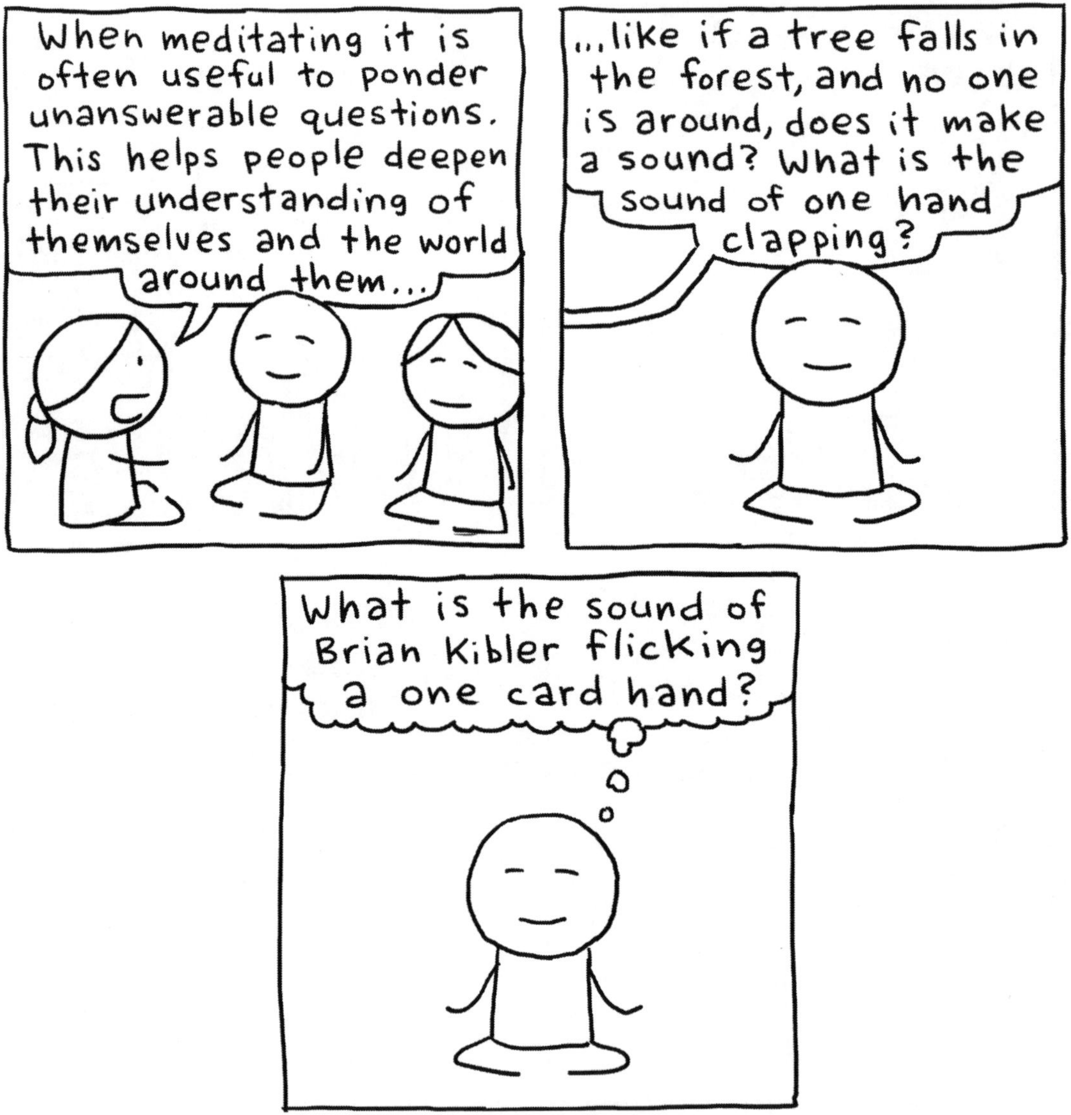
When meditating it is often useful to ponder unanswerable questions. This helps people deepen their understanding of themselves and the world around them...
...like if a tree falls in the forest, and no one is around, does it make a sound? What is the sound of one hand clapping?
What is the sound of Brian Kibler flicking a one card hand?

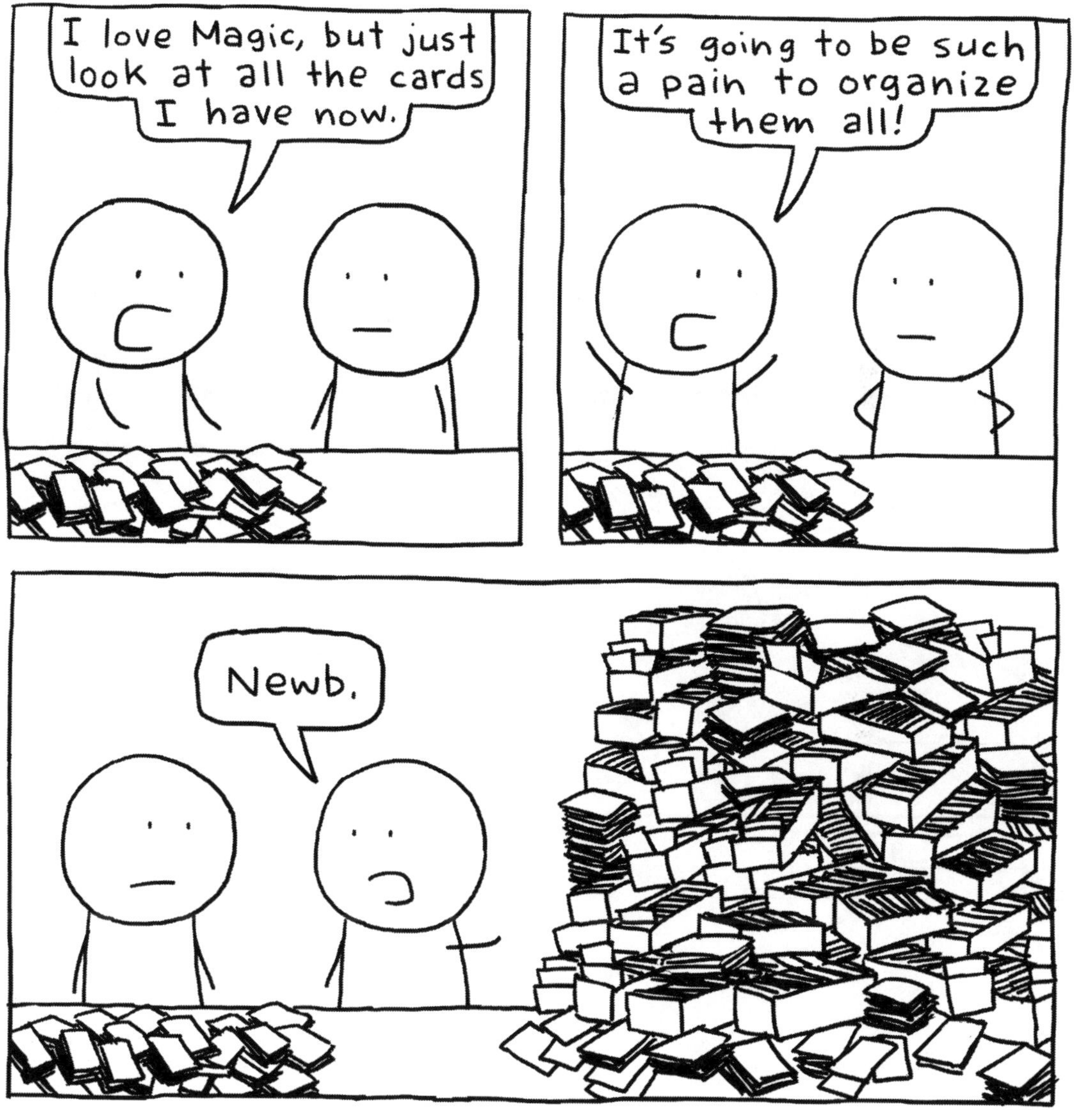
I love Magic, but just look at all the cards I have now.
It's going to be such a pain to organize them all!
Newb.

Hey baby, I love your curves!
I mean seriously, the mana cost distributions in your decks are perfect!

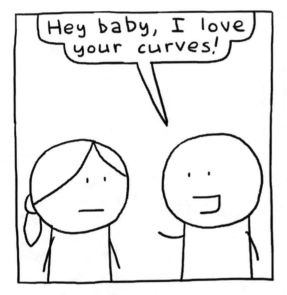

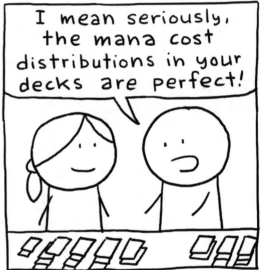

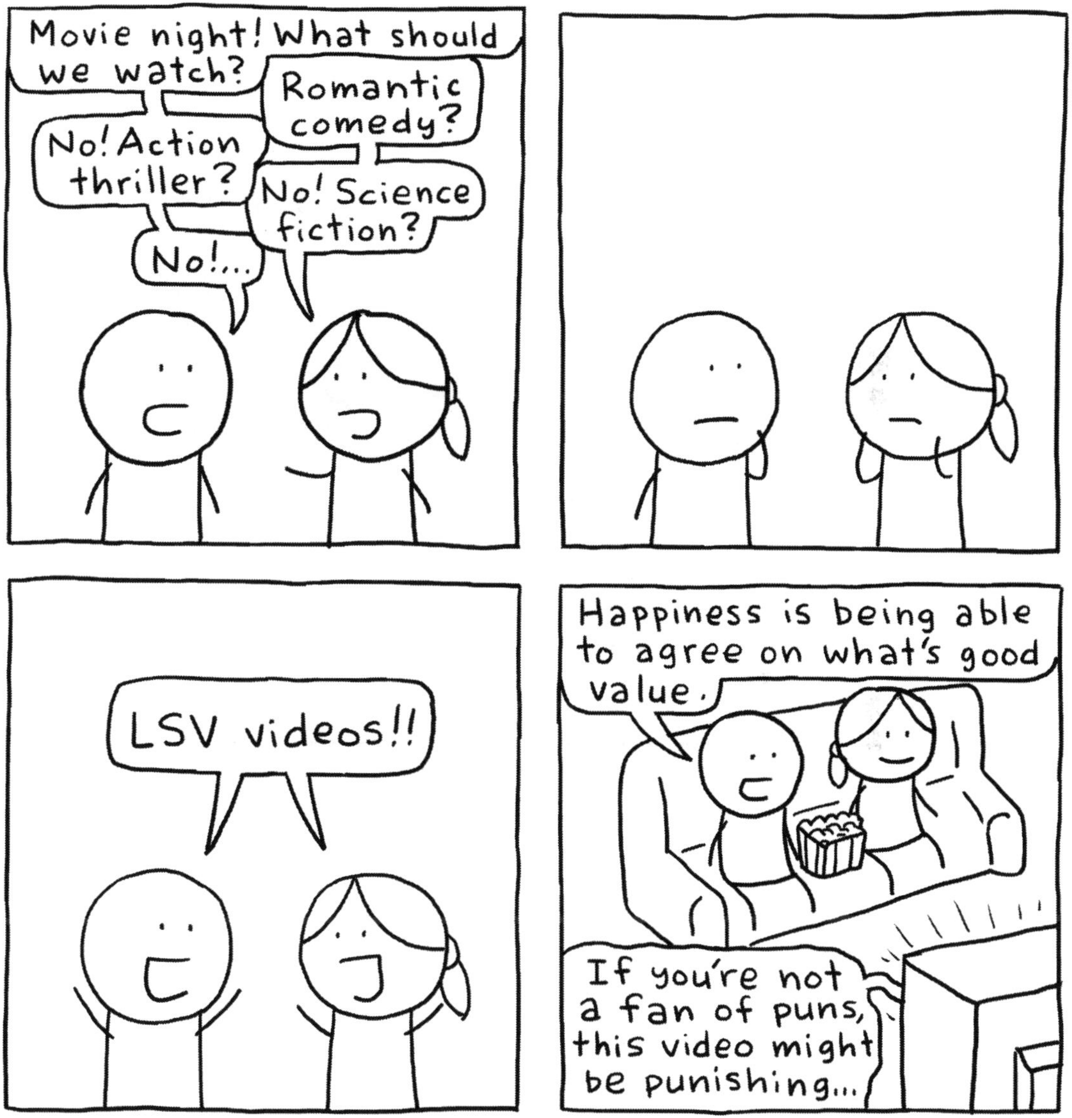
Movie night! What should we watch?
Romantic comedy?
No! Action thriller?
No! Science fiction?
No!...
LSV videos!!
Happiness is being able to agree on what's good value.
If you're not a fan of puns, this video might be punishing...

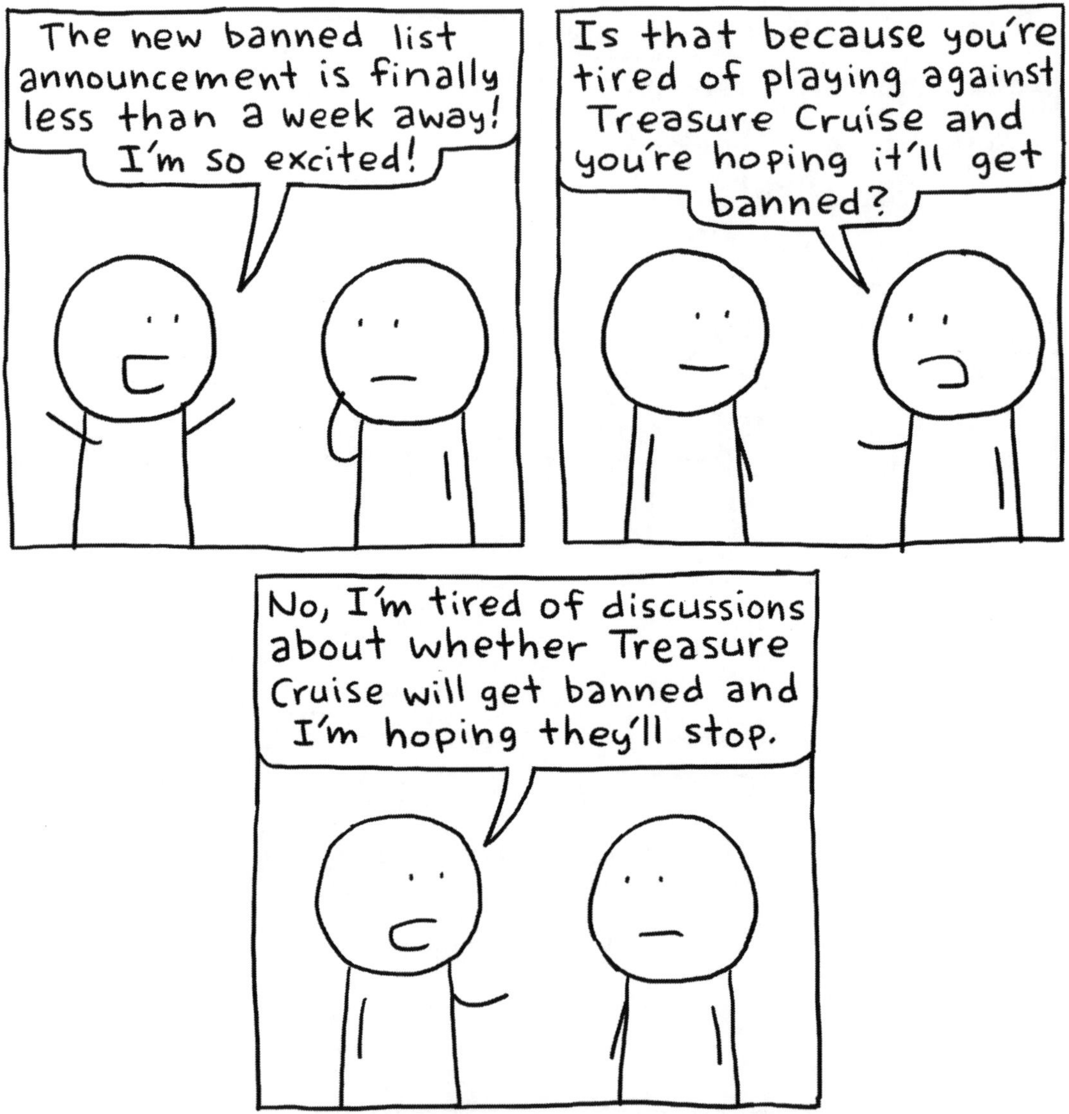
The new banned list announcement is finally less than a week away! I'm so excited!
Is that because you're tired of playing against Treasure Cruise and you're hoping it'll get banned?
No, I'm tired of discussions about whether Treasure Cruise will get banned and I'm hoping they'll stop.

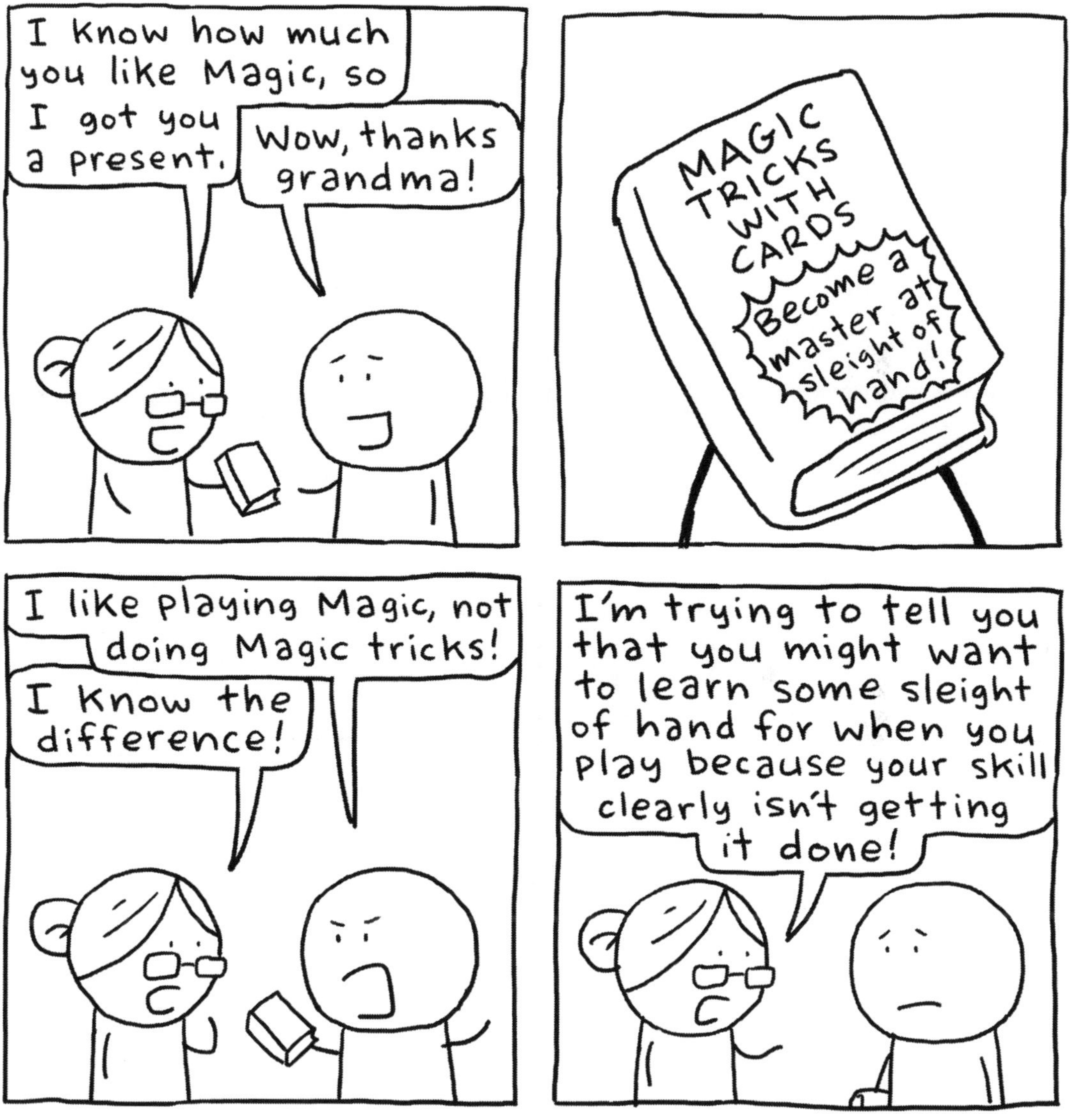
I know how much you like Magic, so I got you a present.
Wow, thanks grandma!
MAGIC TRICKS WITH CARDS
Become a master at sleight of hand!
I like playing Magic, not doing Magic tricks!
I know the difference!
I'm trying to tell you that you might want to learn some sleight of hand for when you play because your skill clearly isn't getting it done!

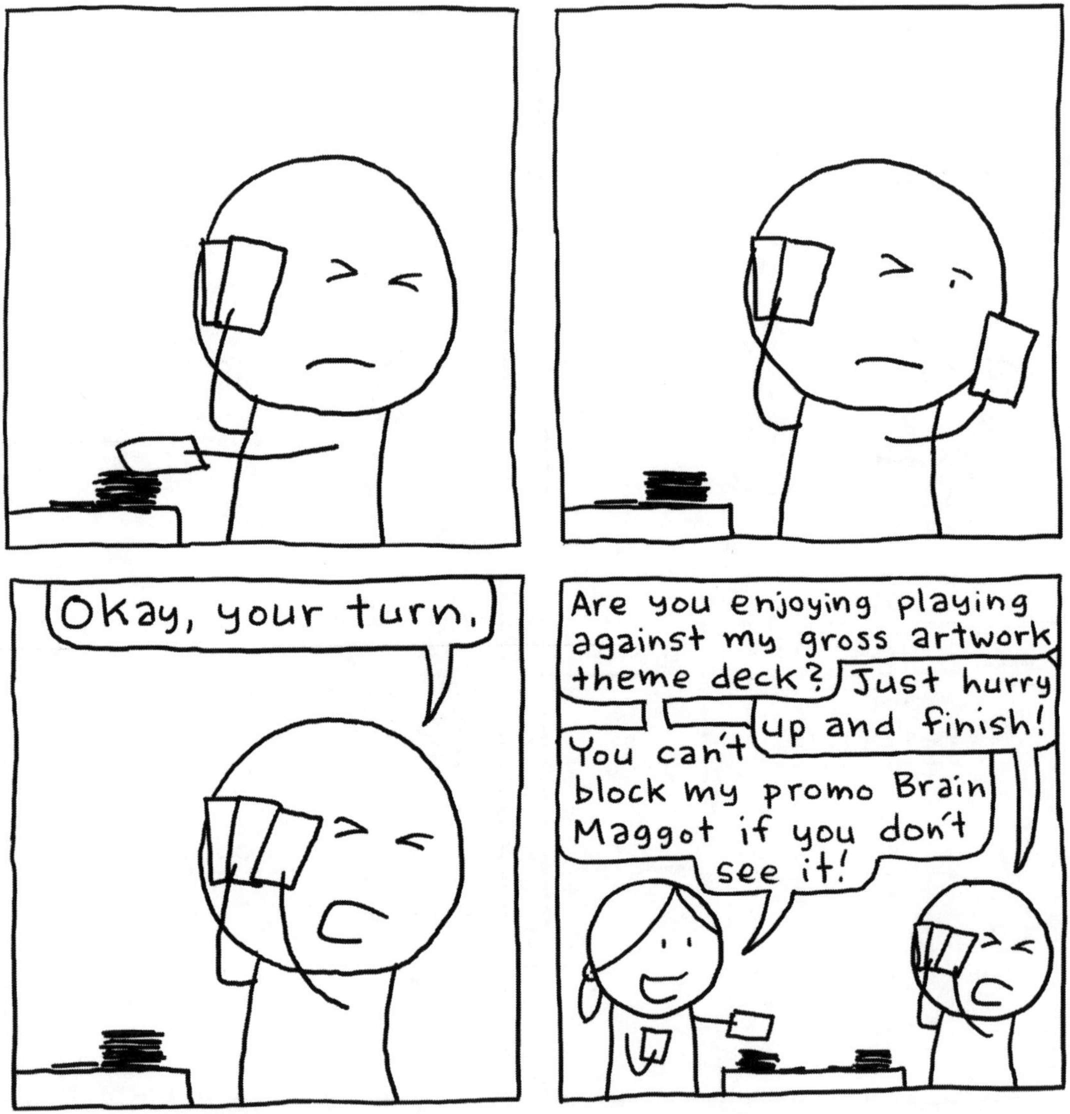
Okay, your turn.
Are you enjoying playing against my gross artwork theme deck?
Just hurry up and finish!
You can't block my promo Brain Maggot if you don't see it!

People say Magic is like drugs, but at least you can sell Magic cards after you use them.
Have you ever sold your Magic cards?
Hell no! I love them all too much!

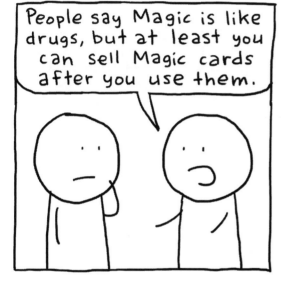

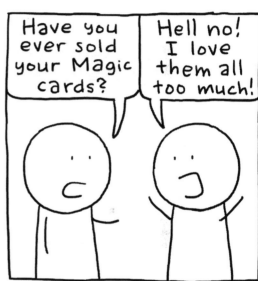

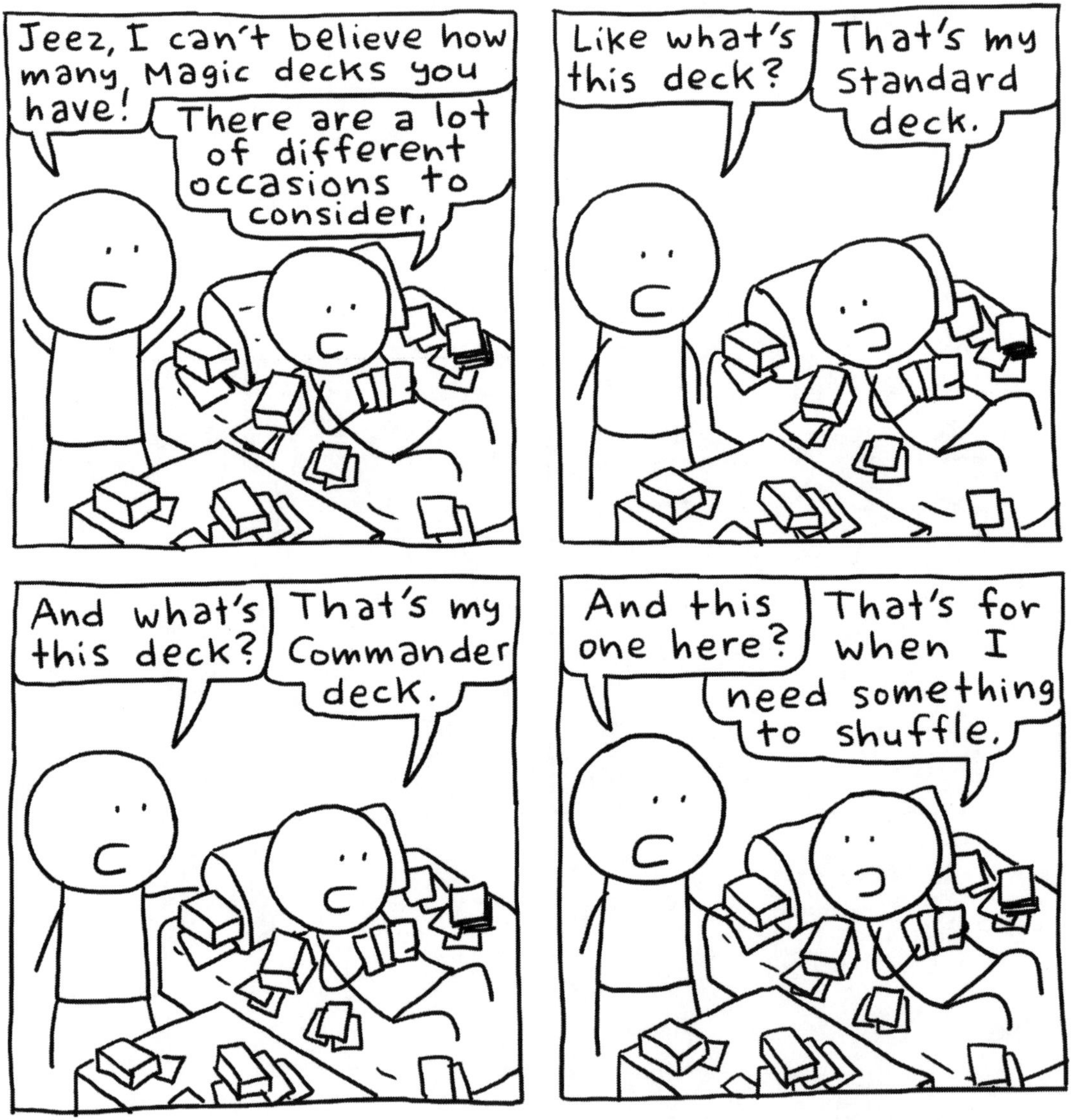
Jeez, I can't believe how many Magic decks you have!
There are a lot of different occasions to consider.
Like what's this deck?
That's my Standard deck.
And what's this deck?
That's my Commander deck.
And this one here?
That's for when I need something to shuffle.

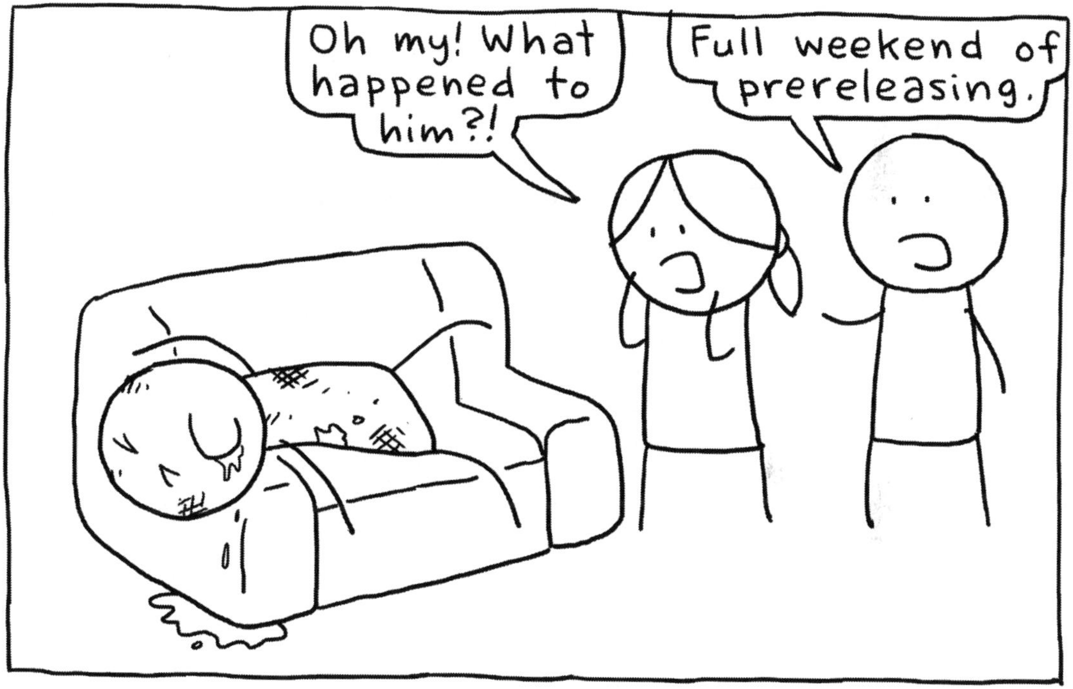
Oh my! What happened to him?!
Full weekend of prereleasing.

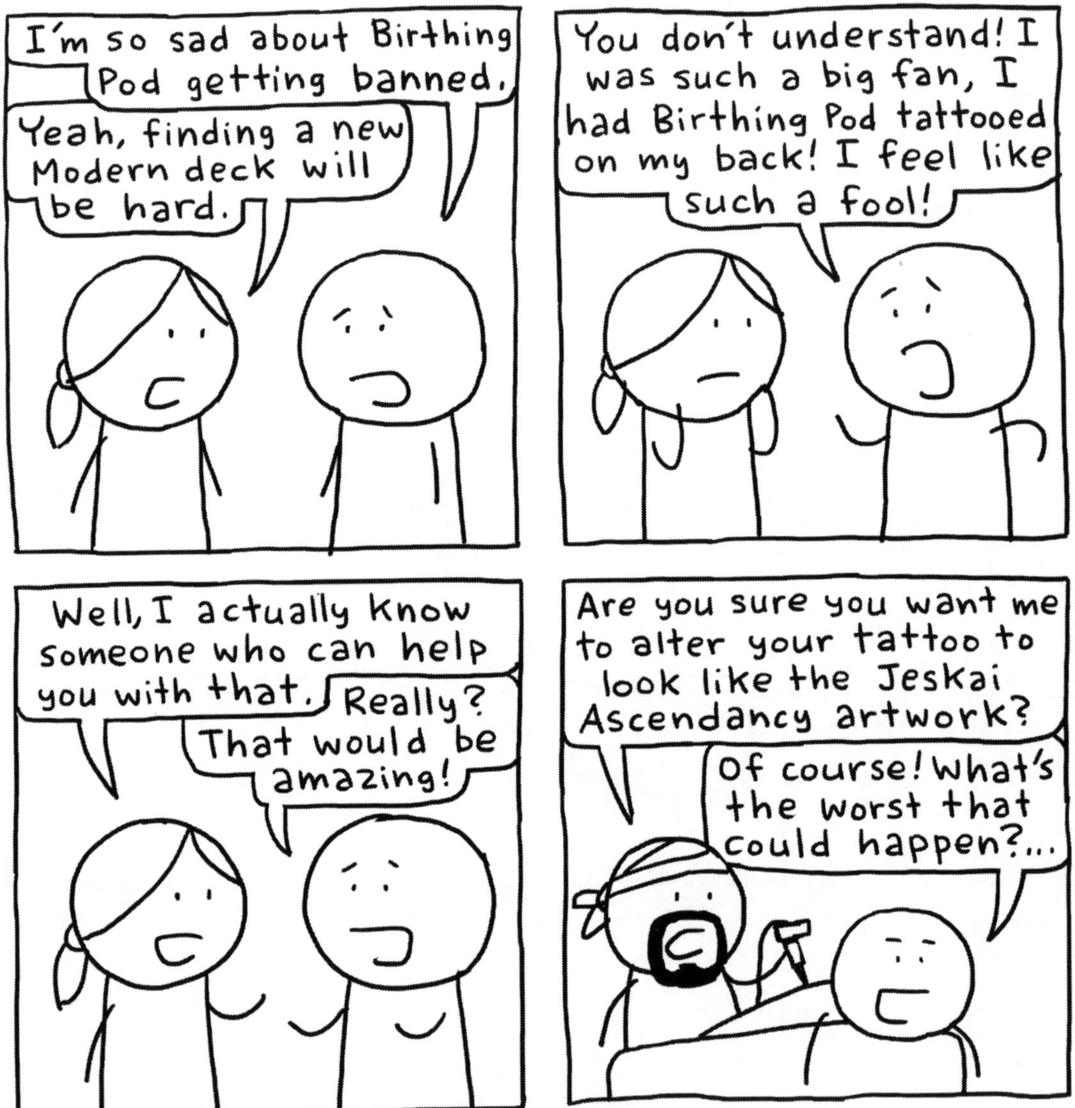
I'm so sad about Birthing Pod getting banned.
Yeah, finding a new Modern deck will be hard.
You don't understand! I was such a big fan, I had Birthing Pod tattooed on my back! I feel like such a fool!
Well, I actually know someone who can help you with that.
Really? That would be amazing!
Are you sure you want me to alter your tattoo to look like the Jeskai Ascendancy artwork?
Of course! What's the worst that could happen?...

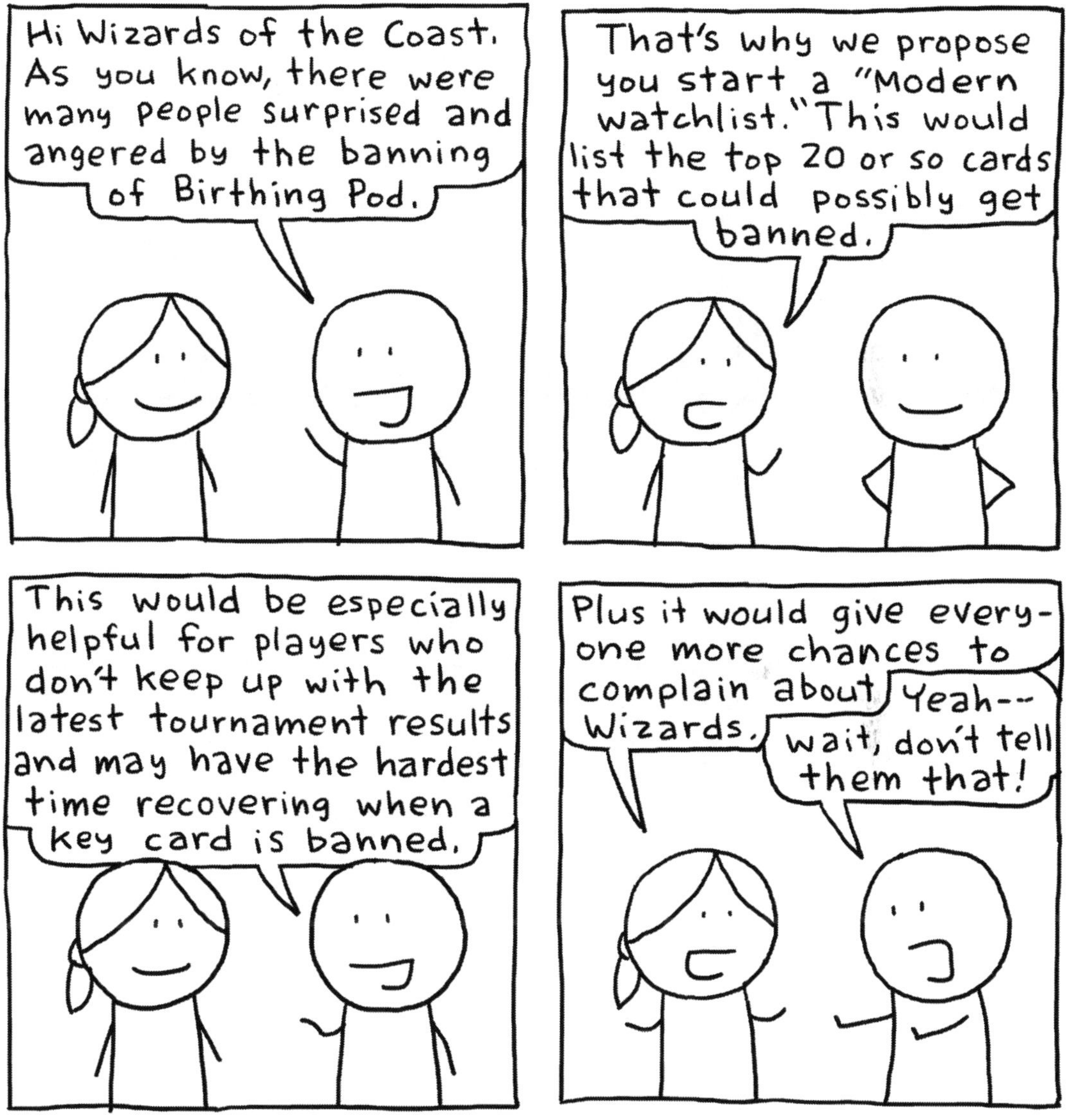
Hi Wizards of the Coast. As you know, there were many people surprised and angered by the banning of Birthing Pod.
That's why we propose you start a "Modern watchlist." This would list the top 20 or so cards that could possibly get banned.
This would be especially helpful for players who don't keep up with the latest tournament results and may have the hardest time recovering when a key card is banned.
Plus it would give everyone more chances to complain about Wizards.
Yeah-- wait, don't tell them that!

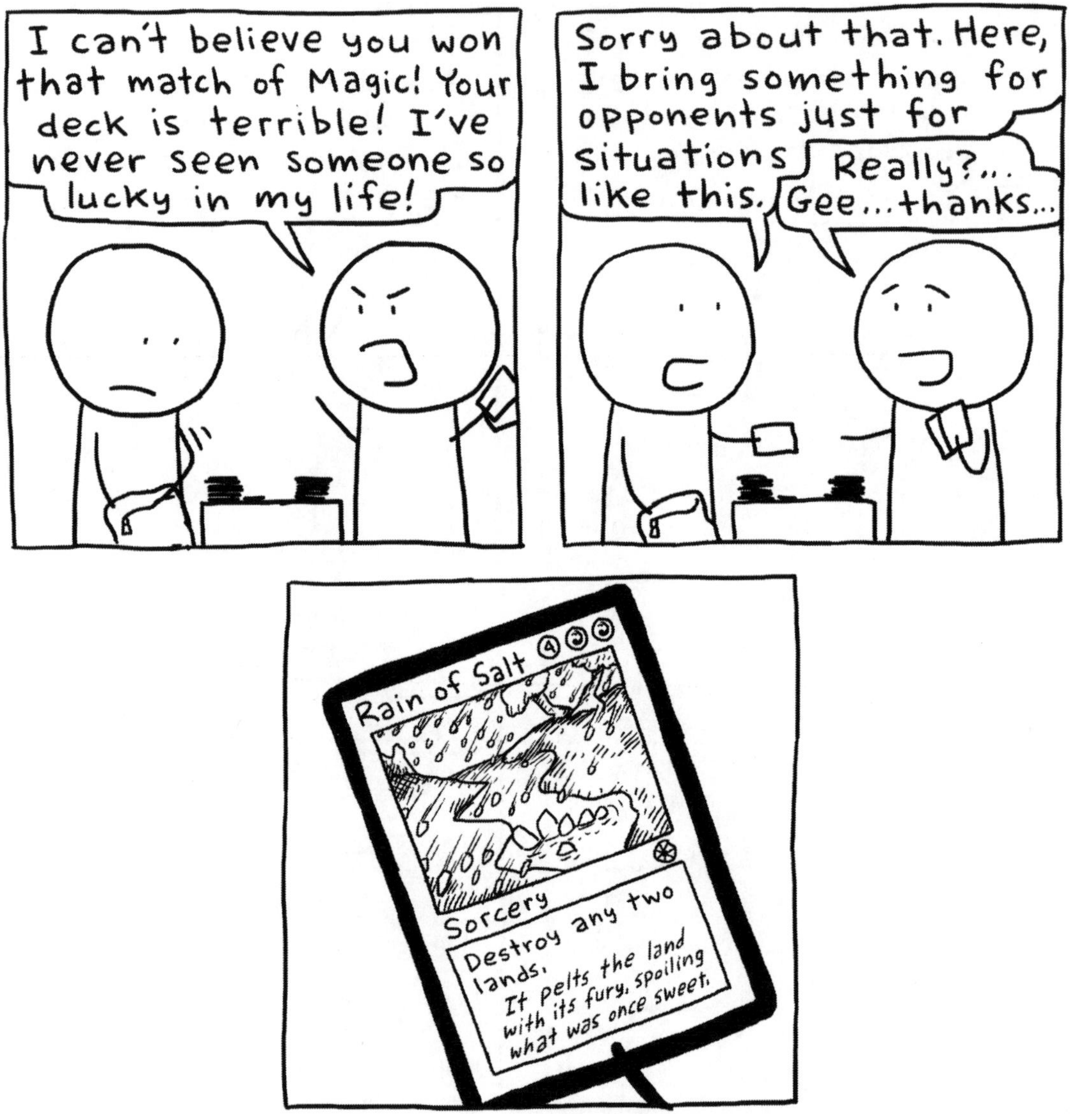
I can't believe you won that match of Magic! Your deck is terrible! I've never seen someone so lucky in my life!
Sorry about that. Here, I bring something for opponents just for situations like this.
Really?... Gee...thanks...
Rain of Salt
Sorcery
Destroy any two lands.
It pelts the land with its fury, spoiling what was once sweet.

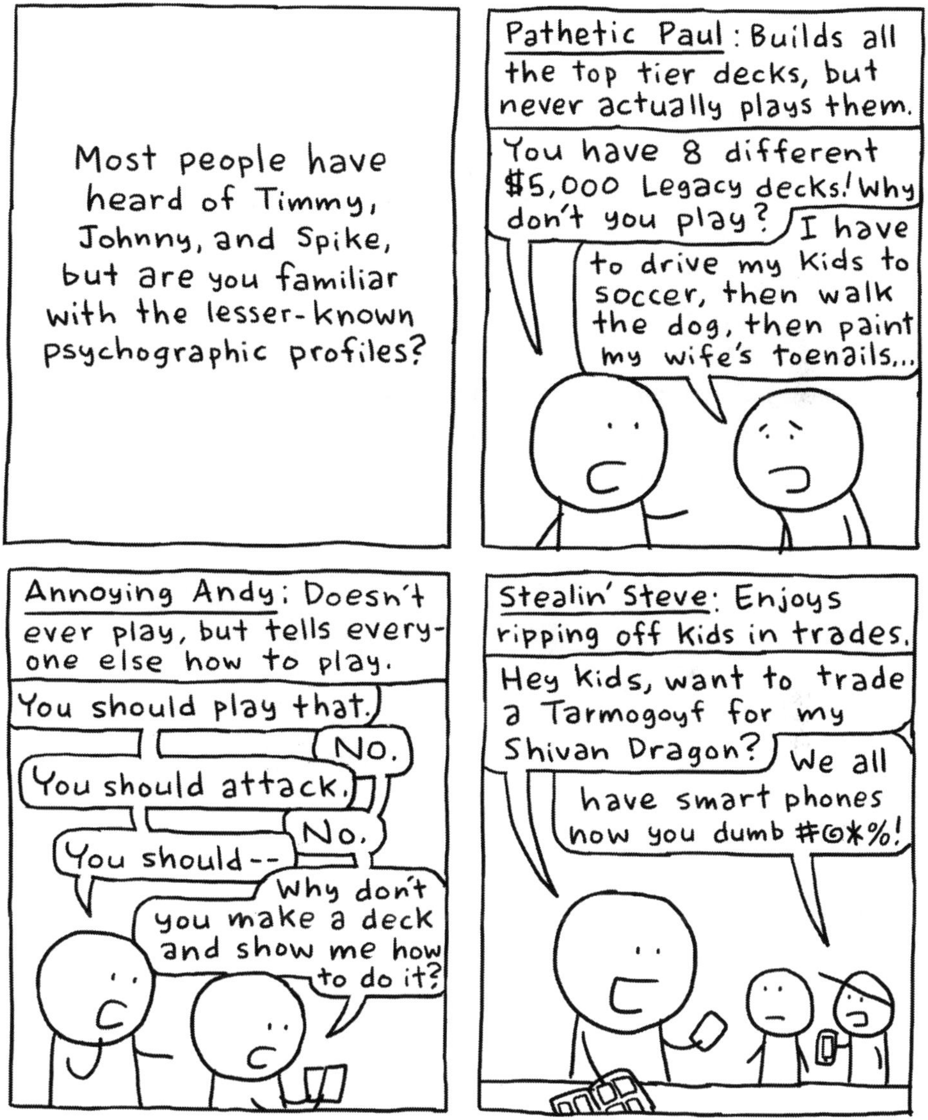

Most people have heard of Timmy, Johnny, and Spike, but are you familiar with the lesser-known psychographic profiles?
Pathetic Paul: Builds all the top tier decks, but never actually plays them.
You have 8 different $5,000 Legacy decks! Why don't you play?
I have to drive my kids to soccer, then walk the dog, then paint my wife's toenails...
Annoying Andy: Doesn't ever play, but tells every-one else how to play.
You should play that.
No.
You should attack.
No.
You should--
Why don't you make a deck and show me how to do it?
Stealin' Steve: Enjoys ripping off kids in trades.
Hey kids, want to trade a Tarmogoyf for my Shivan Dragon?
We all have smart phones now you dumb #@*%!

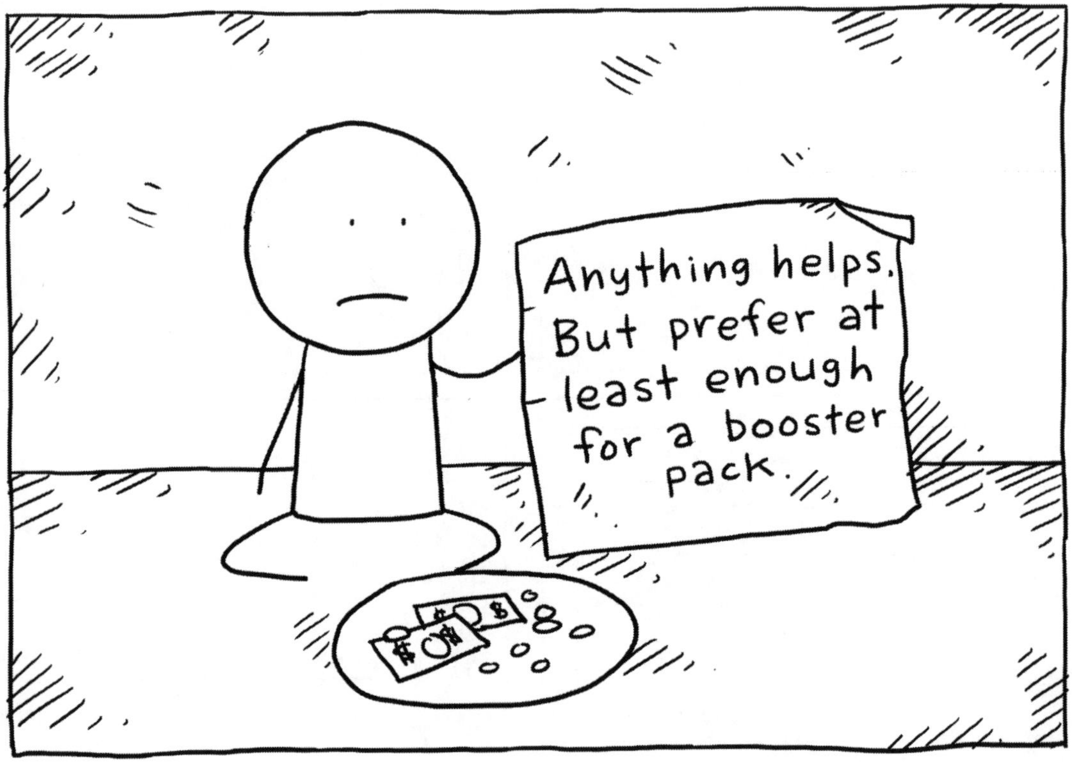
Anything helps. But prefer at least enough for a booster pack.

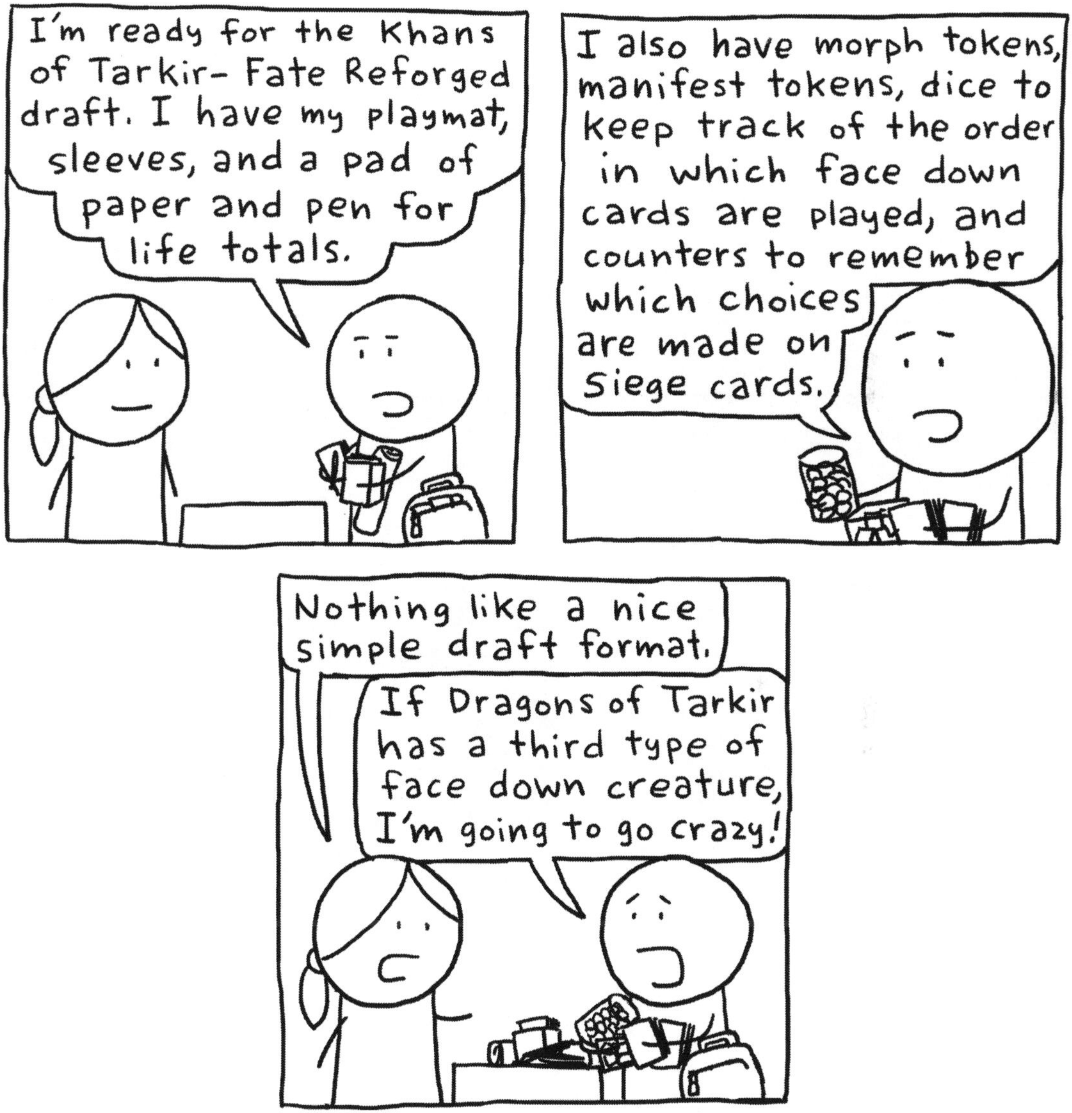
I'm ready for the Khans of Tarkir- Fate Reforged draft. I have my playmat, sleeves, and a pad of paper and pen for life totals.
I also have morph tokens, manifest tokens, dice to keep track of the order in which face down cards are played, and counters to remember which choices are made on Siege cards.
Nothing like a nice simple draft format.
If Dragons of Tarkir has a third type of face down creature, I'm going to go crazy!

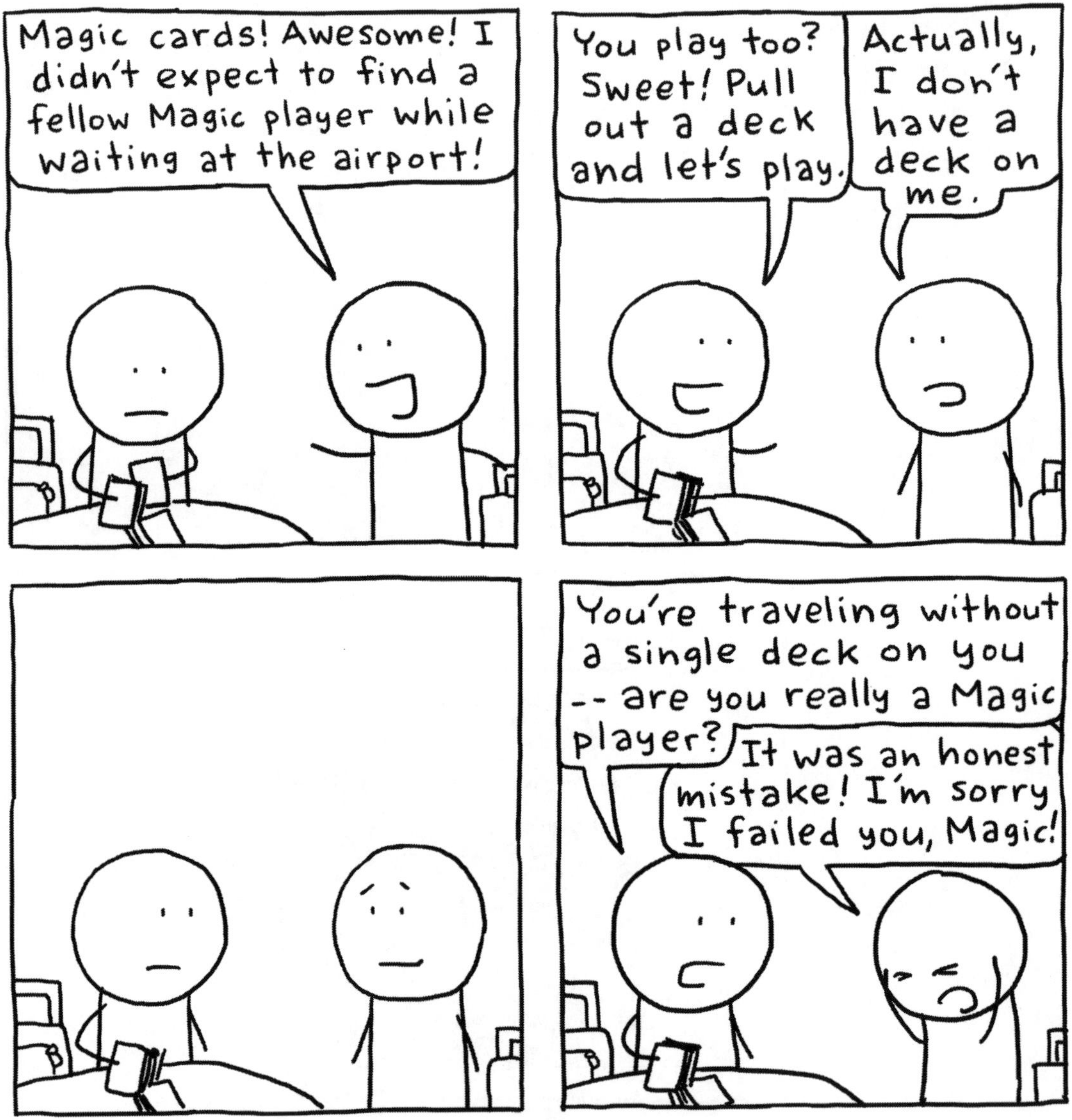
Magic cards! Awesome! I didn't expect to find a fellow Magic player while waiting at the airport!
You play too? Sweet! Pull out a deck and let's play.
Actually, I don't have a deck on me.
You're traveling without a single deck on you -- are you really a Magic player?
It was an honest mistake! I'm sorry I failed you, Magic!

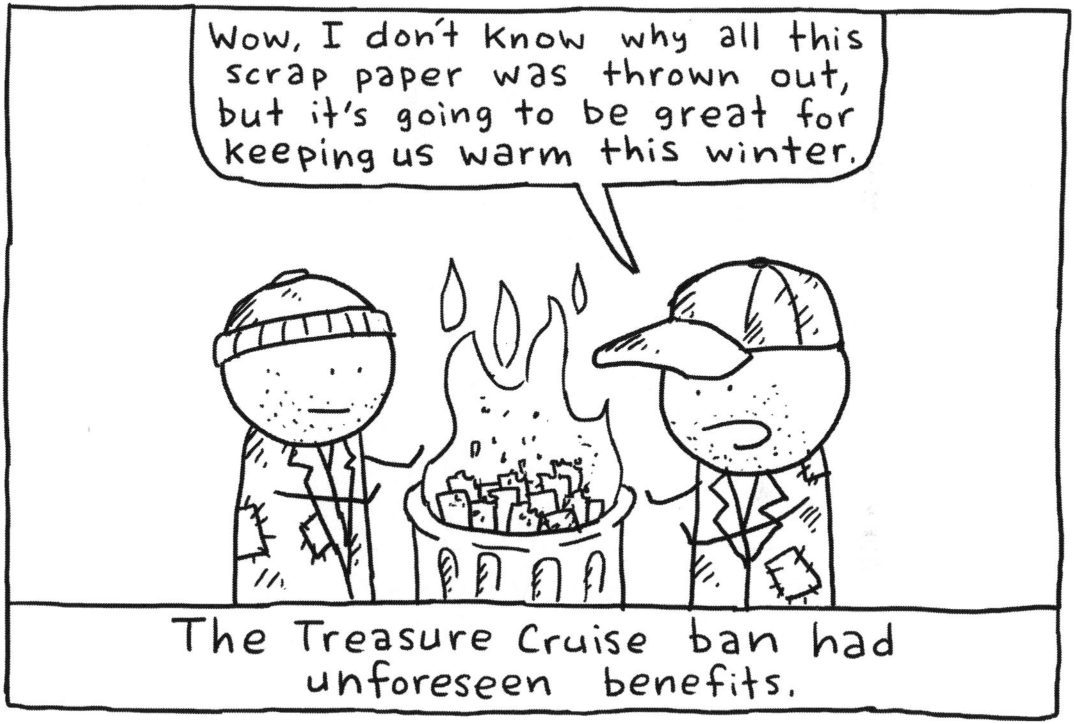
Wow, I don't know why all this scrap paper was thrown out, but it's going to be great for keeping us warm this winter.
The Treasure Cruise ban had unforeseen benefits.

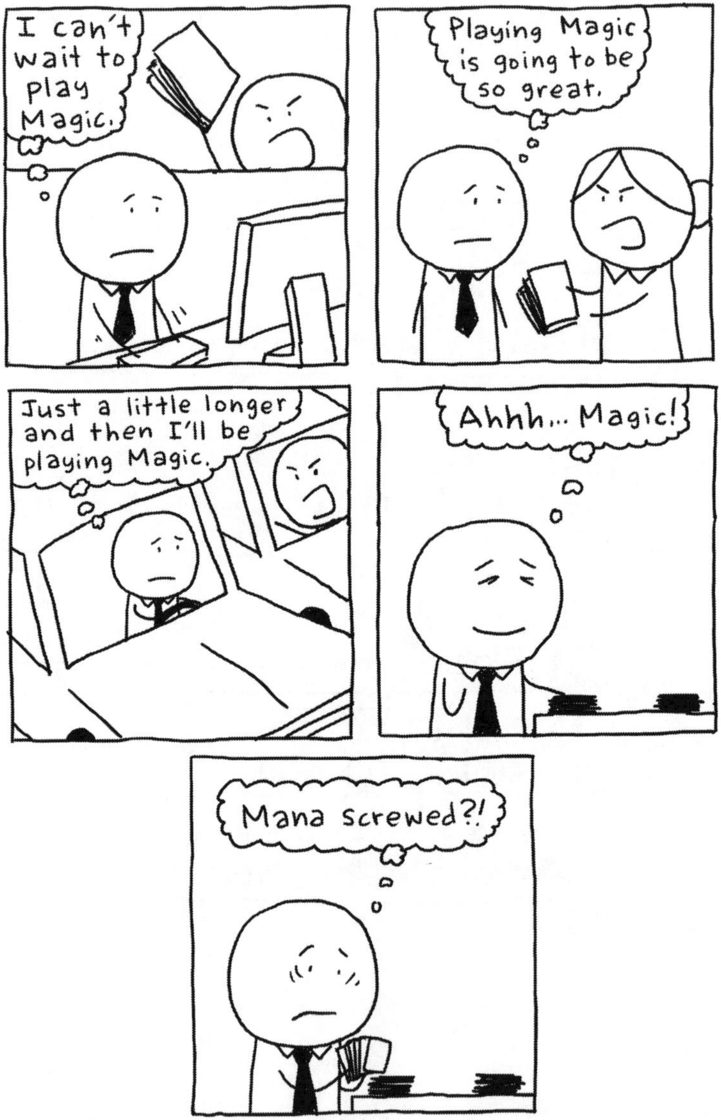
I can't wait to play Magic.
Playing Magic is going to be so great.
Just a little longer and then I'll be playing Magic.
Ahhh... Magic!
Mana screwed?!

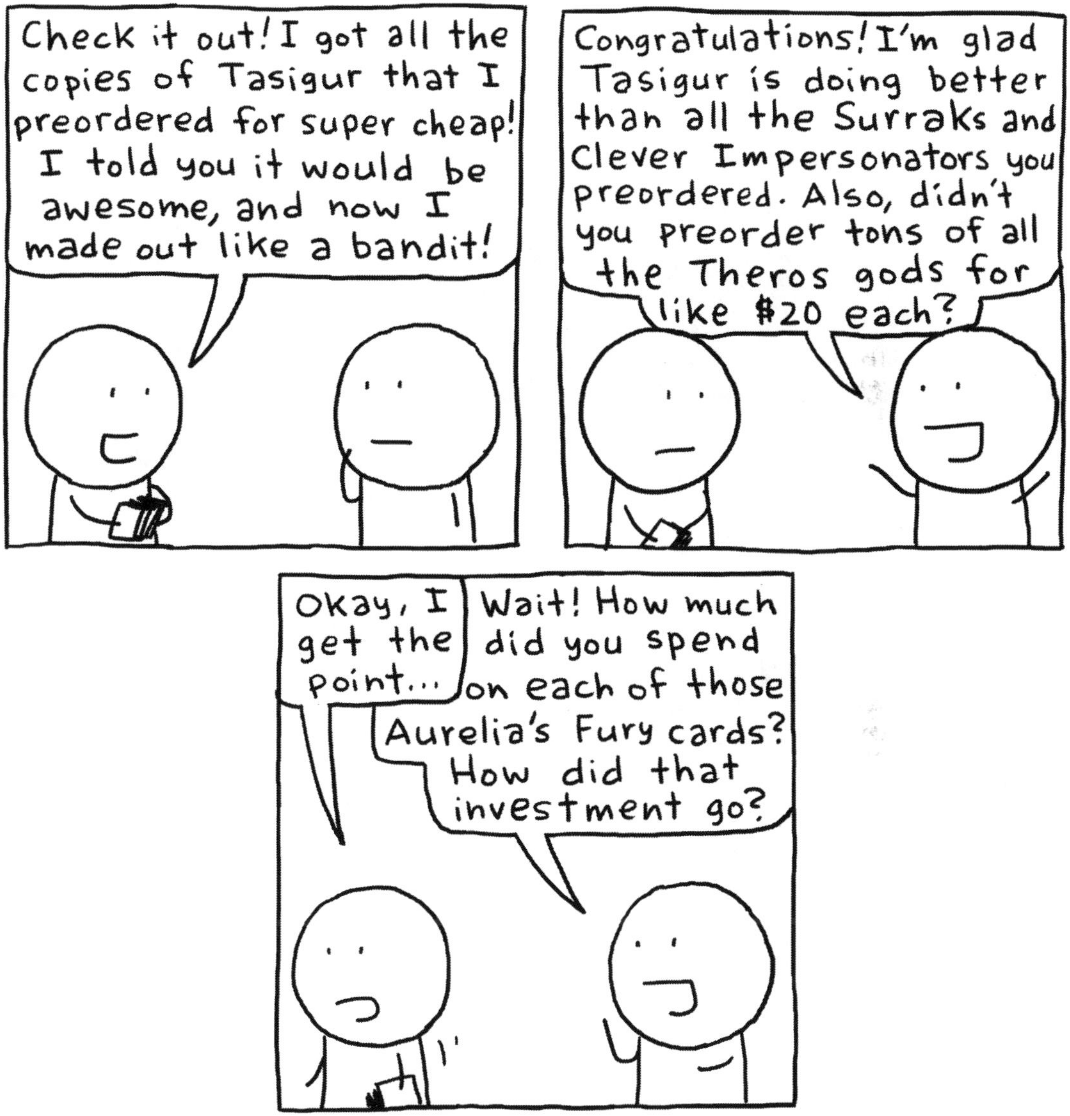
Check it out! I got all the copies of Tasigur that I preordered for super cheap! I told you it would be awesome, and now I made out like a bandit!
Congratulations! I'm glad Tasigur is doing better than all the Surraks and Clever Impersonators you preordered. Also, didn't you preorder tons of all the Theros gods for like $20 each?
Wait! How much did you spend on each of those Aurelia's Fury cards? How did that investment go?
Okay, I get the point...

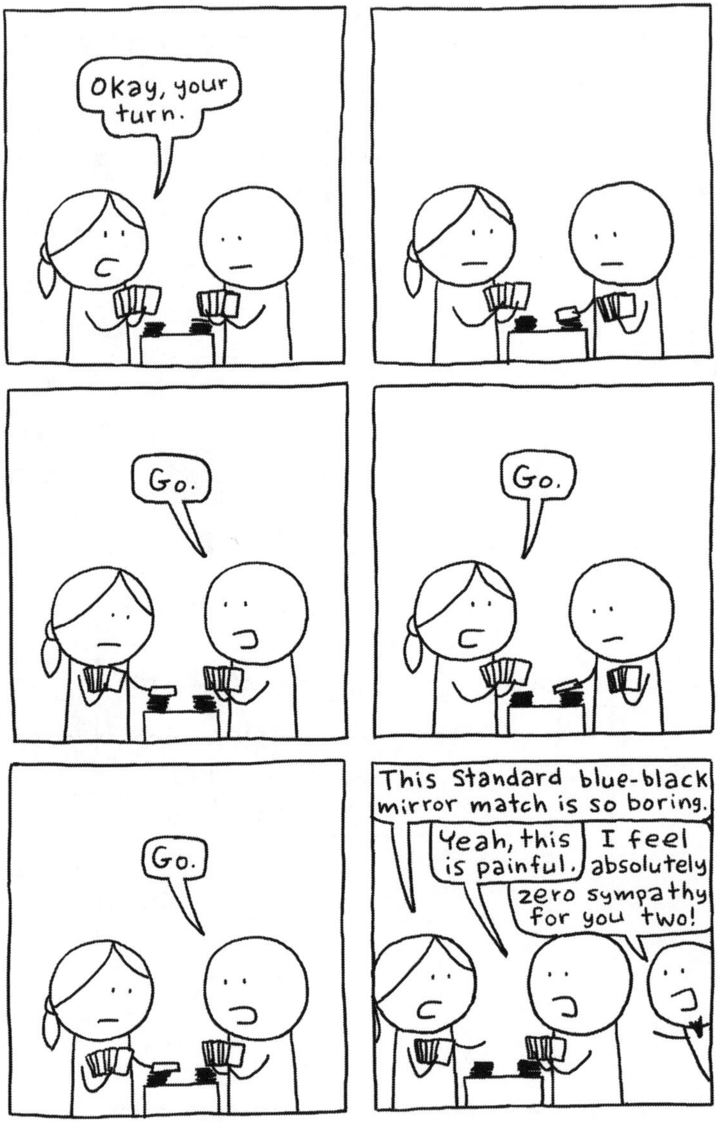

Okay, your turn.
Go.
Go.
Go.
This Standard blue-black mirror match is so boring.
Yeah, this is painful.
I feel absolutely zero sympathy for you two!

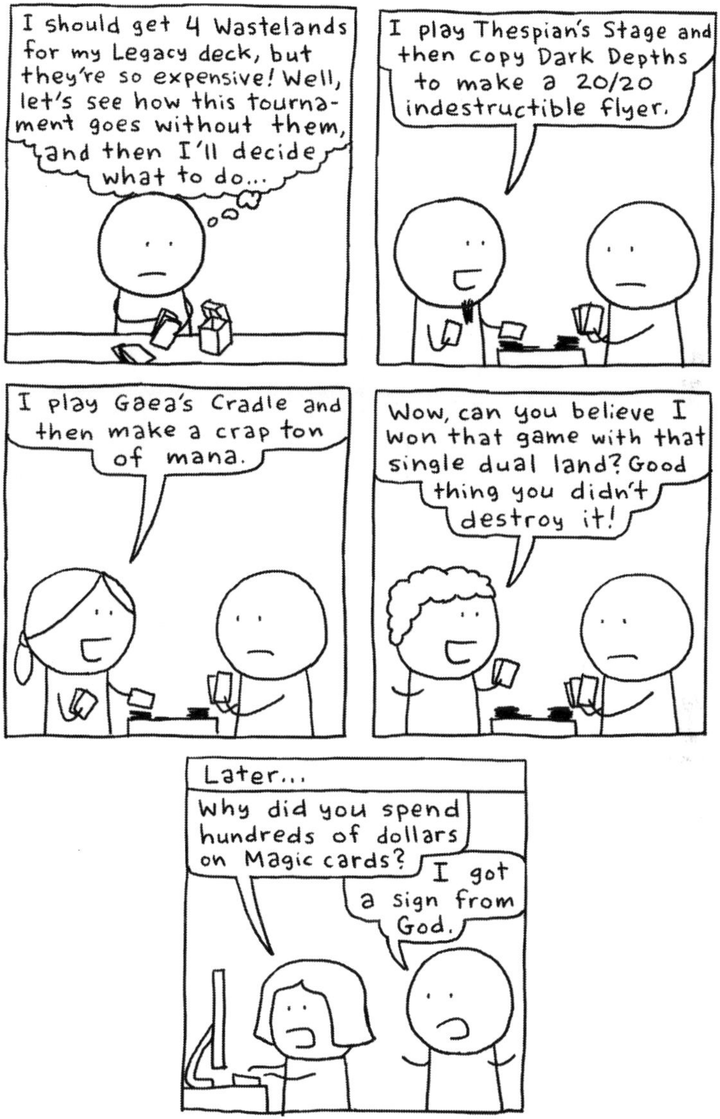
I should get 4 Wastelands for my Legacy deck, but they're so expensive! Well, let's see how this tournament goes without them, and then I'll decide what to do...
I play Thespian's Stage and then copy Dark Depths to make a 20/20 indestructible flyer.
I play Gaea's Cradle and then make a crap ton of mana.
Wow, can you believe I won that game with that single dual land? Good thing you didn't destroy it!
Later...
Why did you spend hundreds of dollars on Magic cards?
I got a sign from God.

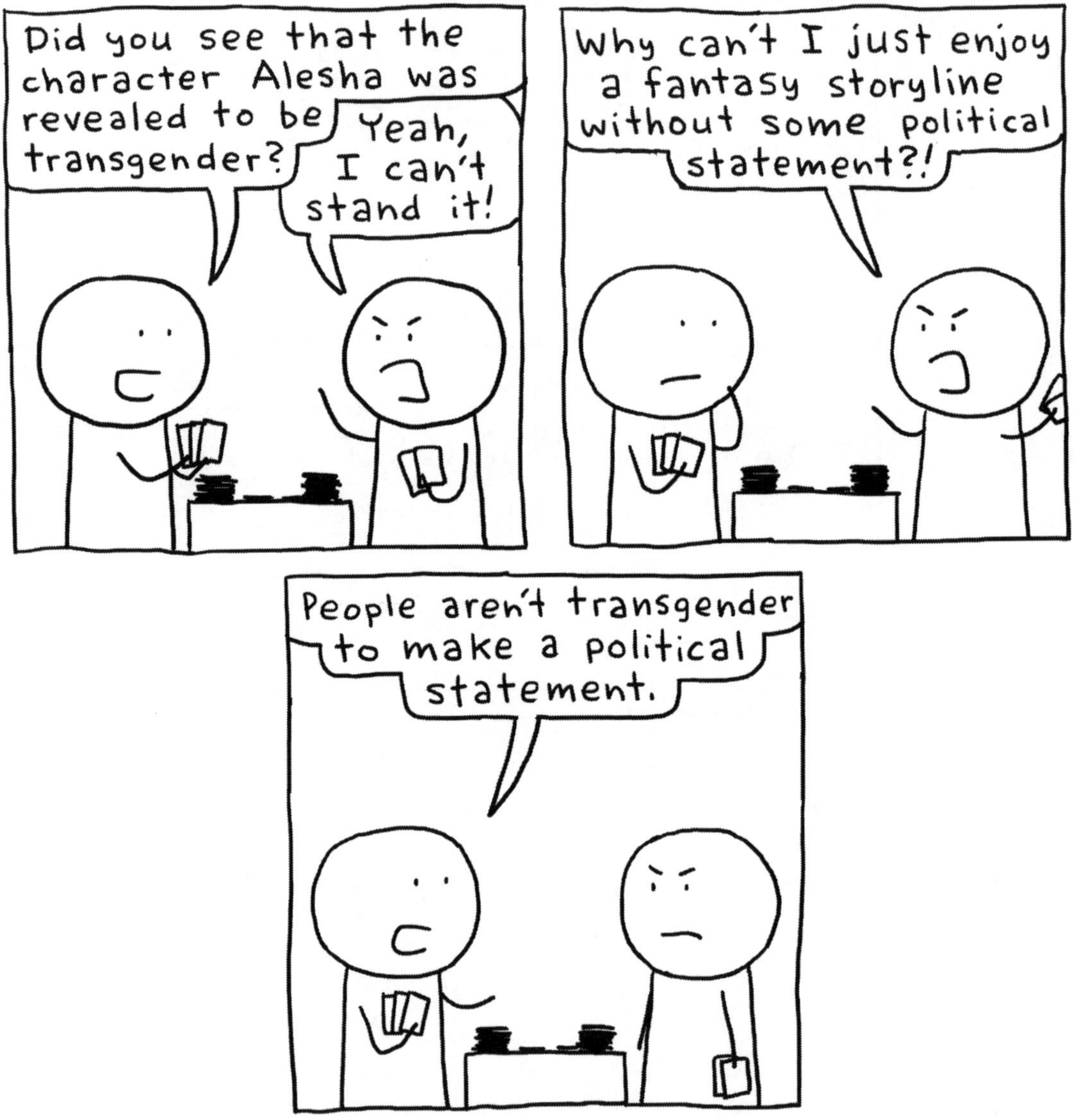
Did you see that the character Alesha was revealed to be transgender?
Yeah, I can't stand it!
Why can't I just enjoy a fantasy storyline without some political statement?!
People aren't transgender to make a political statement.

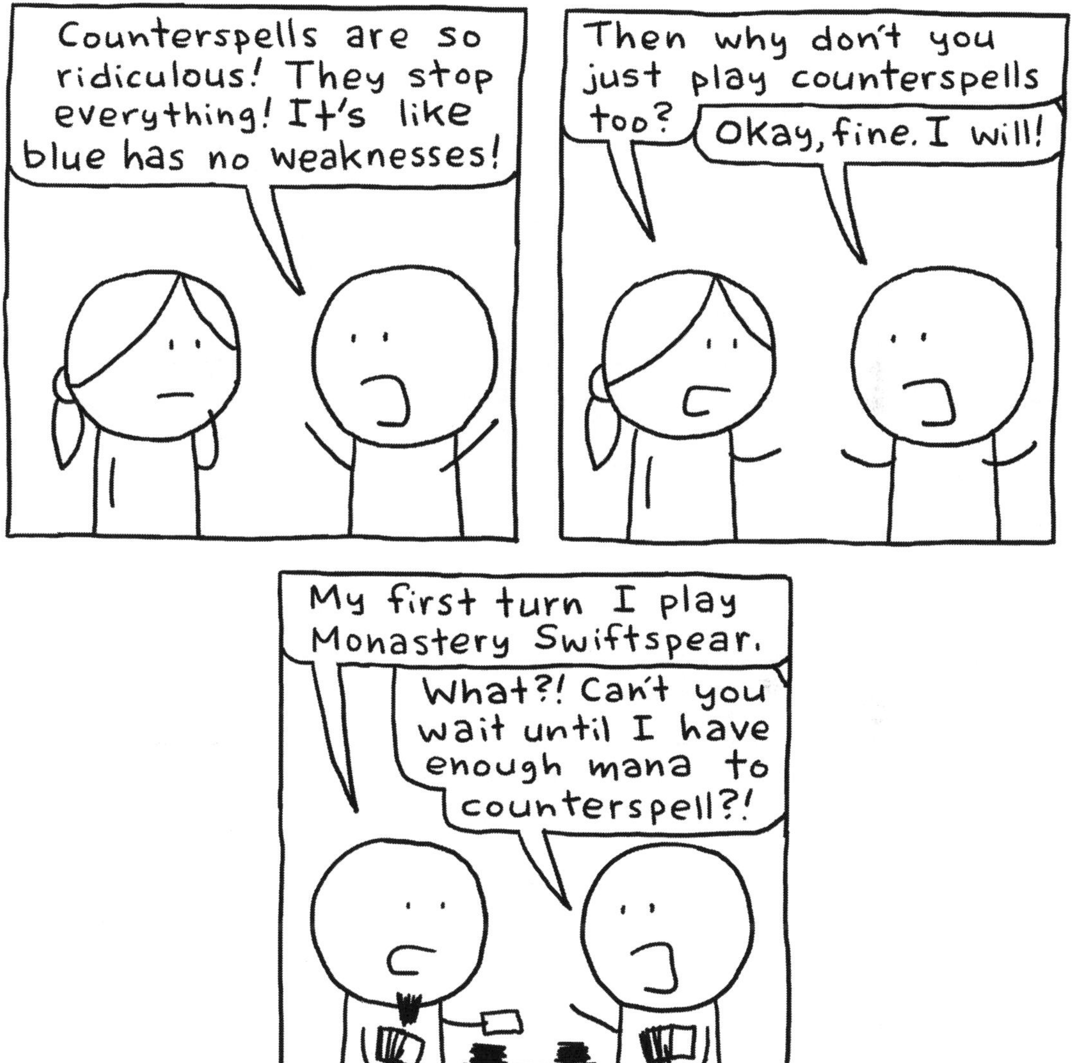
Counterspells are so ridiculous! They stop everything! It's like blue has no weaknesses!
Then why don't you just play counterspells too?
Okay, fine. I will!
My first turn I play Monastery Swiftspear.
What?! Can't you wait until I have enough mana to counterspell?!

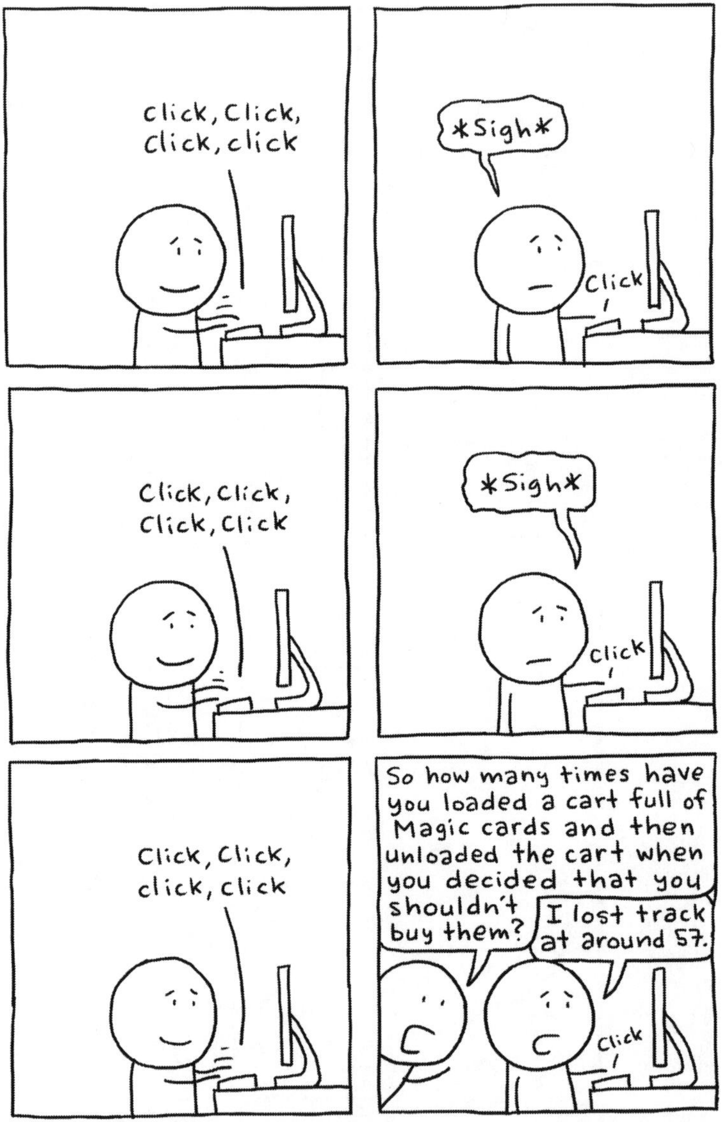
Click, Click,
Click, click
Sigh
Click
Click, Click,
Click, Click
Sigh
Click
Click, Click,
click, click
So how many times have you loaded a cart full of Magic cards and then unloaded the cart when you decided that you shouldn't buy them?
I lost track at around 57.
Click

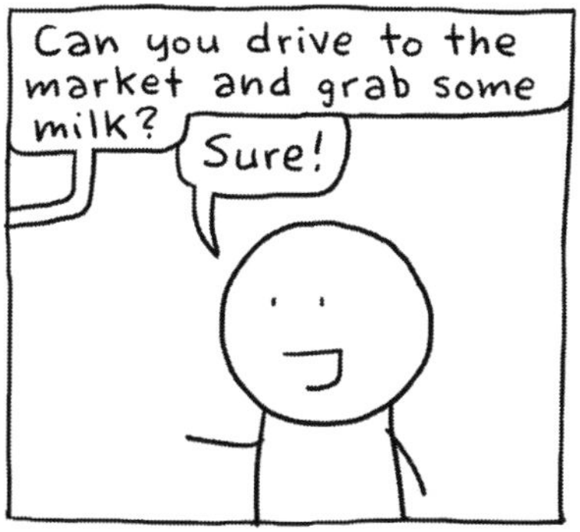
Can you drive to the market and grab some milk?
Sure!

How long will it take a Magic player to run an errand? Use this handy formula to find out!

$$\text{Total time} = 2 \times \left(\frac{D}{s} + N \times A\right) + t$$

↑ Assuming a round trip

D = Distance to destination
s = Driving speed
t = Time at destination
N = Number of Magic shops on the way
A = Average time looking at Magic cards

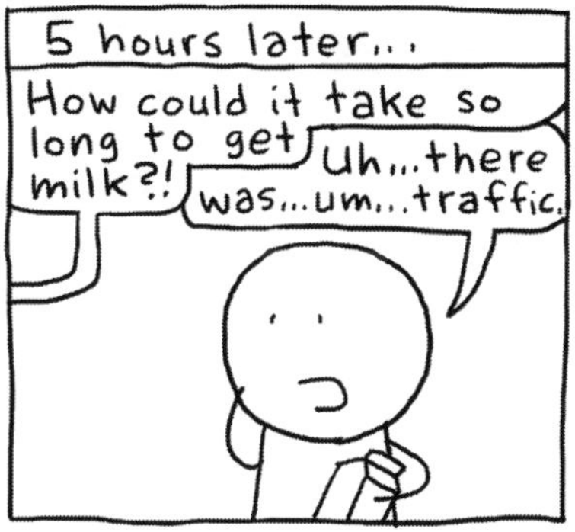
5 hours later...
How could it take so long to get milk?!
Uh...there was...um...traffic.

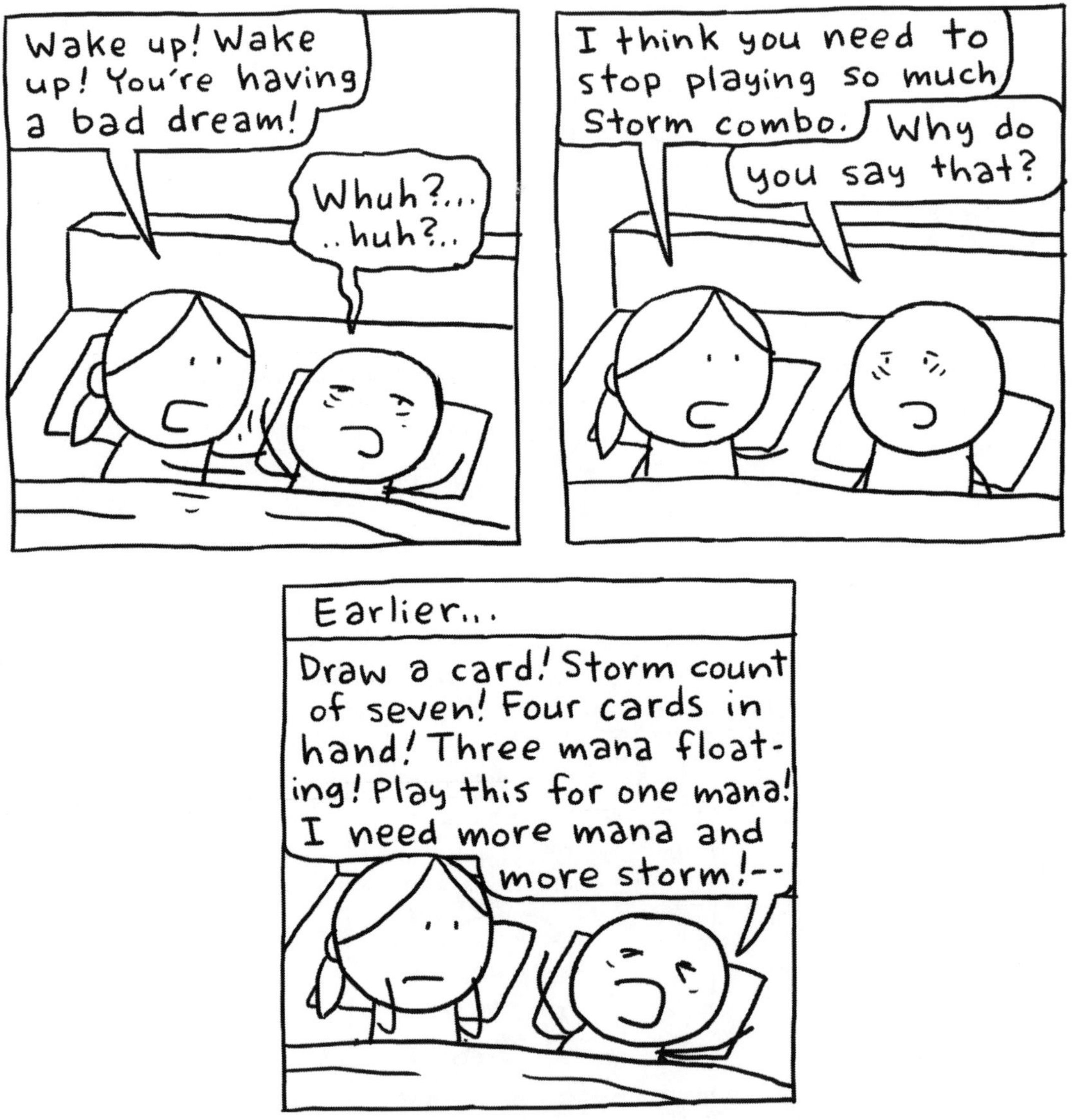
Wake up! Wake up! You're having a bad dream!
Whuh?... ..huh?..
I think you need to stop playing so much Storm combo.
Why do you say that?
Earlier...
Draw a card! Storm count of seven! Four cards in hand! Three mana floating! Play this for one mana! I need more mana and more storm!--

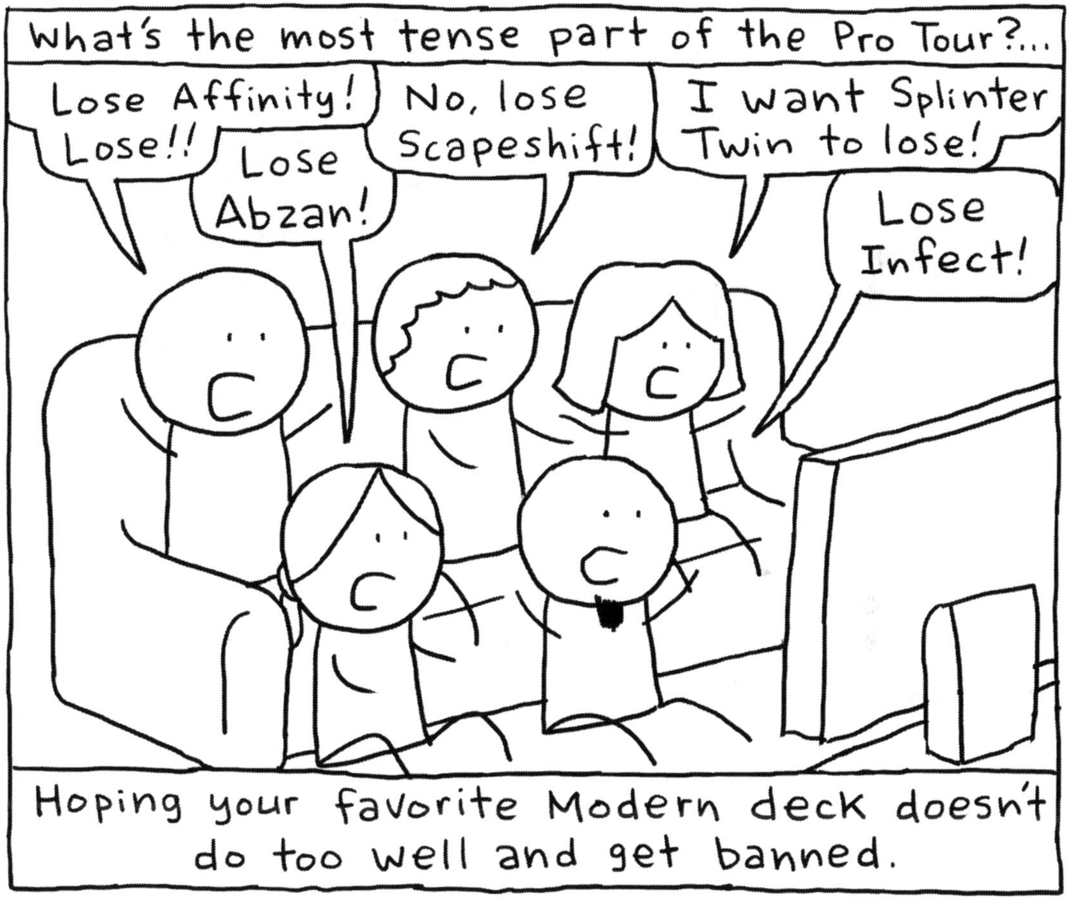

What's the most tense part of the Pro Tour?...
Lose Affinity! Lose!!
Lose Abzan!
No, lose Scapeshift!
I want Splinter Twin to lose!
Lose Infect!
Hoping your favorite Modern deck doesn't do too well and get banned.

Son, if you value your Magic collection, remember to always use protection.
Don't worry Dad, I always use card sleeves.
Sleeves?! I meant use a condom! Do you know how many Magic cards I could afford if I didn't have you?!

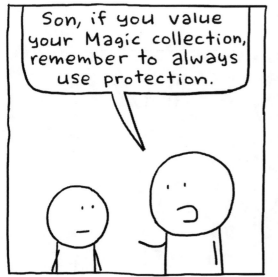

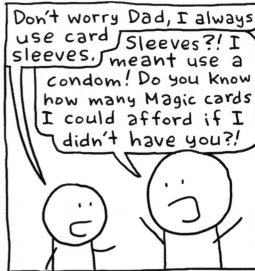

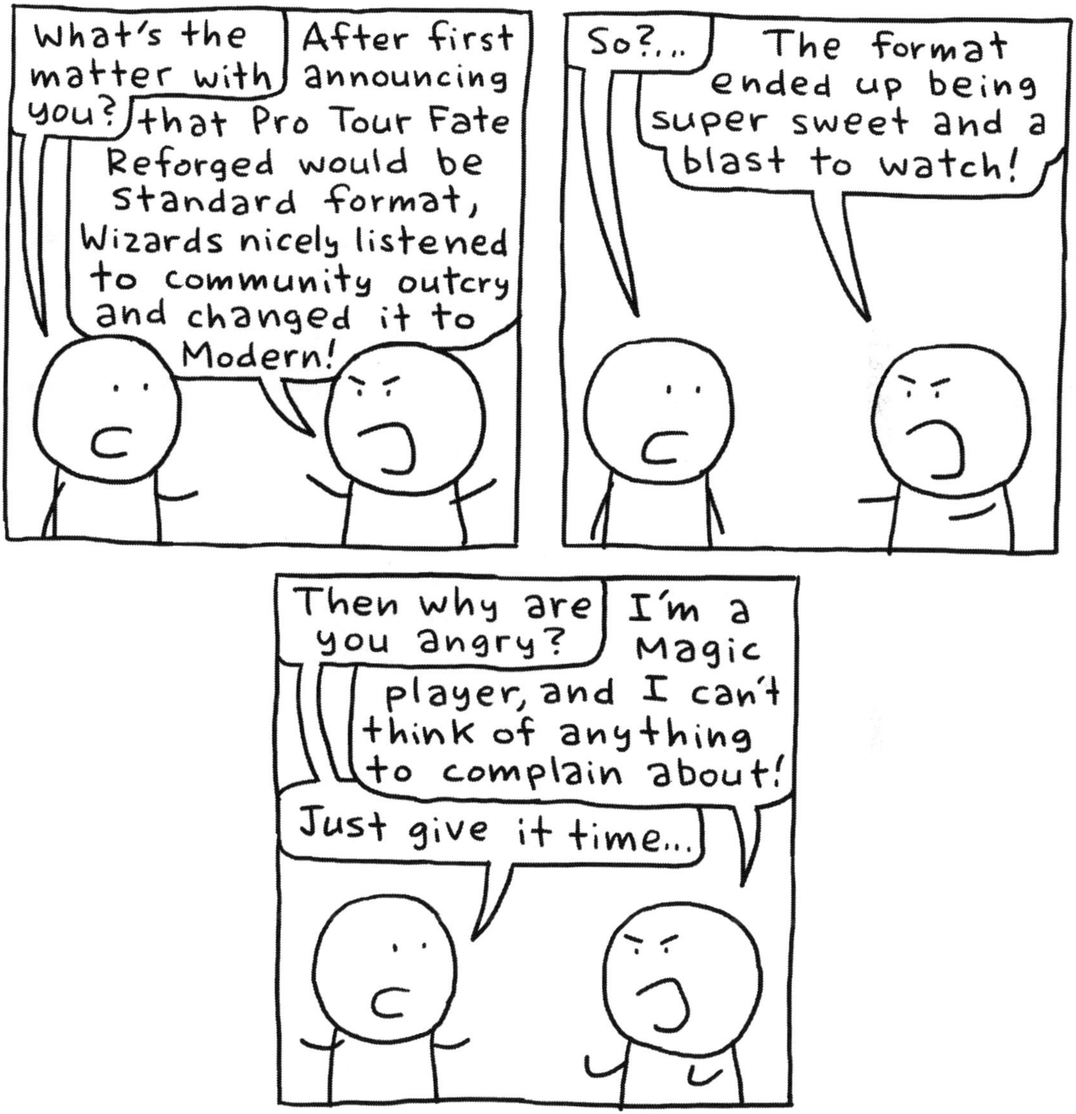
What's the matter with you?
After first announcing that Pro Tour Fate Reforged would be Standard format, Wizards nicely listened to community outcry and changed it to Modern!
So?...
The format ended up being super sweet and a blast to watch!
Then why are you angry?
I'm a Magic player, and I can't think of anything to complain about!
Just give it time...

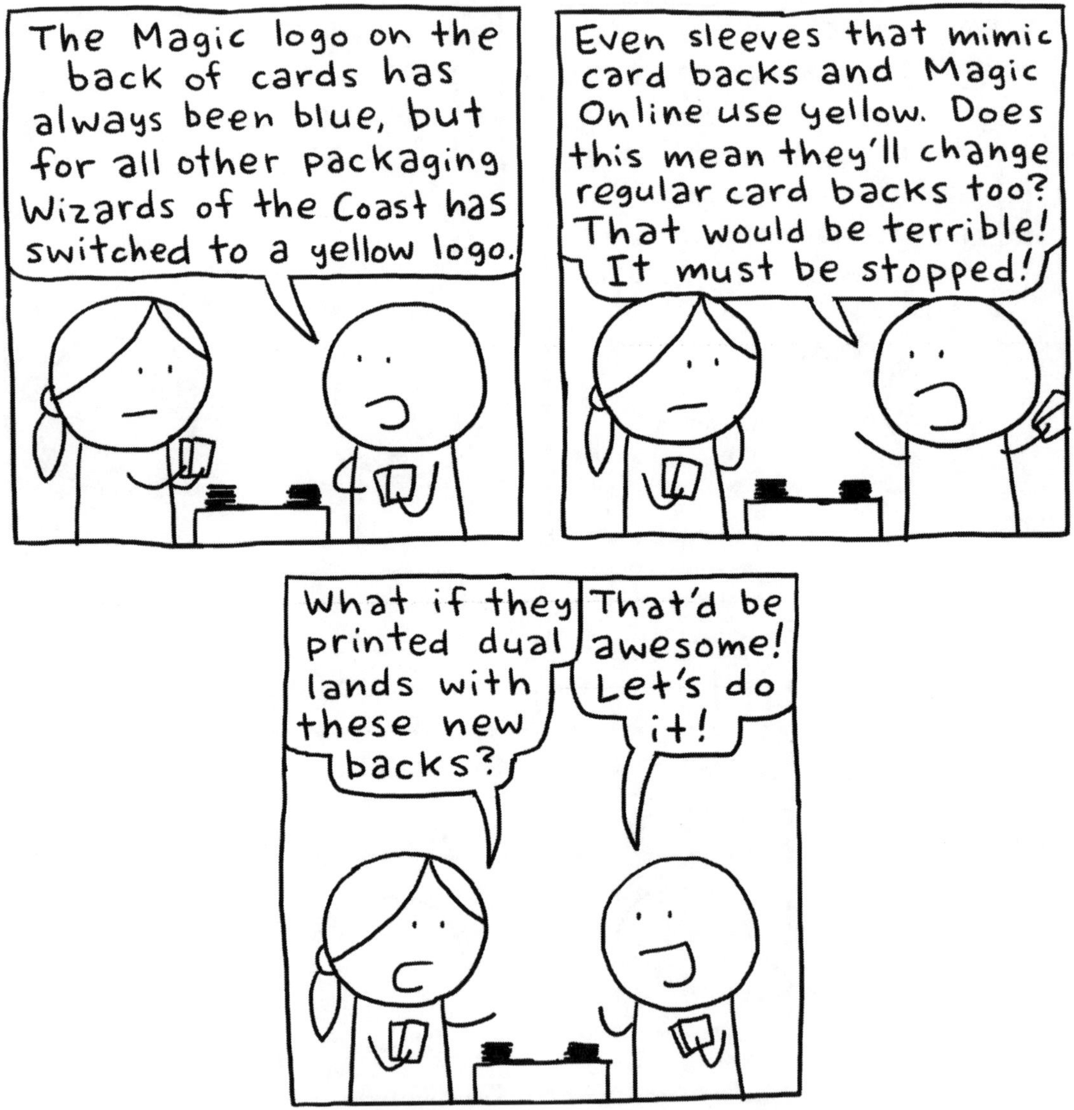
The Magic logo on the back of cards has always been blue, but for all other packaging Wizards of the Coast has switched to a yellow logo.
Even sleeves that mimic card backs and Magic Online use yellow. Does this mean they'll change regular card backs too? That would be terrible! It must be stopped!
What if they printed dual lands with these new backs?
That'd be awesome! Let's do it!

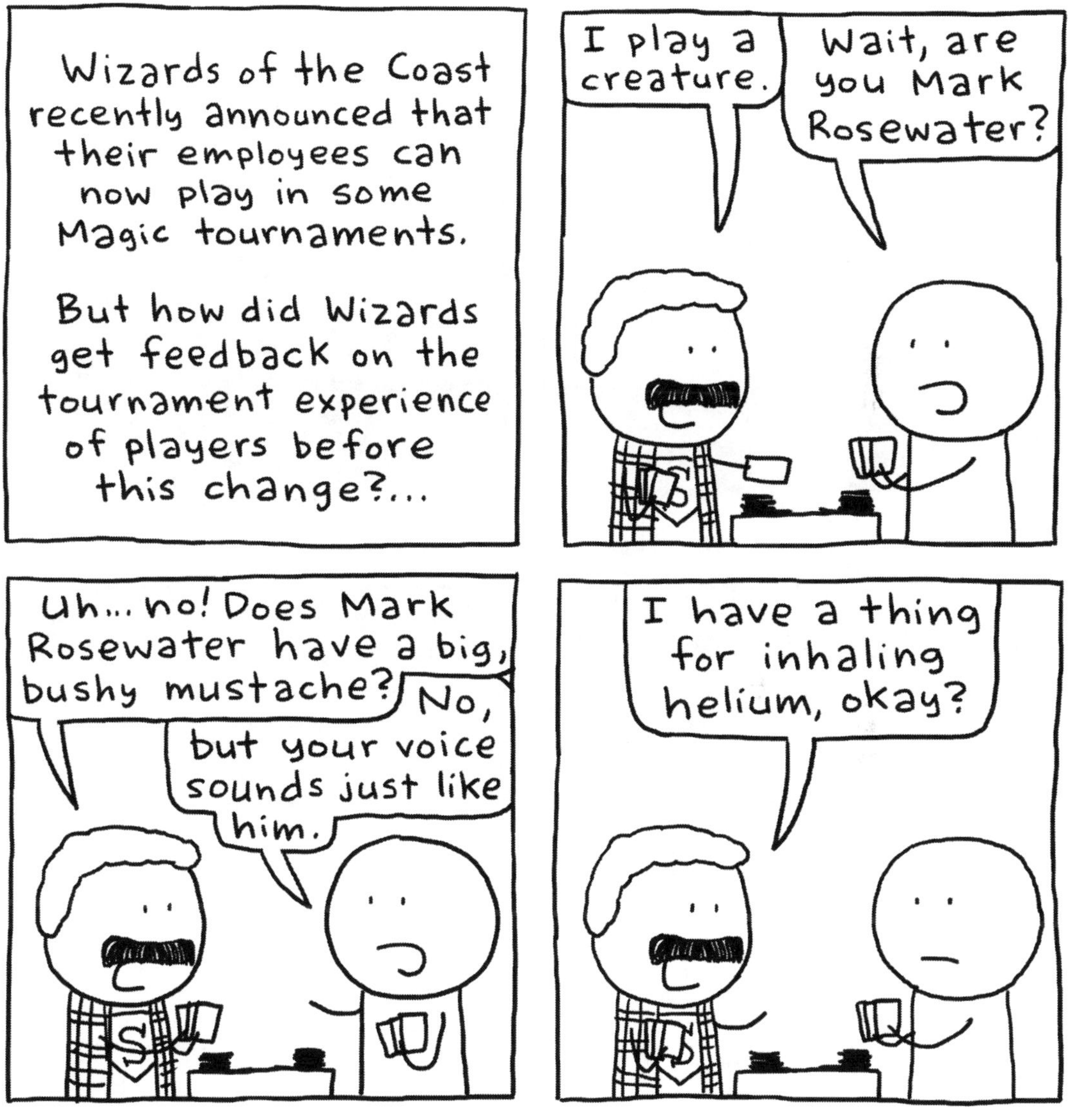
Wizards of the Coast recently announced that their employees can now play in some Magic tournaments.
But how did Wizards get feedback on the tournament experience of players before this change?...
I play a creature.
Wait, are you Mark Rosewater?
Uh... no! Does Mark Rosewater have a big, bushy mustache?
No, but your voice sounds just like him.
I have a thing for inhaling helium, okay?

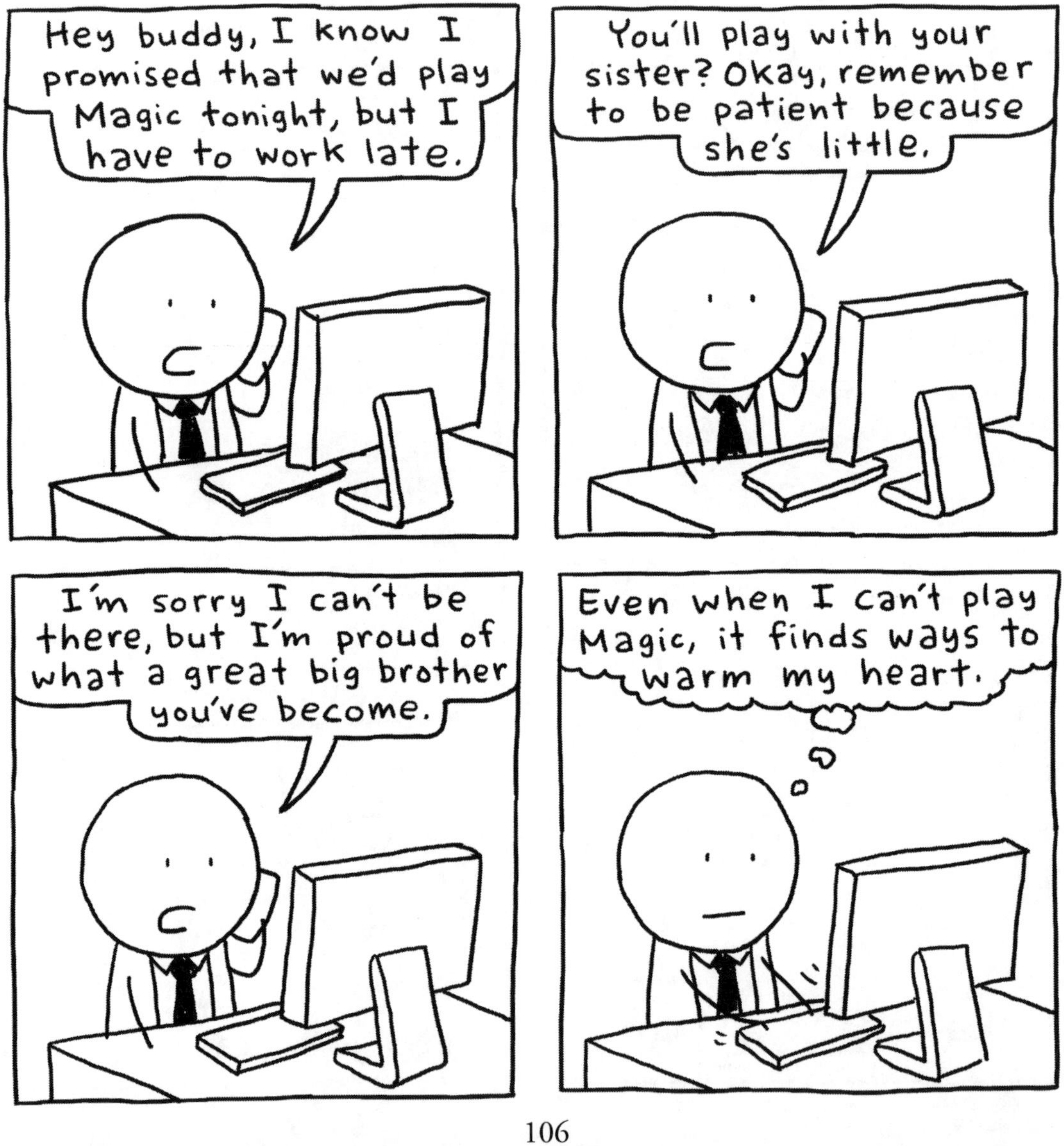
Hey buddy, I know I promised that we'd play Magic tonight, but I have to work late.
You'll play with your sister? Okay, remember to be patient because she's little.
I'm sorry I can't be there, but I'm proud of what a great big brother you've become.
Even when I can't play Magic, it finds ways to warm my heart.

Did you hear there's going to be a Magic board game? I wonder what that will be like.
It's just like chess, except the queen is a mythic rare.

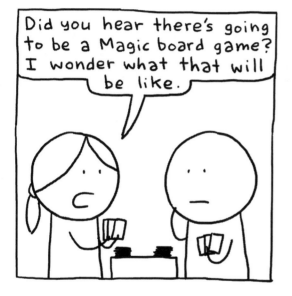

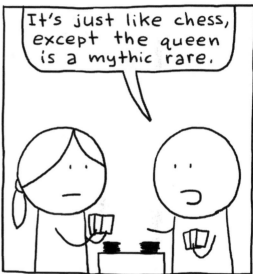

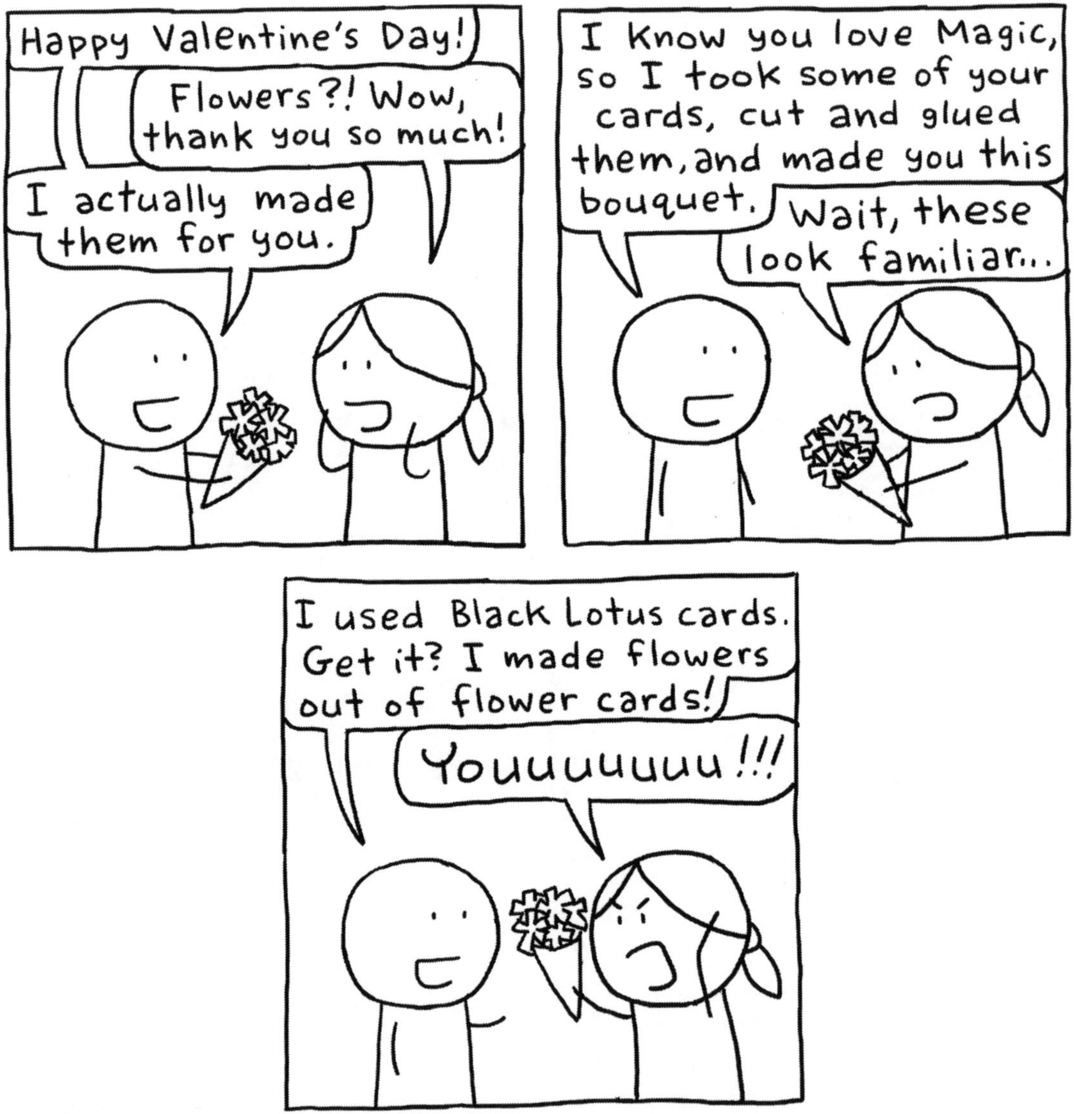
Happy Valentine's Day!
Flowers?! Wow, thank you so much!
I actually made them for you.
I know you love Magic, so I took some of your cards, cut and glued them, and made you this bouquet.
Wait, these look familiar...
I used Black Lotus cards. Get it? I made flowers out of flower cards!
Youuuuuuu!!!

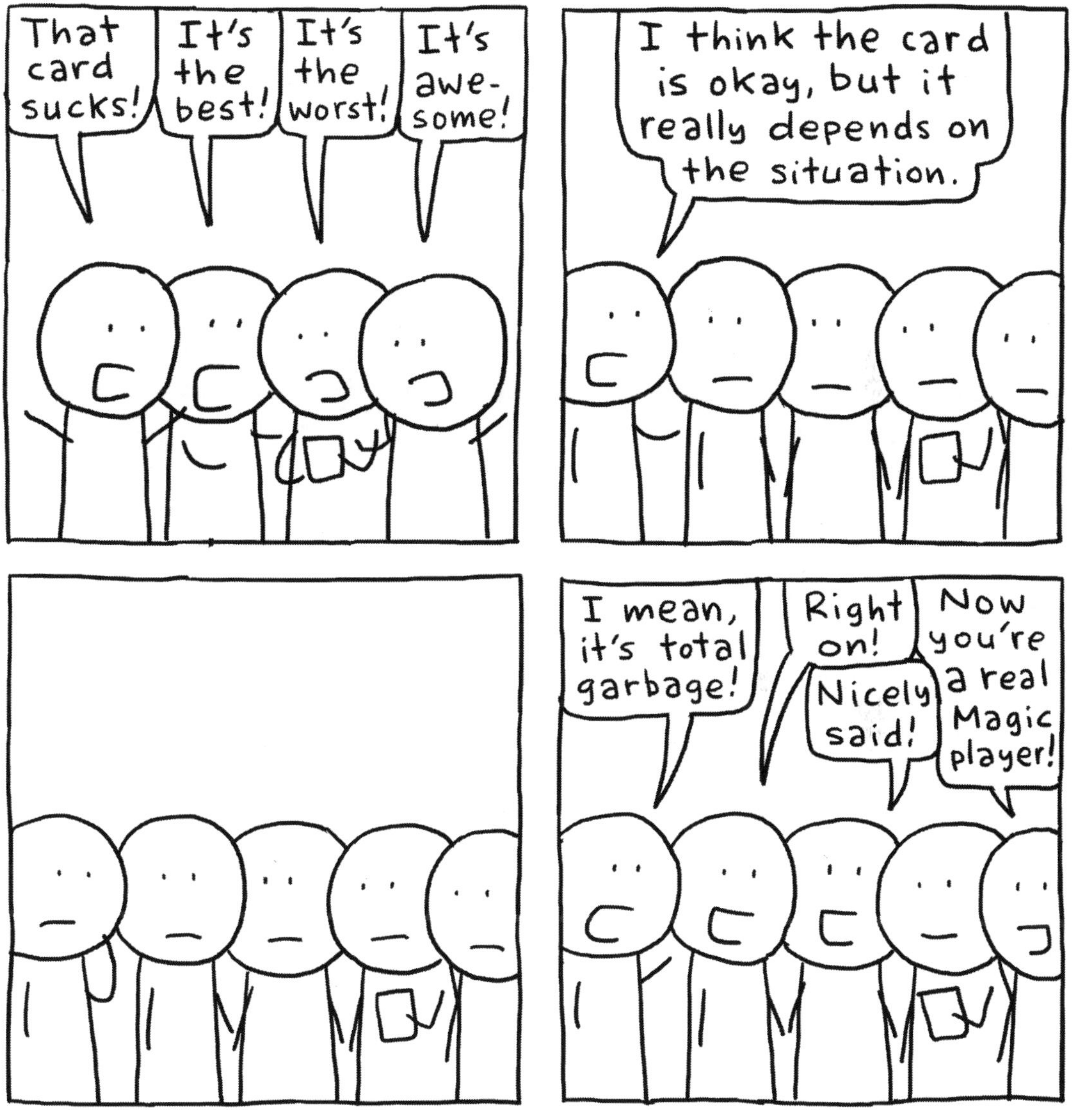
That card sucks!
It's the best!
It's the worst!
It's awe-some!
I think the card is okay, but it really depends on the situation.
I mean, it's total garbage!
Right on!
Nicely said!
Now you're a real Magic player!

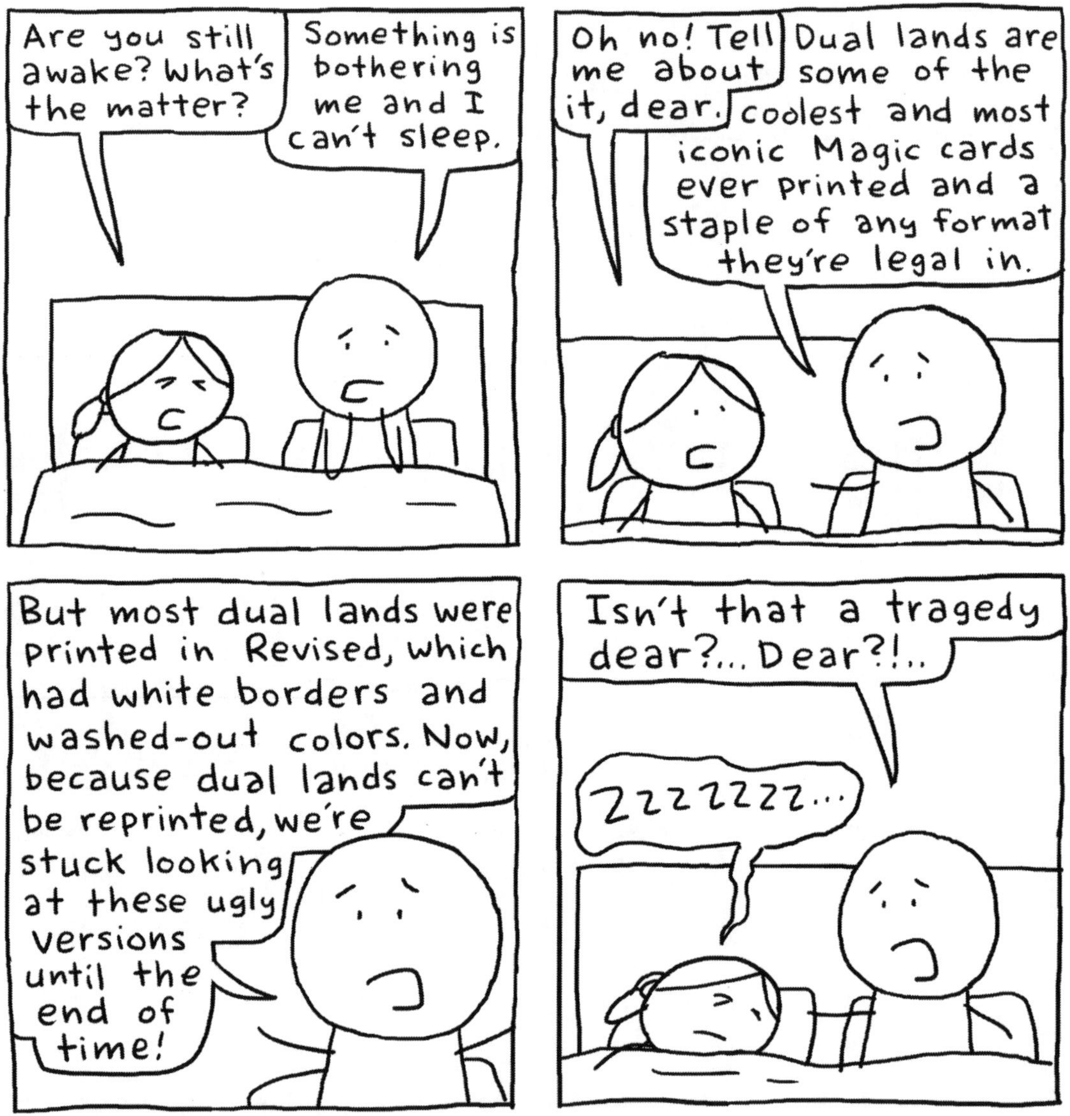
Are you still awake? What's the matter?
Something is bothering me and I can't sleep.
Oh no! Tell me about it, dear.
Dual lands are some of the coolest and most iconic Magic cards ever printed and a staple of any format they're legal in.
But most dual lands were printed in Revised, which had white borders and washed-out colors. Now, because dual lands can't be reprinted, we're stuck looking at these ugly versions until the end of time!
Isn't that a tragedy dear?... Dear?!..
Zzzzzzz...

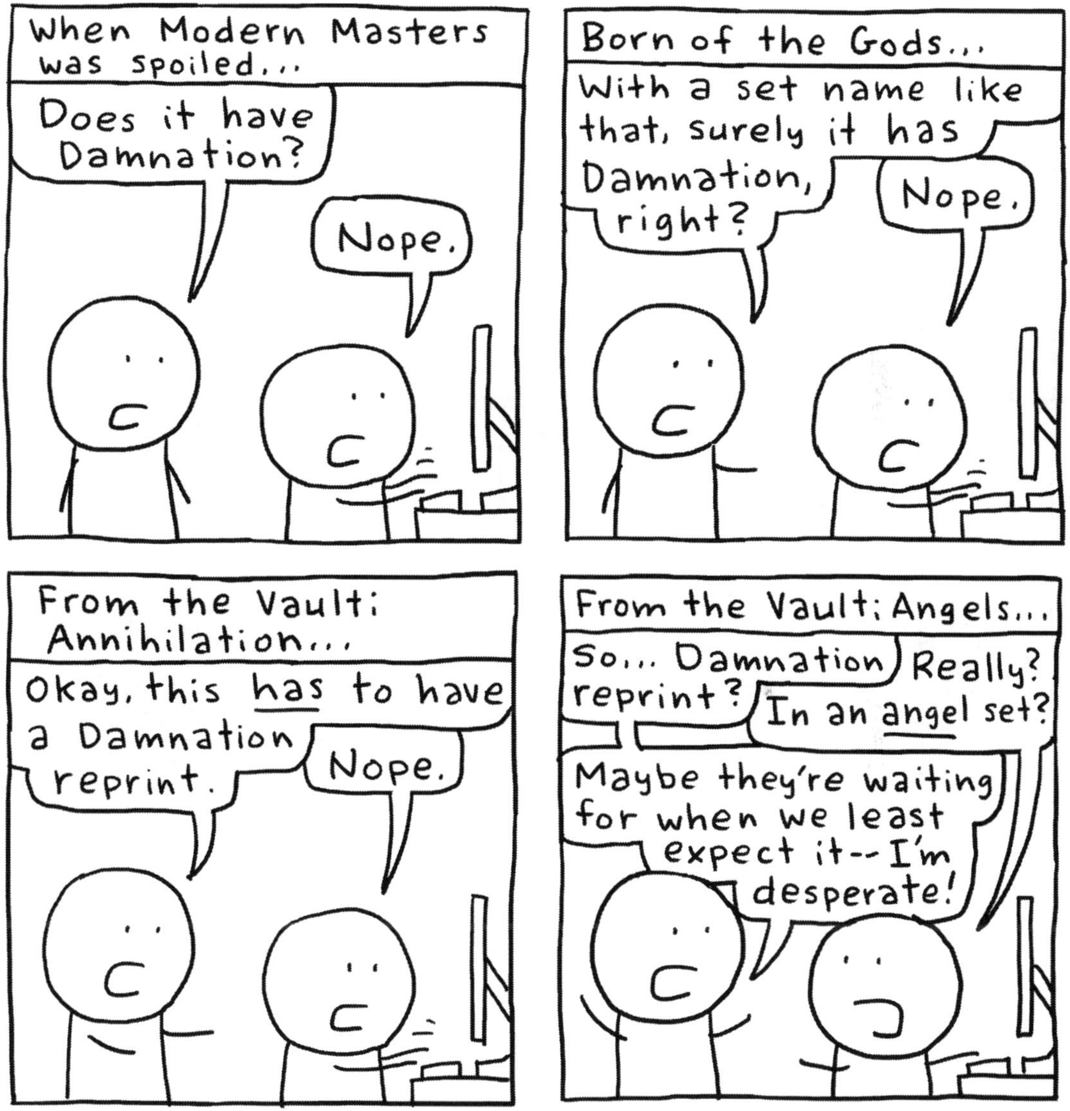
When Modern Masters was spoiled...
Does it have Damnation?
Nope.
Born of the Gods...
With a set name like that, surely it has Damnation, right?
Nope.
From the Vault: Annihilation...
Okay, this has to have a Damnation reprint.
Nope.
From the Vault: Angels...
So... Damnation reprint?
Really? In an angel set?
Maybe they're waiting for when we least expect it-- I'm desperate!

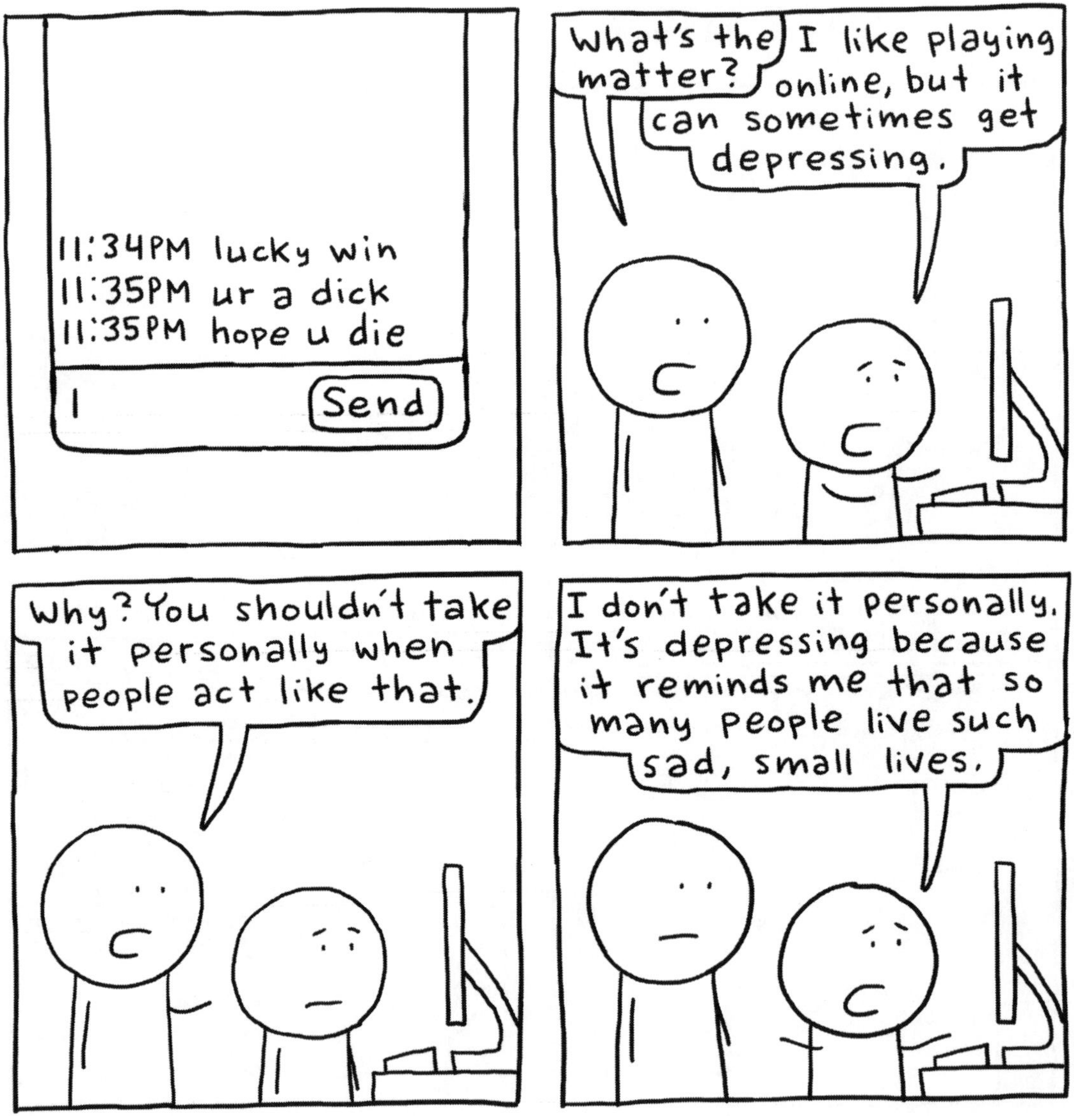
11:34PM lucky win
11:35PM ur a dick
11:35PM hope u die
Send
What's the matter?
I like playing online, but it can sometimes get depressing.
Why? You shouldn't take it personally when people act like that.
I don't take it personally. It's depressing because it reminds me that so many people live such sad, small lives.

I have a list of things I need. Could you pick them up at the store for me?
No problem!
Later...
Thanks, but what's this extra charge?
That's the Magic tax.

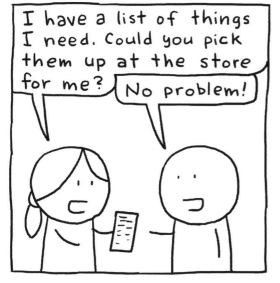

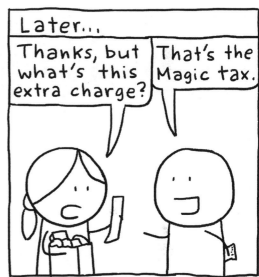

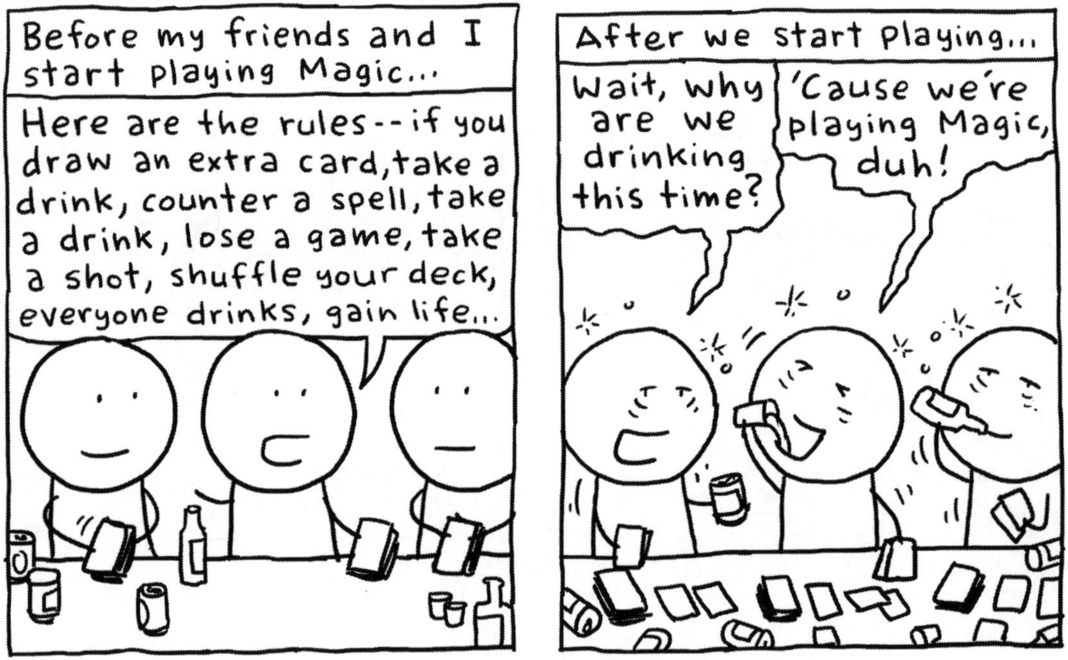
Before my friends and I start playing Magic...
Here are the rules--if you draw an extra card, take a drink, counter a spell, take a drink, lose a game, take a shot, shuffle your deck, everyone drinks, gain life...
After we start playing...
Wait, why are we drinking this time?
'Cause we're playing Magic, duh!

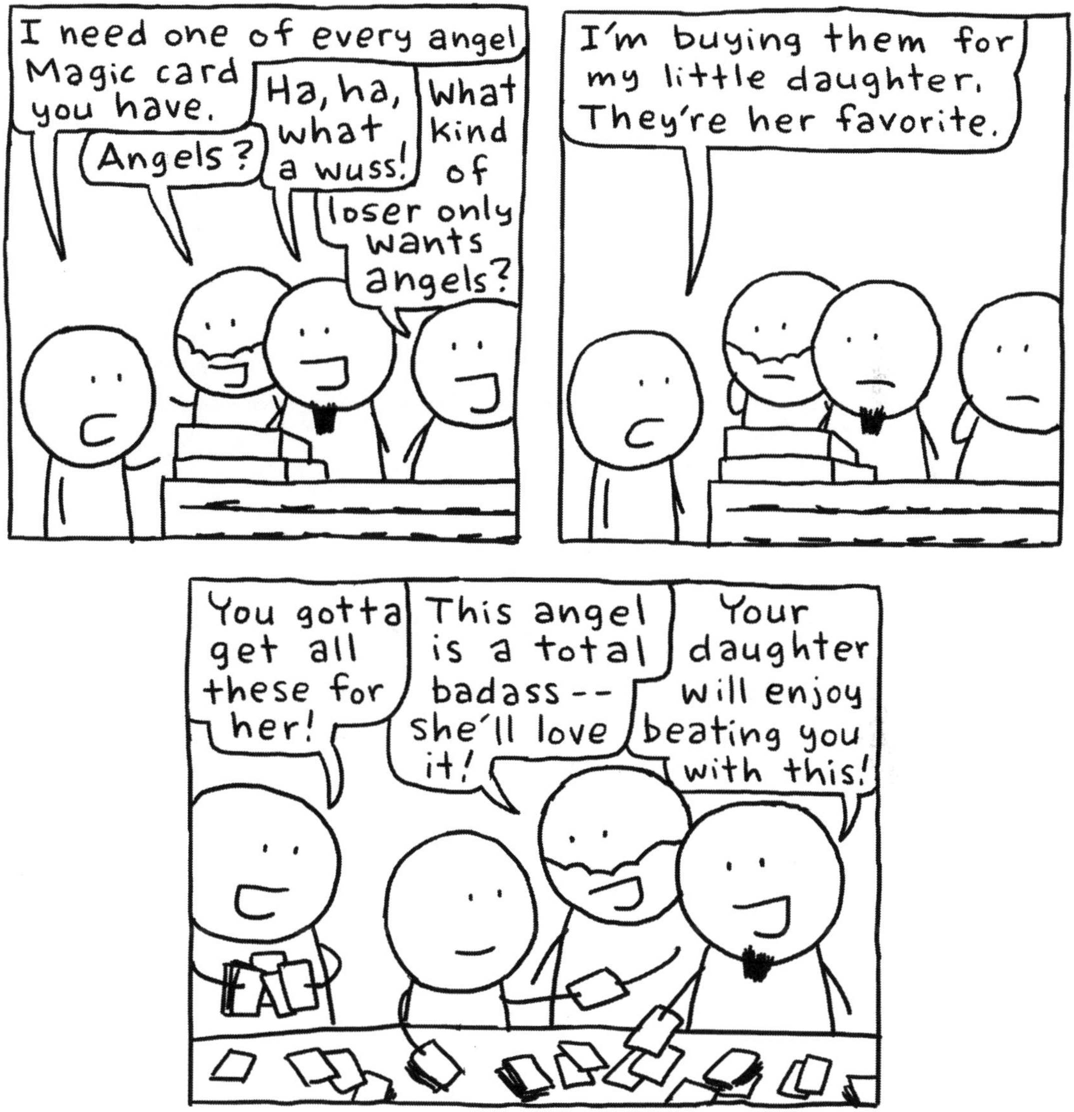
I need one of every angel Magic card you have.
Angels?
Ha, ha, what a wuss!
What kind of loser only wants angels?
I'm buying them for my little daughter. They're her favorite.
You gotta get all these for her!
This angel is a total badass -- she'll love it!
Your daughter will enjoy beating you with this!

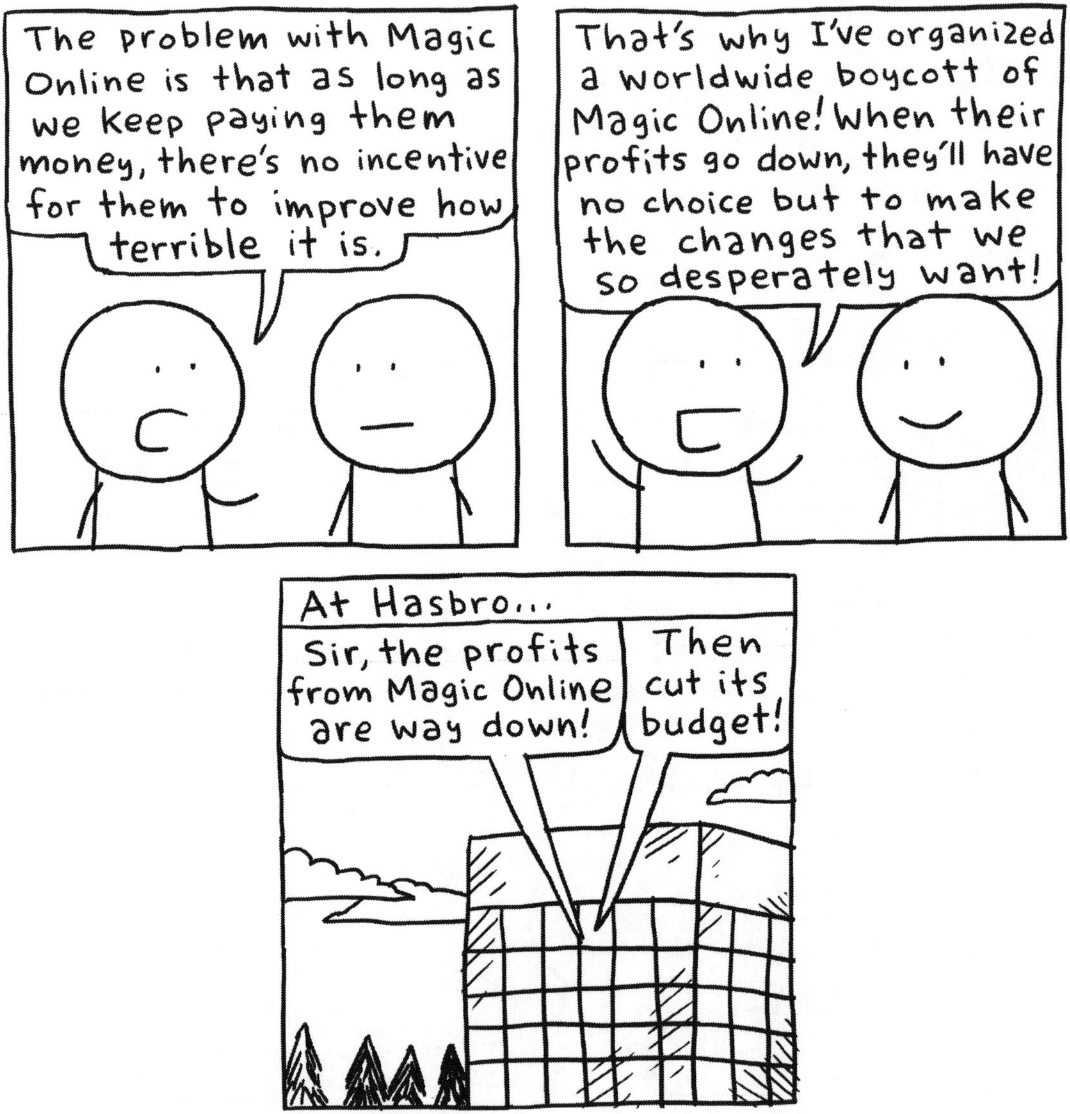
The problem with Magic Online is that as long as we keep paying them money, there's no incentive for them to improve how terrible it is.
That's why I've organized a worldwide boycott of Magic Online! When their profits go down, they'll have no choice but to make the changes that we so desperately want!
At Hasbro...
Sir, the profits from Magic Online are way down!
Then cut its budget!

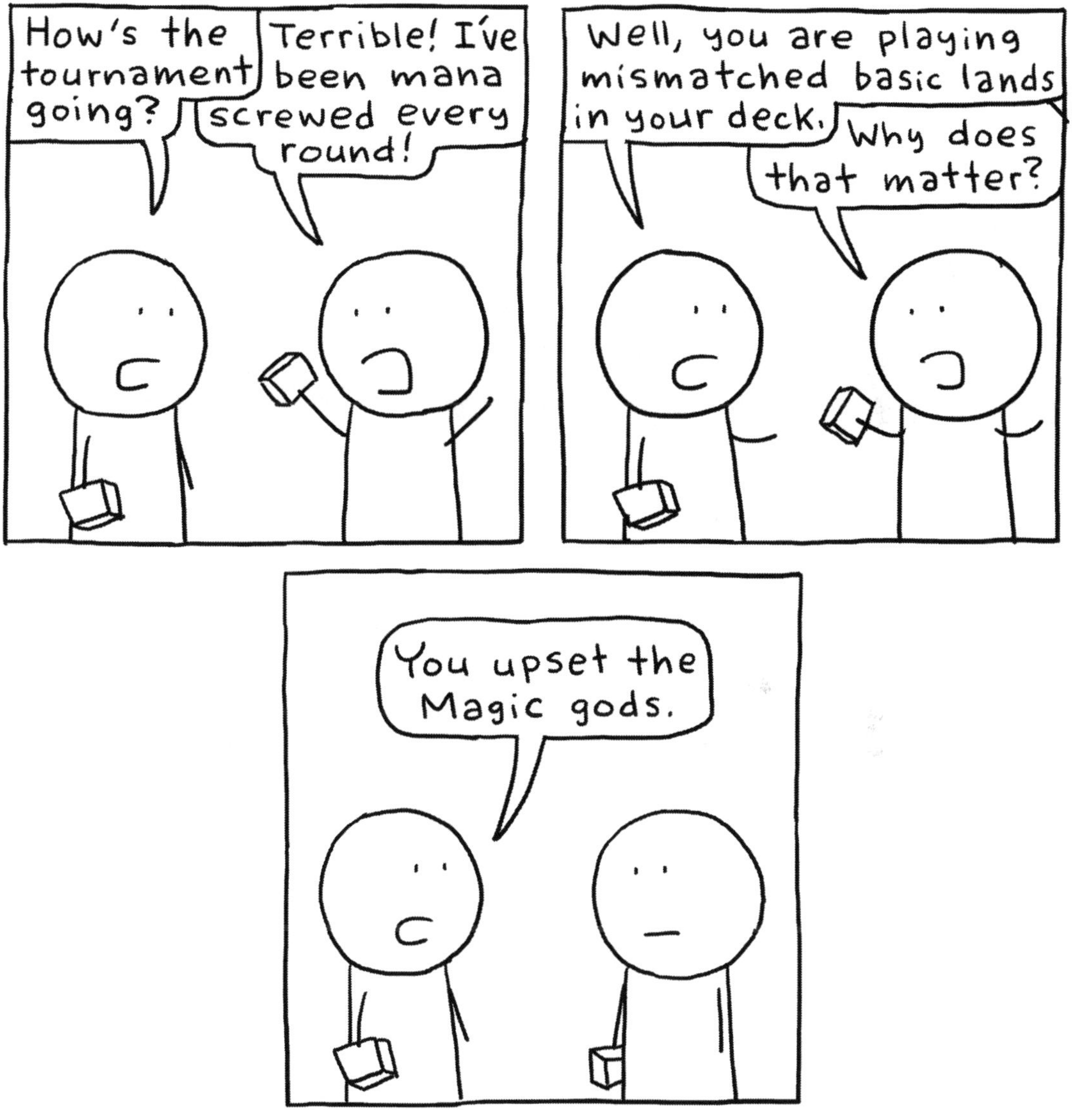
How's the tournament going?
Terrible! I've been mana screwed every round!
Well, you are playing mismatched basic lands in your deck.
Why does that matter?
You upset the Magic gods.

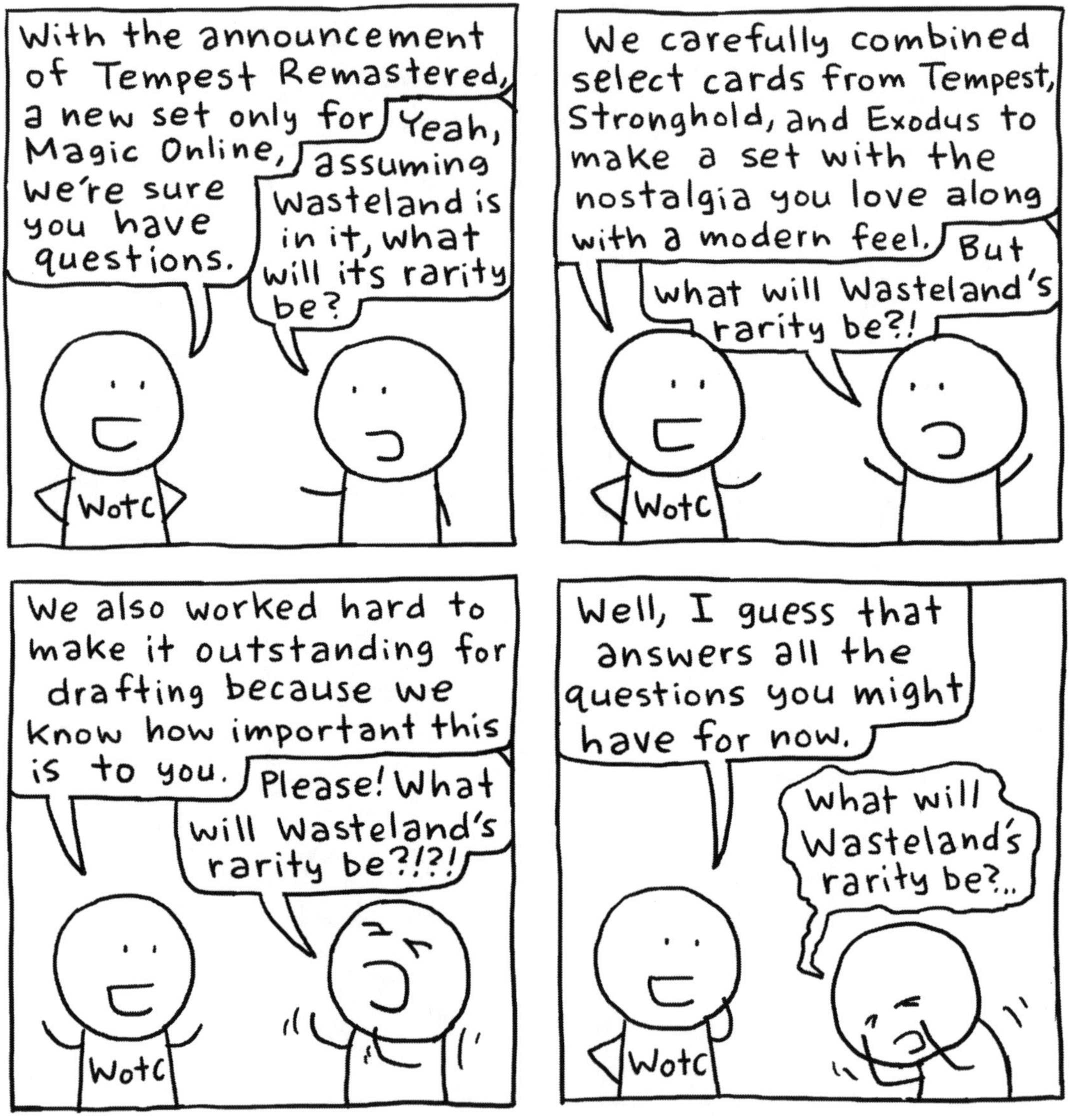
With the announcement of Tempest Remastered, a new set only for Magic Online, we're sure you have questions.
Yeah, assuming Wasteland is in it, what will its rarity be?
WotC
We carefully combined select cards from Tempest, Stronghold, and Exodus to make a set with the nostalgia you love along with a modern feel.
But what will Wasteland's rarity be?!
WotC
We also worked hard to make it outstanding for drafting because we know how important this is to you.
Please! What will Wasteland's rarity be?!?!
WotC
Well, I guess that answers all the questions you might have for now.
What will Wasteland's rarity be?..
WotC

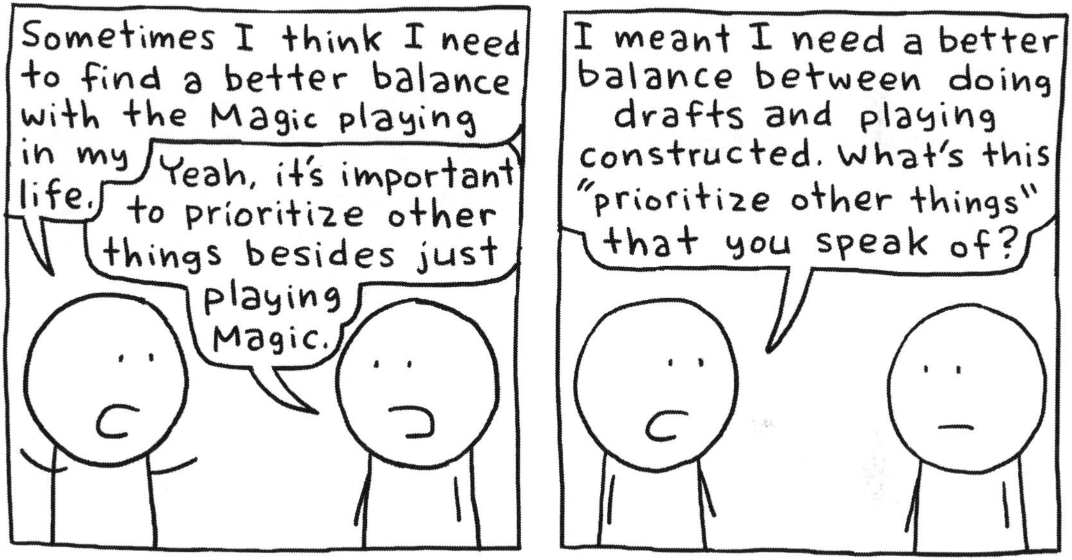
Sometimes I think I need to find a better balance with the Magic playing in my life.
Yeah, it's important to prioritize other things besides just playing Magic.
I meant I need a better balance between doing drafts and playing constructed. What's this "prioritize other things" that you speak of?

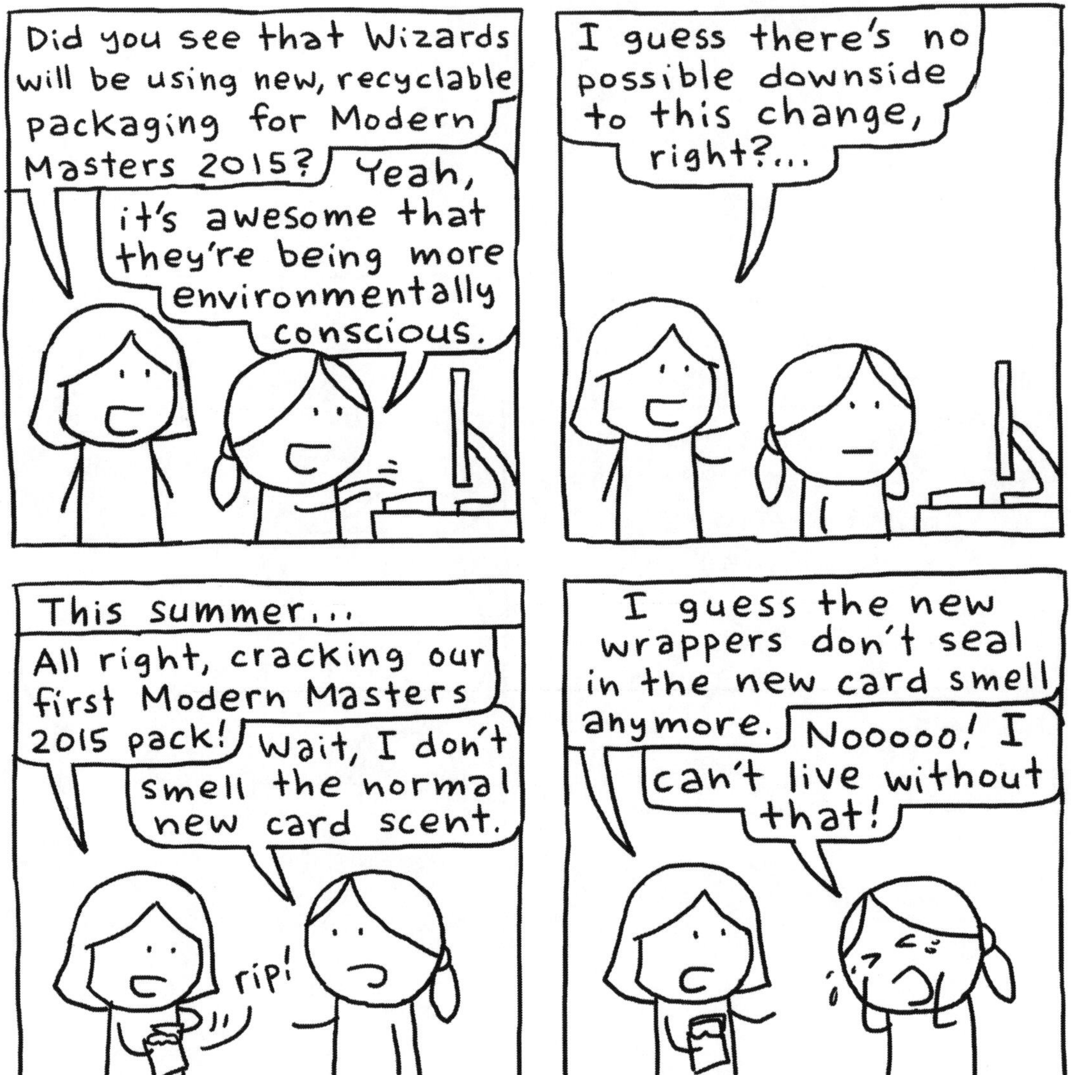
Did you see that Wizards will be using new, recyclable packaging for Modern Masters 2015?
Yeah, it's awesome that they're being more environmentally conscious.
I guess there's no possible downside to this change, right?...
This summer...
All right, cracking our first Modern Masters 2015 pack!
Wait, I don't smell the normal new card scent.
rip!
I guess the new wrappers don't seal in the new card smell anymore.
Nooooo! I can't live without that!

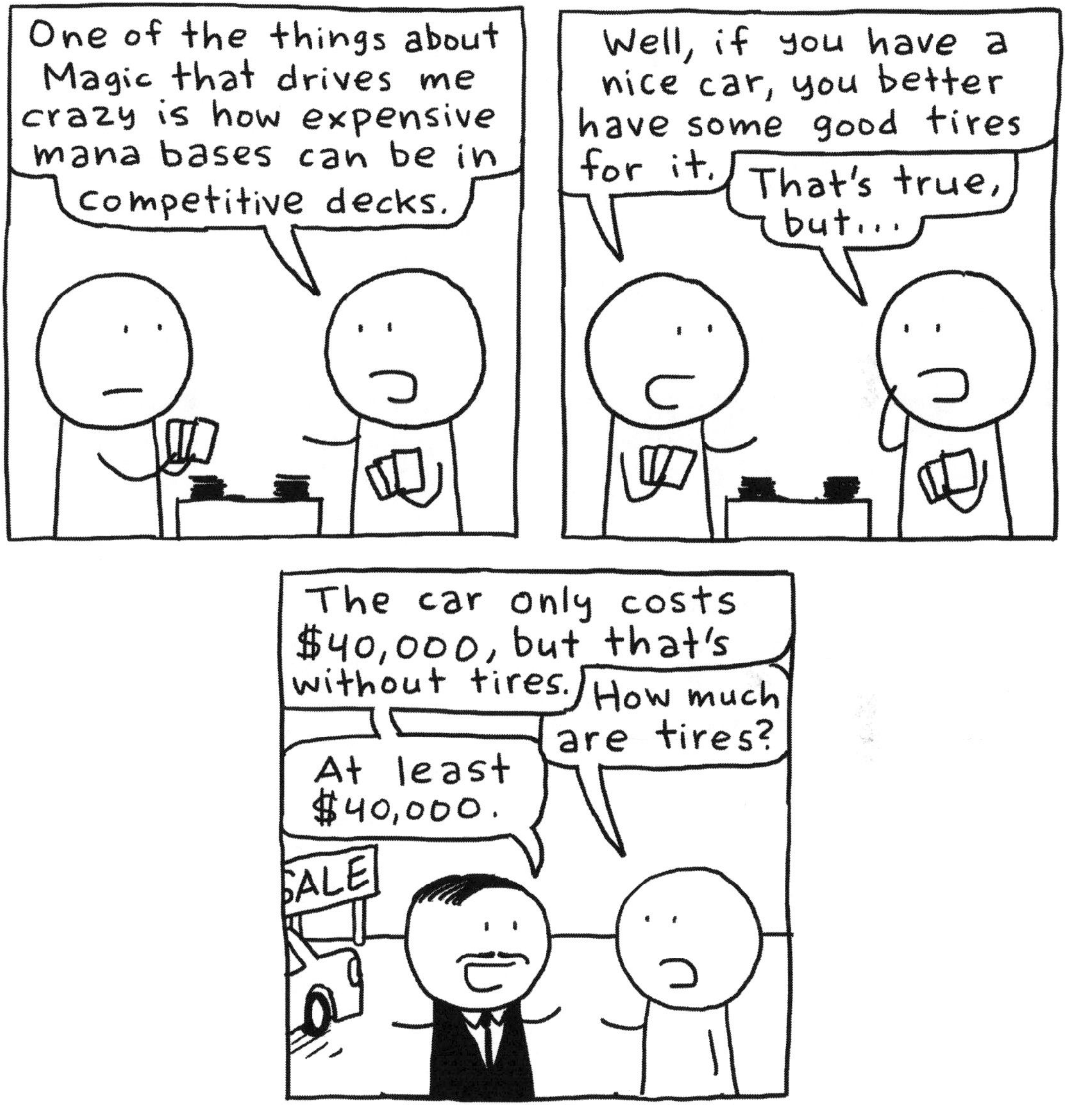
One of the things about Magic that drives me crazy is how expensive mana bases can be in competitive decks.
Well, if you have a nice car, you better have some good tires for it.
That's true, but...
The car only costs $40,000, but that's without tires.
How much are tires?
At least $40,000.
SALE

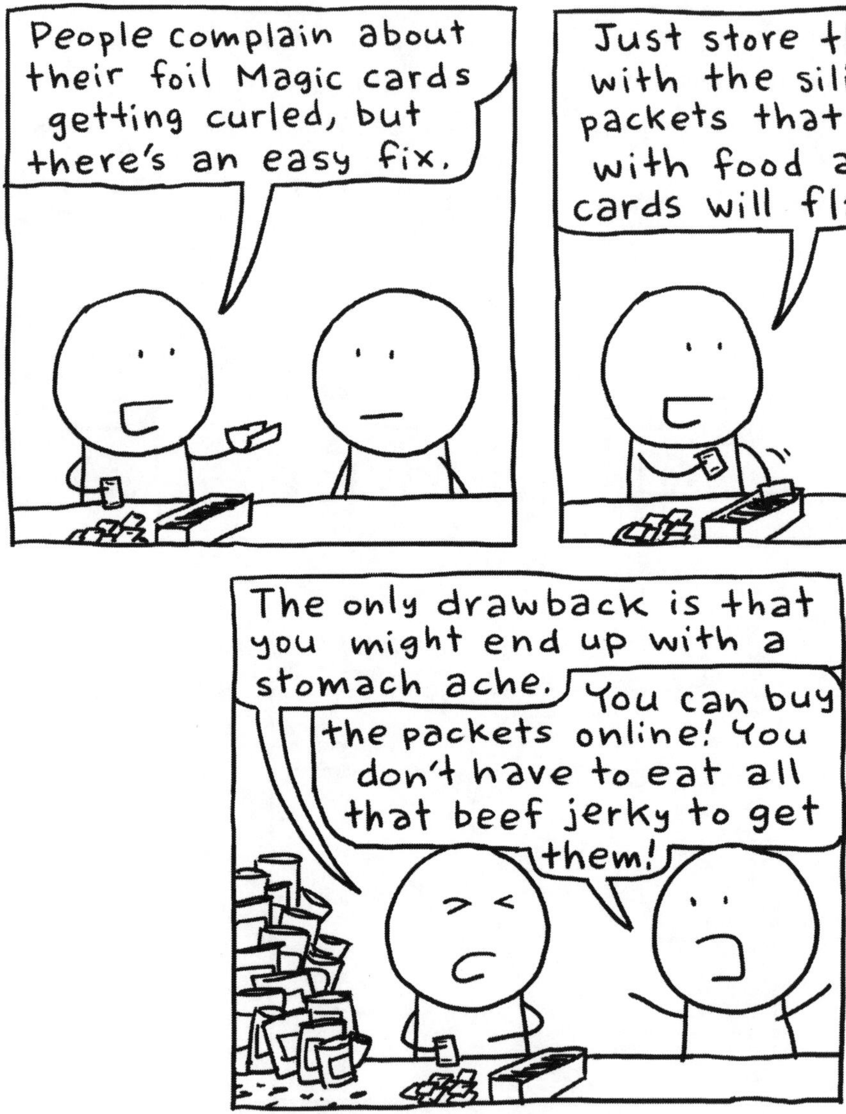
People complain about their foil Magic cards getting curled, but there's an easy fix.
Just store the foils with the silica gel packets that you find with food and the cards will flatten out.
The only drawback is that you might end up with a stomach ache.
You can buy the packets online! You don't have to eat all that beef jerky to get them!

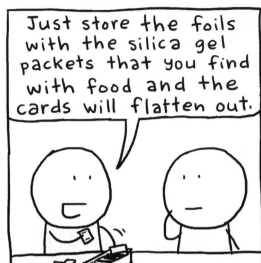

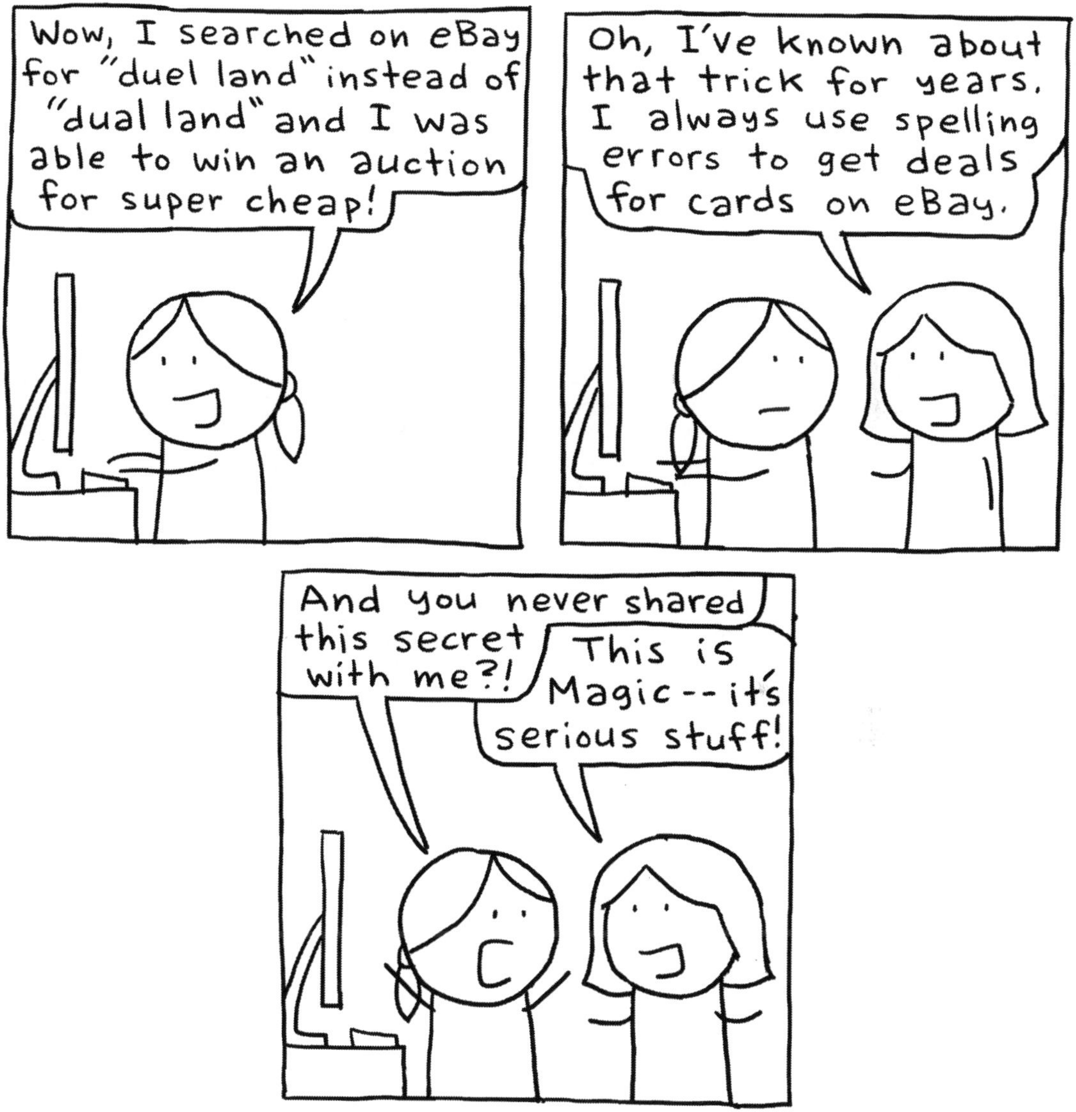
Wow, I searched on eBay for "duel land" instead of "dual land" and I was able to win an auction for super cheap!
Oh, I've known about that trick for years. I always use spelling errors to get deals for cards on eBay.
And you never shared this secret with me?!
This is Magic--it's serious stuff!

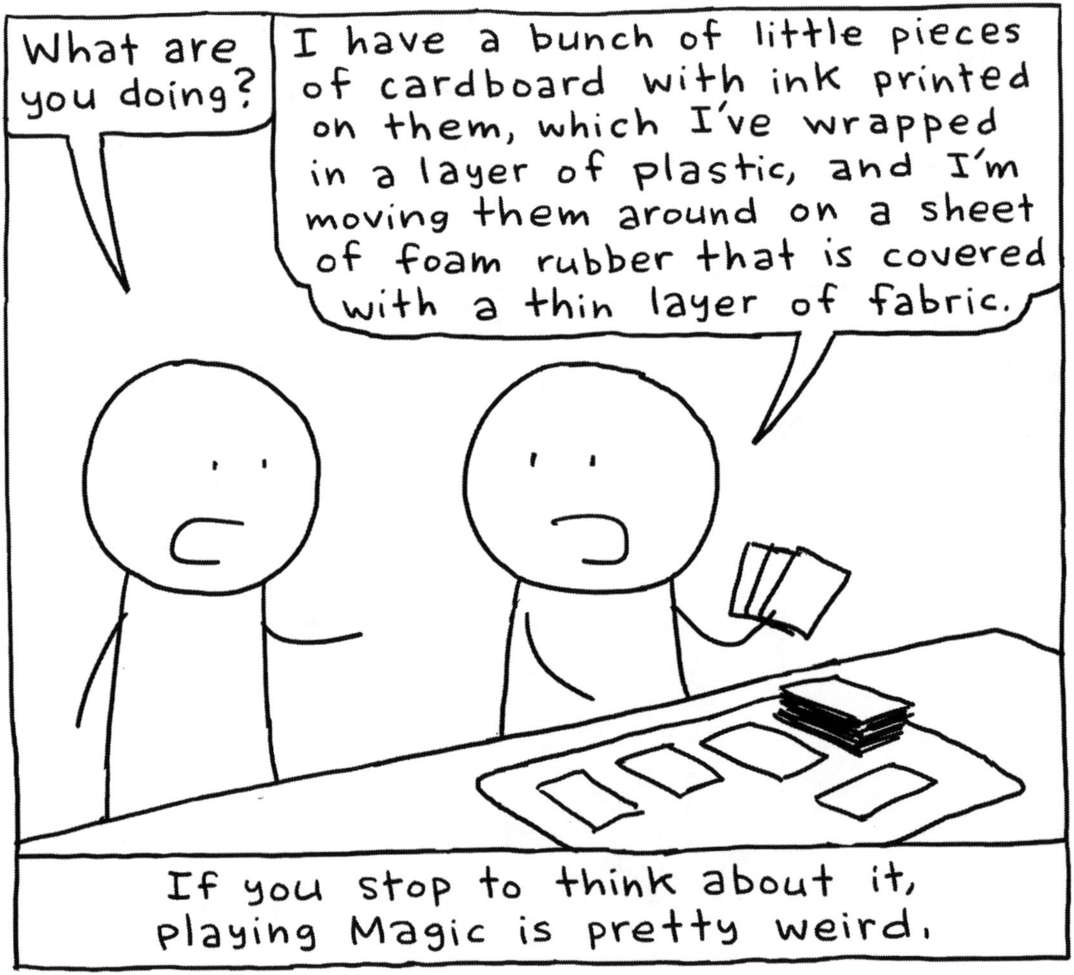
What are you doing?
I have a bunch of little pieces of cardboard with ink printed on them, which I've wrapped in a layer of plastic, and I'm moving them around on a sheet of foam rubber that is covered with a thin layer of fabric.
If you stop to think about it, playing Magic is pretty weird.

Did you see that Rebound has come back in Dragons of Tarkir?
Yeah, that's pretty sweet...
...although it's too bad that this is the last time we'll be seeing this mechanic.
Why is that?

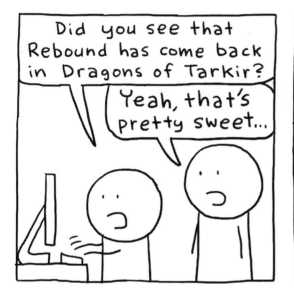

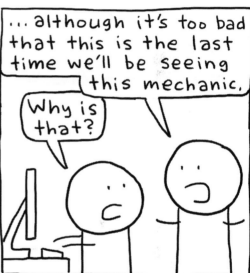

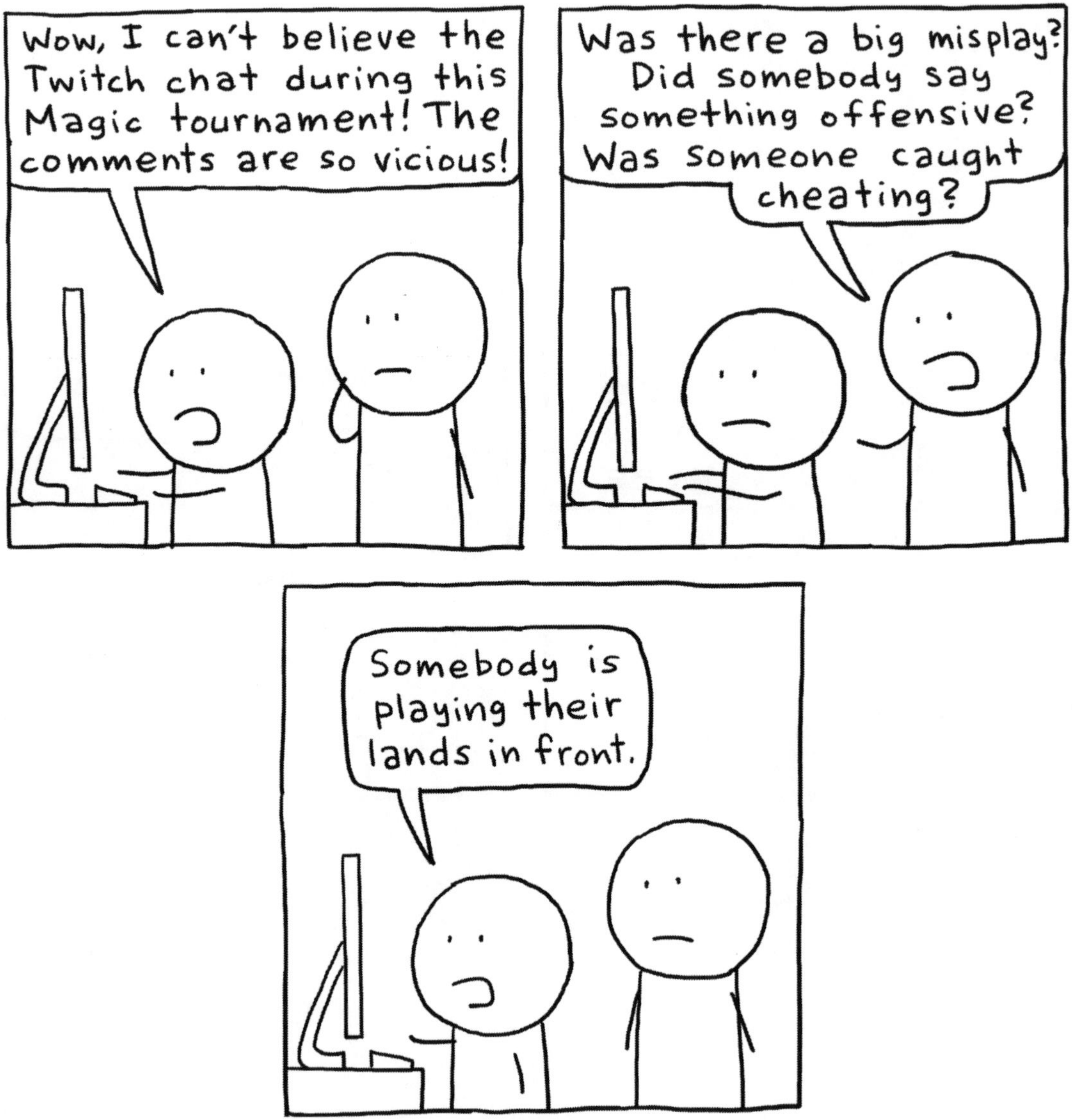
Wow, I can't believe the Twitch chat during this Magic tournament! The comments are so vicious!
Was there a big misplay? Did somebody say something offensive? Was someone caught cheating?
Somebody is playing their lands in front.

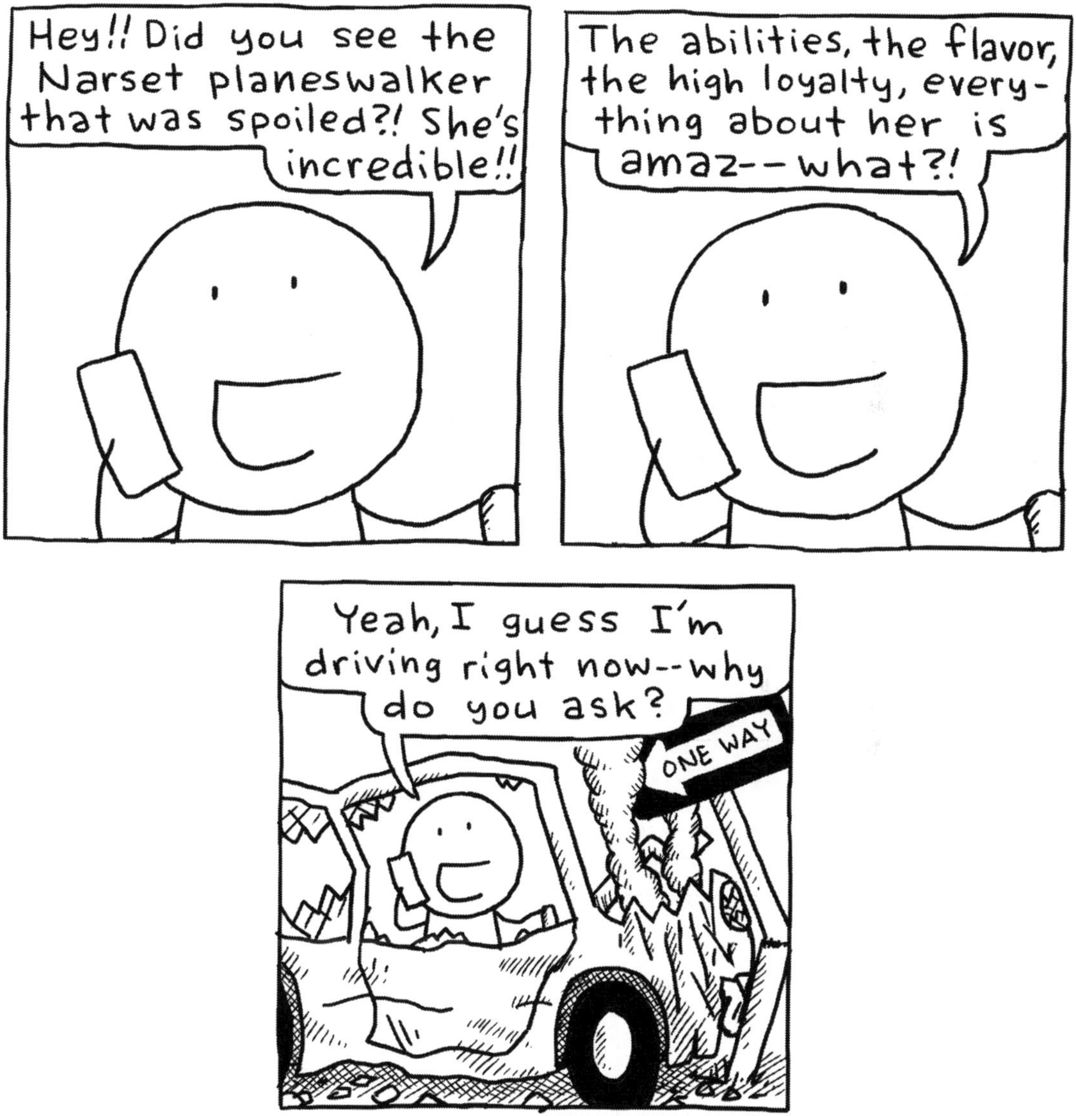
Hey!! Did you see the Narset planeswalker that was spoiled?! She's incredible!!
The abilities, the flavor, the high loyalty, every-thing about her is amaz--what?!
Yeah, I guess I'm driving right now--why do you ask?
ONE WAY

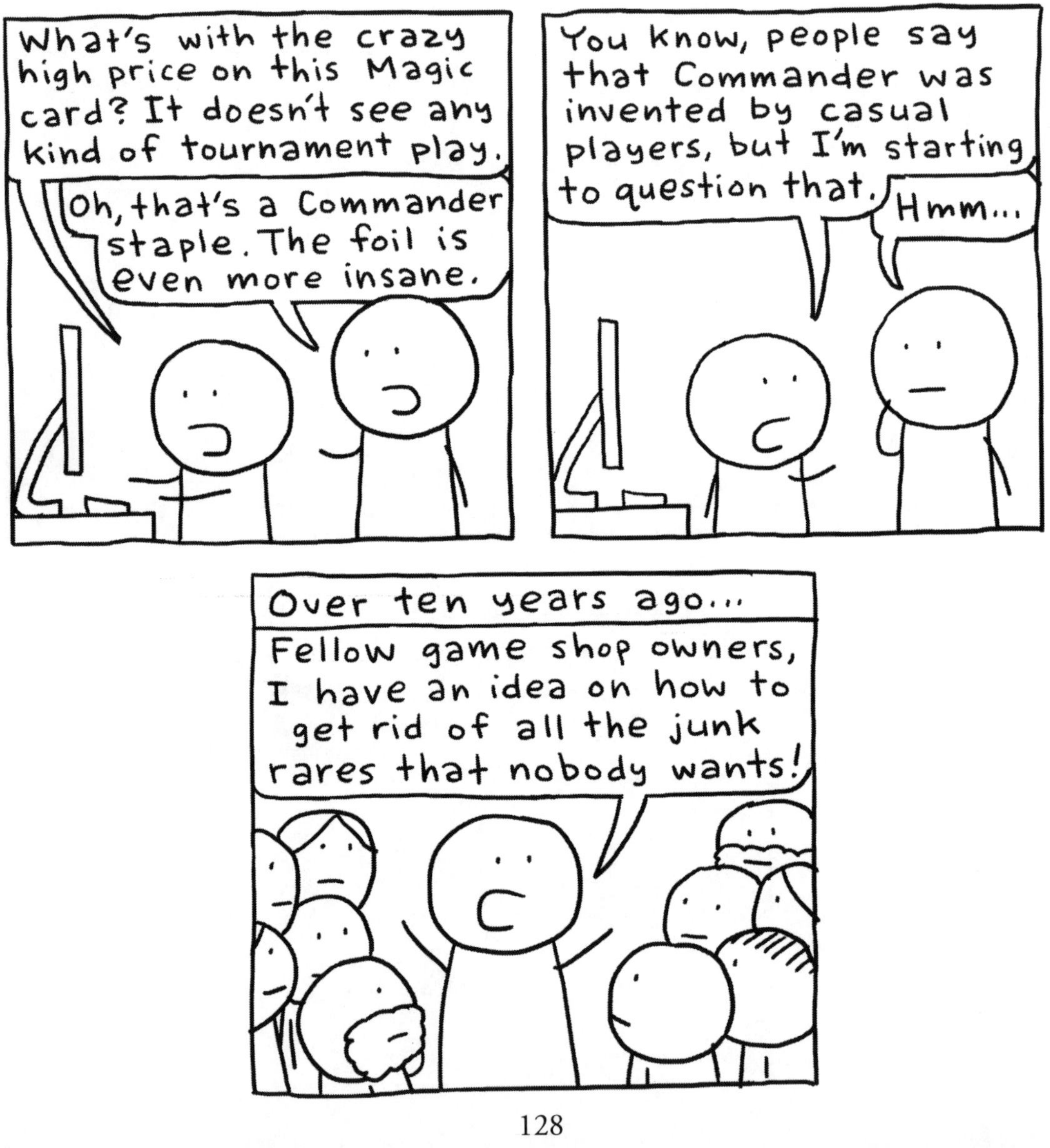
What's with the crazy high price on this Magic card? It doesn't see any kind of tournament play.
Oh, that's a Commander staple. The foil is even more insane.
You know, people say that Commander was invented by casual players, but I'm starting to question that.
Hmm...
Over ten years ago...
Fellow game shop owners, I have an idea on how to get rid of all the junk rares that nobody wants!

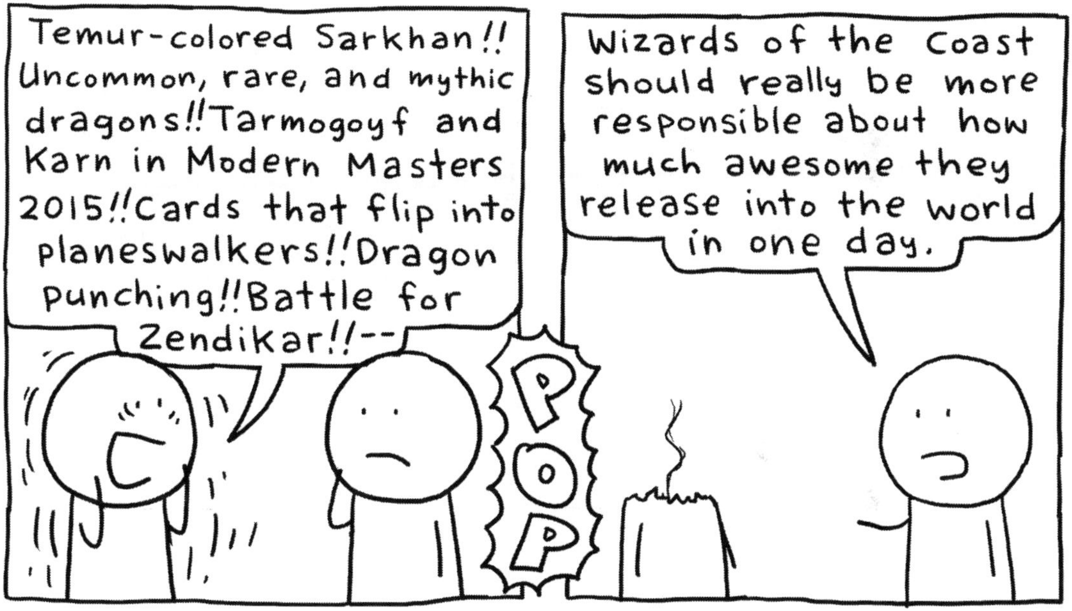
Temur-colored Sarkhan!! Uncommon, rare, and mythic dragons!! Tarmogoyf and Karn in Modern Masters 2015!! Cards that flip into planeswalkers!! Dragon punching!! Battle for Zendikar!!--
POP
Wizards of the Coast should really be more responsible about how much awesome they release into the world in one day.

Bonus Comics

The following pages feature comics that have never appeared on the Cardboard Crack website. I hope you enjoy the chance to see them here for the first time!

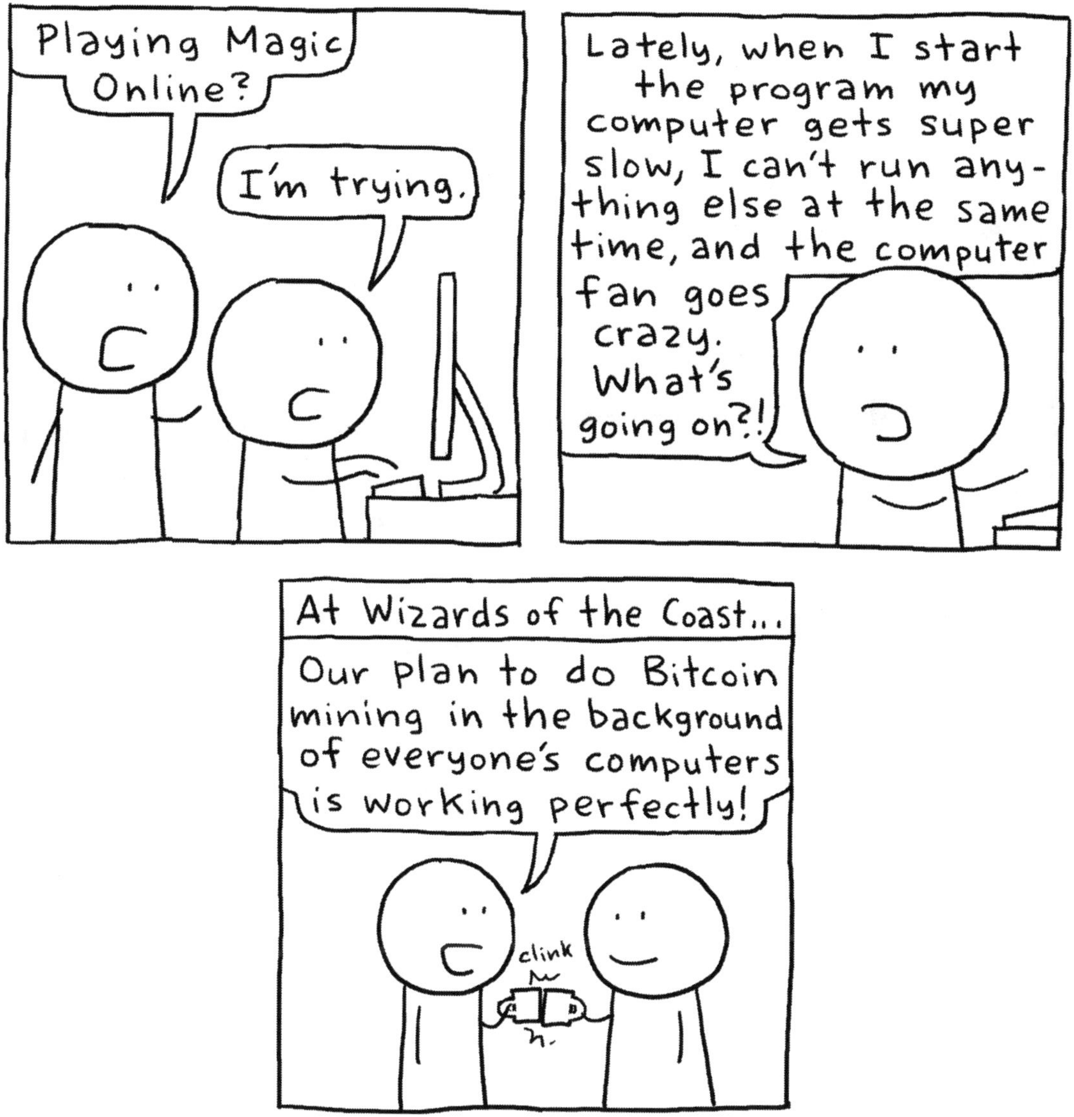
Playing Magic Online?
I'm trying.
Lately, when I start the program my computer gets super slow, I can't run anything else at the same time, and the computer fan goes crazy. What's going on?!
At Wizards of the Coast...
Our plan to do Bitcoin mining in the background of everyone's computers is working perfectly!
clink

It's Christmas! Why aren't you celebrating?!
This year Christmas doesn't begin for me until December 29th.

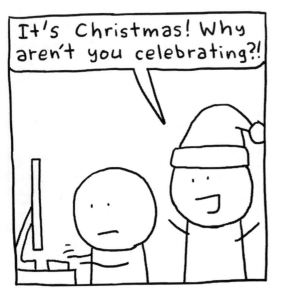

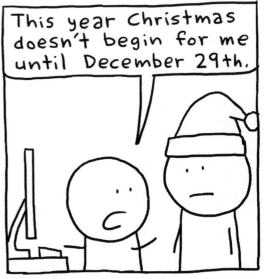

The joke here was that the spoilers for Fate Reforged were scheduled to start on December 29th. At the last minute, I realized that Wizards of the Coast would probably have a special spoiler on Christmas day anyway (which they did, Ugin, the Spirit Dragon). So I made a replacement comic to post on Christmas instead of this one, which you can find on page 59.

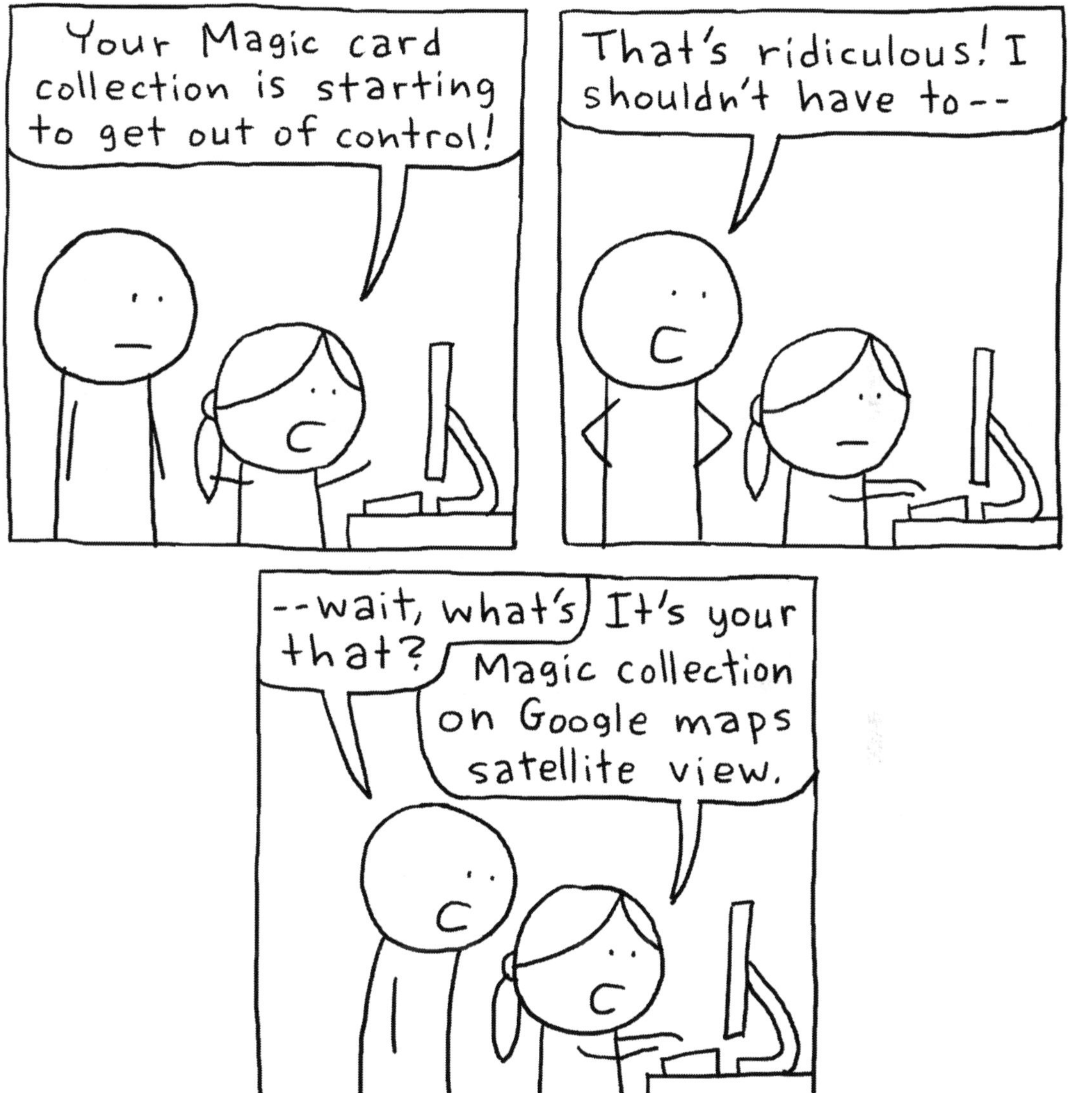
Your Magic card collection is starting to get out of control!
That's ridiculous! I shouldn't have to--
--wait, what's that?
It's your Magic collection on Google maps satellite view.

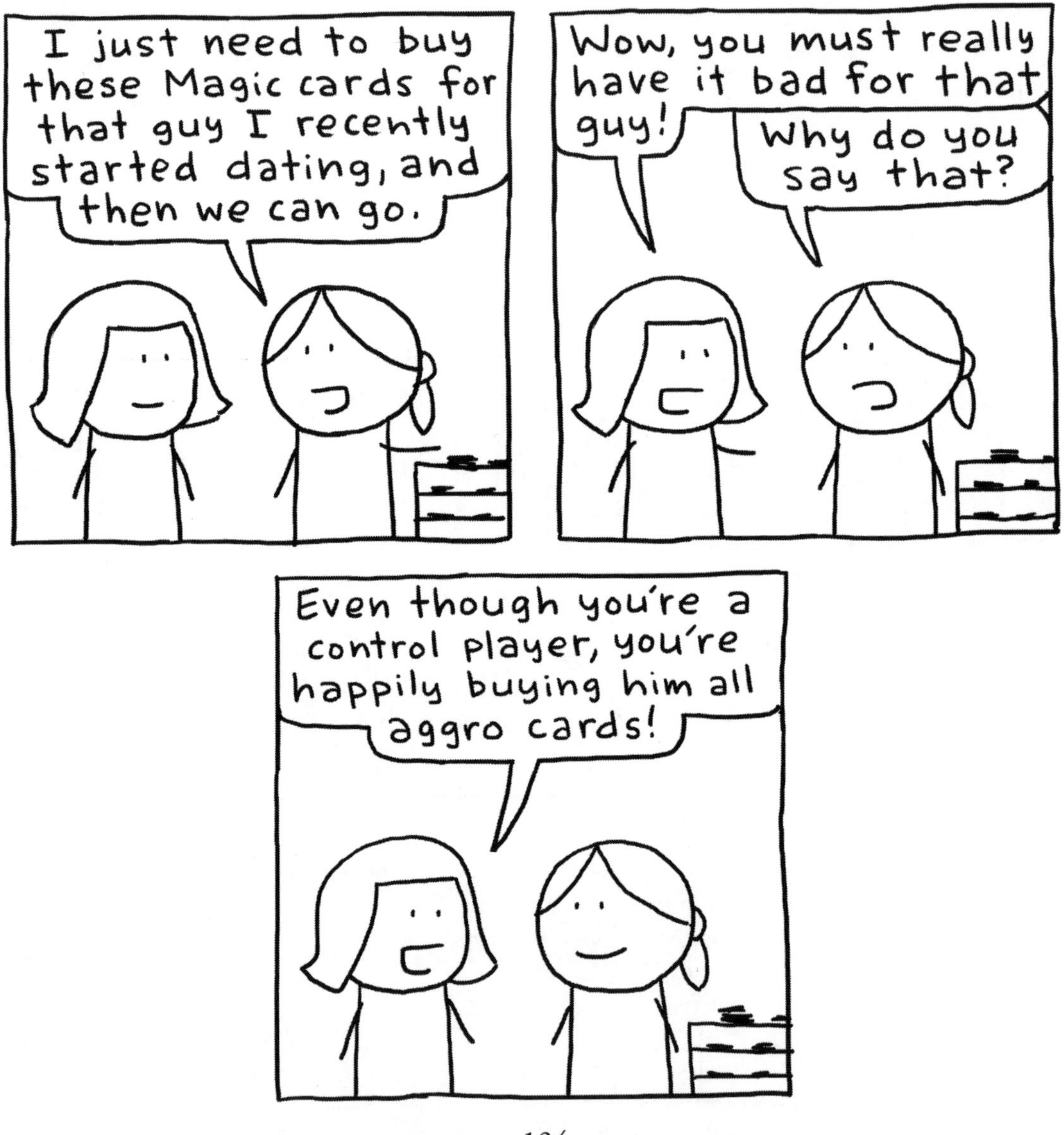
I just need to buy these Magic cards for that guy I recently started dating, and then we can go.
Wow, you must really have it bad for that guy!
Why do you say that?
Even though you're a control player, you're happily buying him all aggro cards!

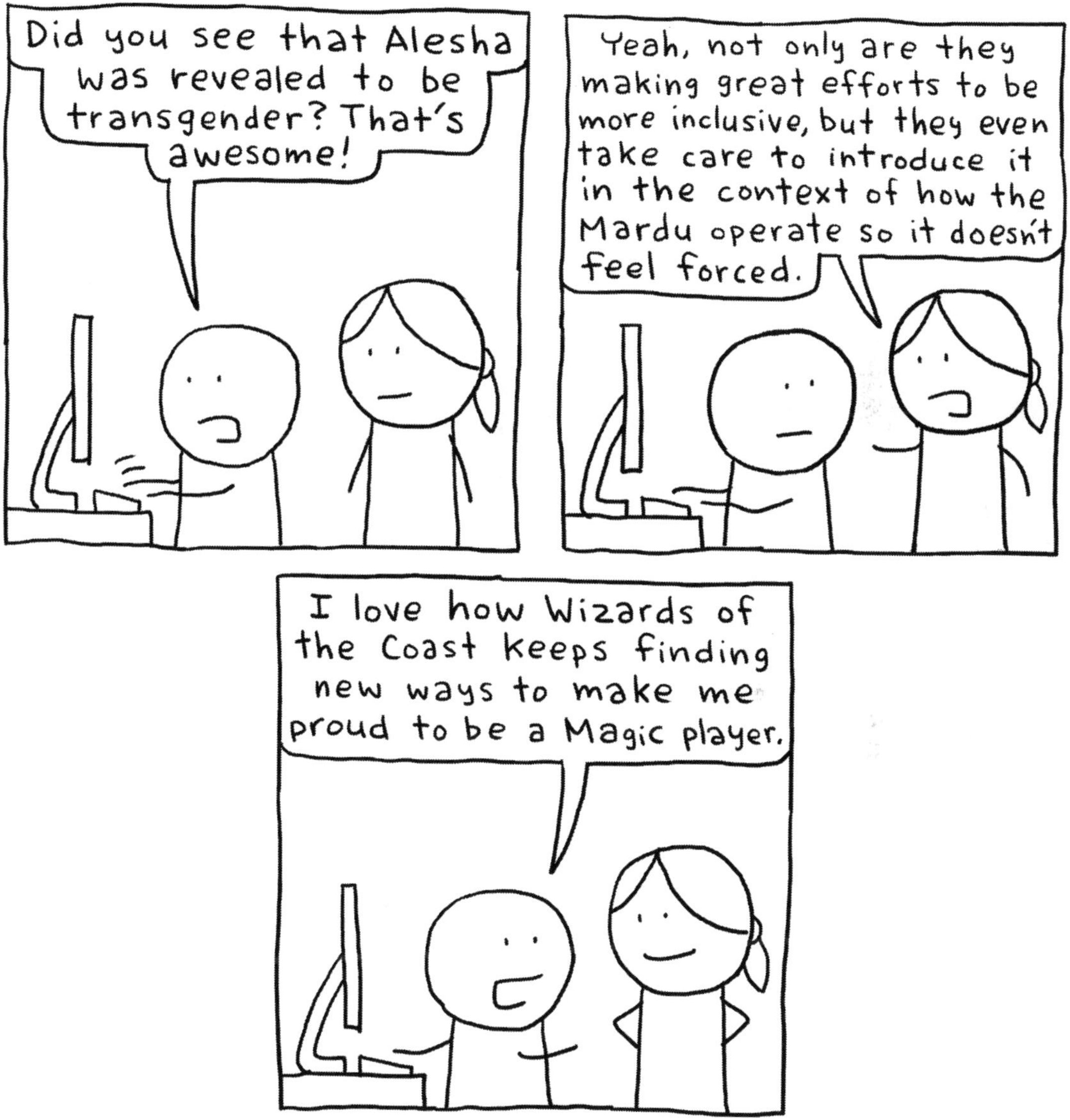
Did you see that Alesha was revealed to be transgender? That's awesome!
Yeah, not only are they making great efforts to be more inclusive, but they even take care to introduce it in the context of how the Mardu operate so it doesn't feel forced.
I love how Wizards of the Coast keeps finding new ways to make me proud to be a Magic player.

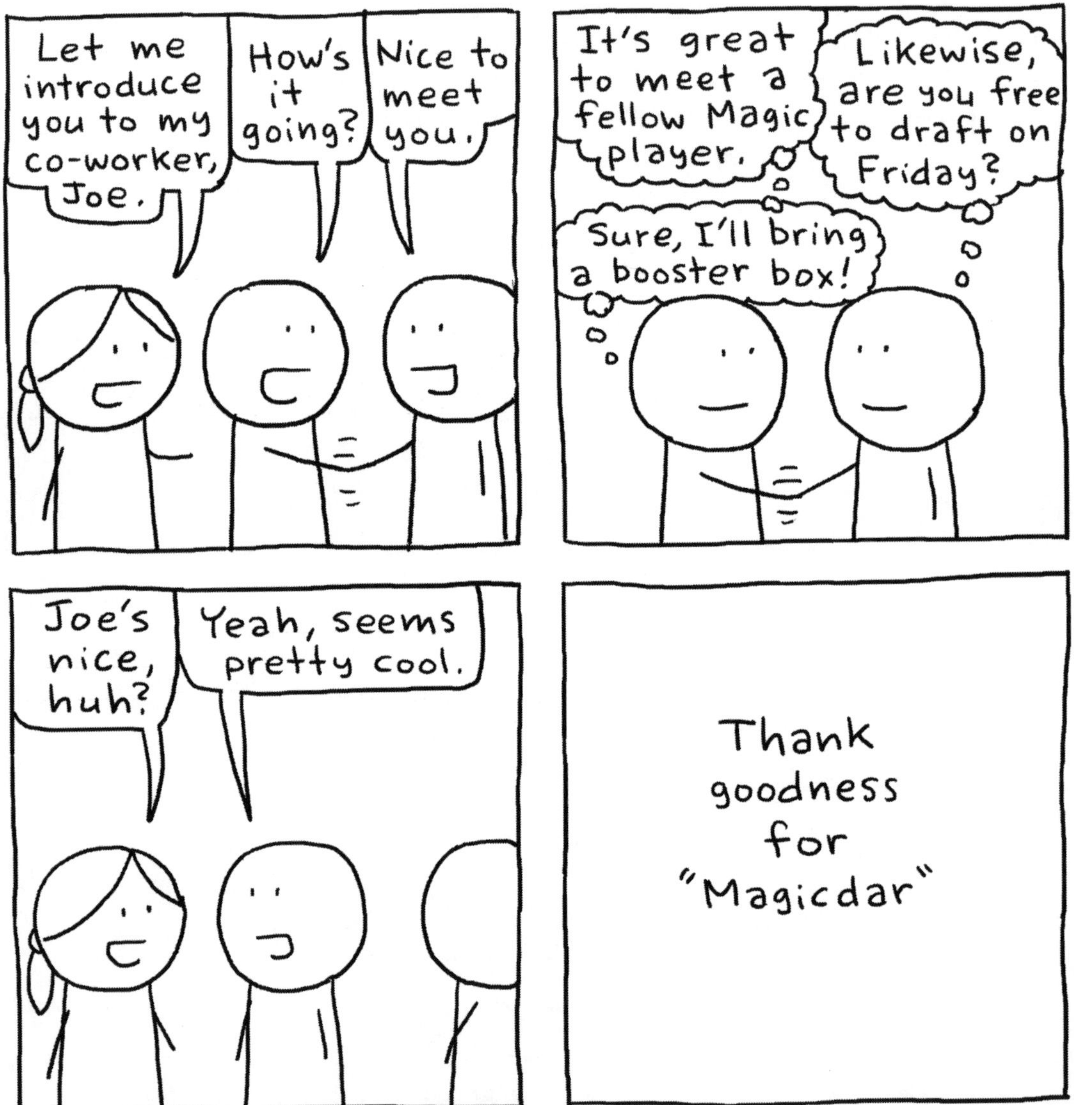
Let me introduce you to my co-worker, Joe.
How's it going?
Nice to meet you.
It's great to meet a fellow Magic player.
Likewise, are you free to draft on Friday?
Sure, I'll bring a booster box!
Joe's nice, huh?
Yeah, seems pretty cool.
Thank goodness for "Magicdar"

Are you ready for the SCG Players' Championship this weekend? Who are you rooting for?
I'm rooting for Chris VanMeter's beard!
I'm rooting for Reid Duke's hair!
That is definitely not what I meant.

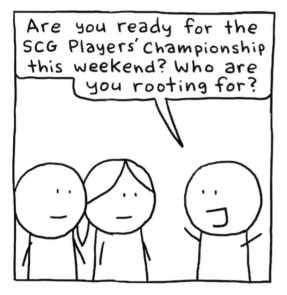

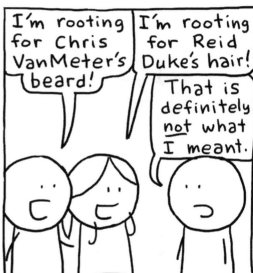

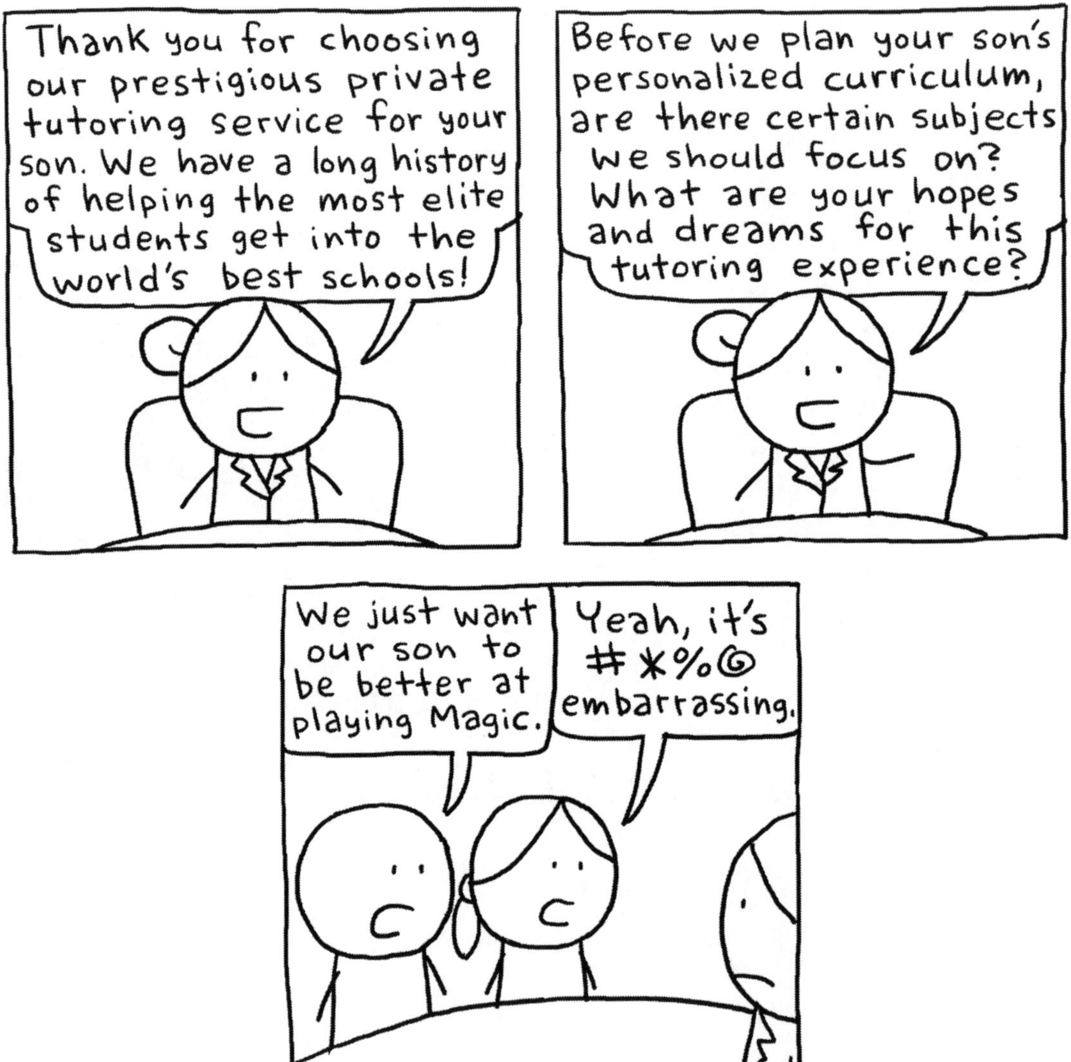
Thank you for choosing our prestigious private tutoring service for your son. We have a long history of helping the most elite students get into the world's best schools!
Before we plan your son's personalized curriculum, are there certain subjects we should focus on? What are your hopes and dreams for this tutoring experience?
We just want our son to be better at playing Magic.
Yeah, it's #*%@ embarrassing.

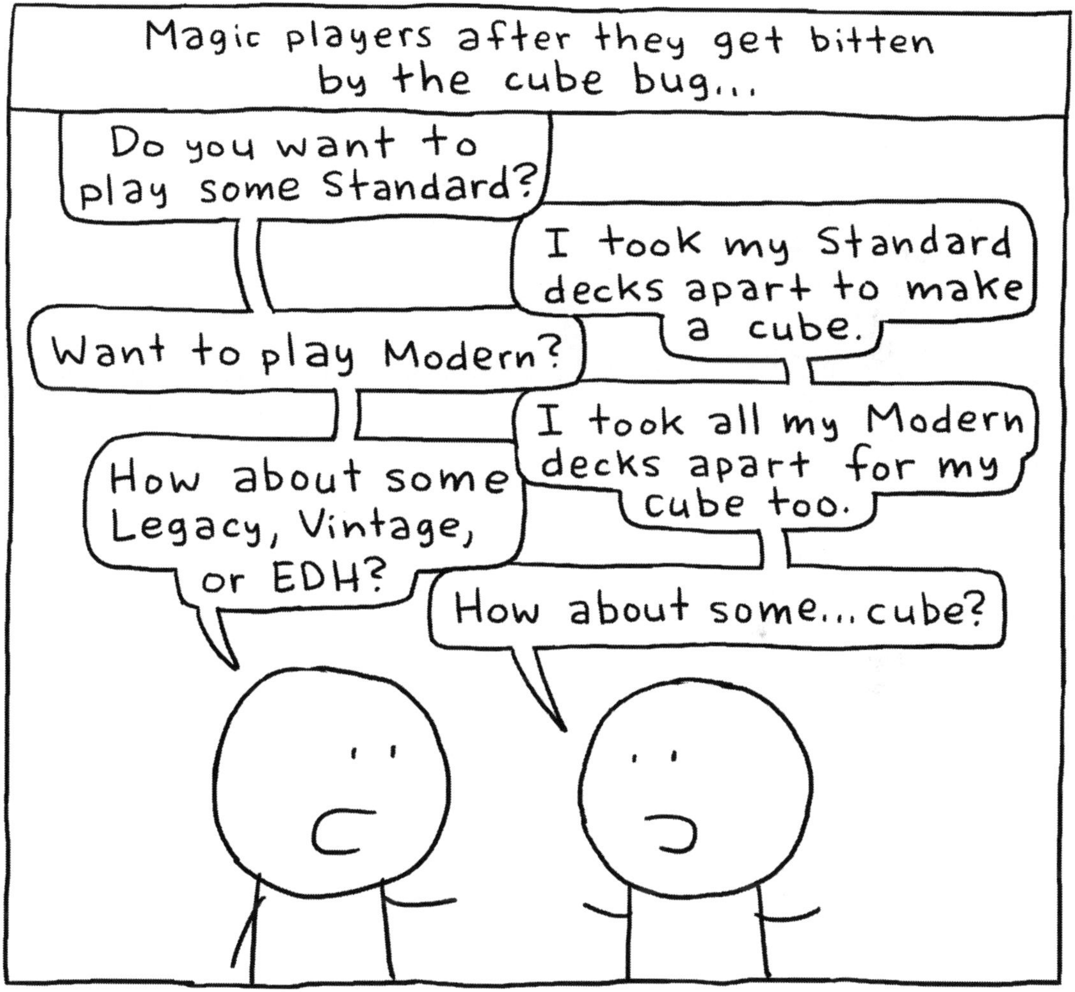
Magic players after they get bitten by the cube bug...
Do you want to play some Standard?
I took my Standard decks apart to make a cube.
Want to play Modern?
I took all my Modern decks apart for my cube too.
How about some Legacy, Vintage, or EDH?
How about some...cube?

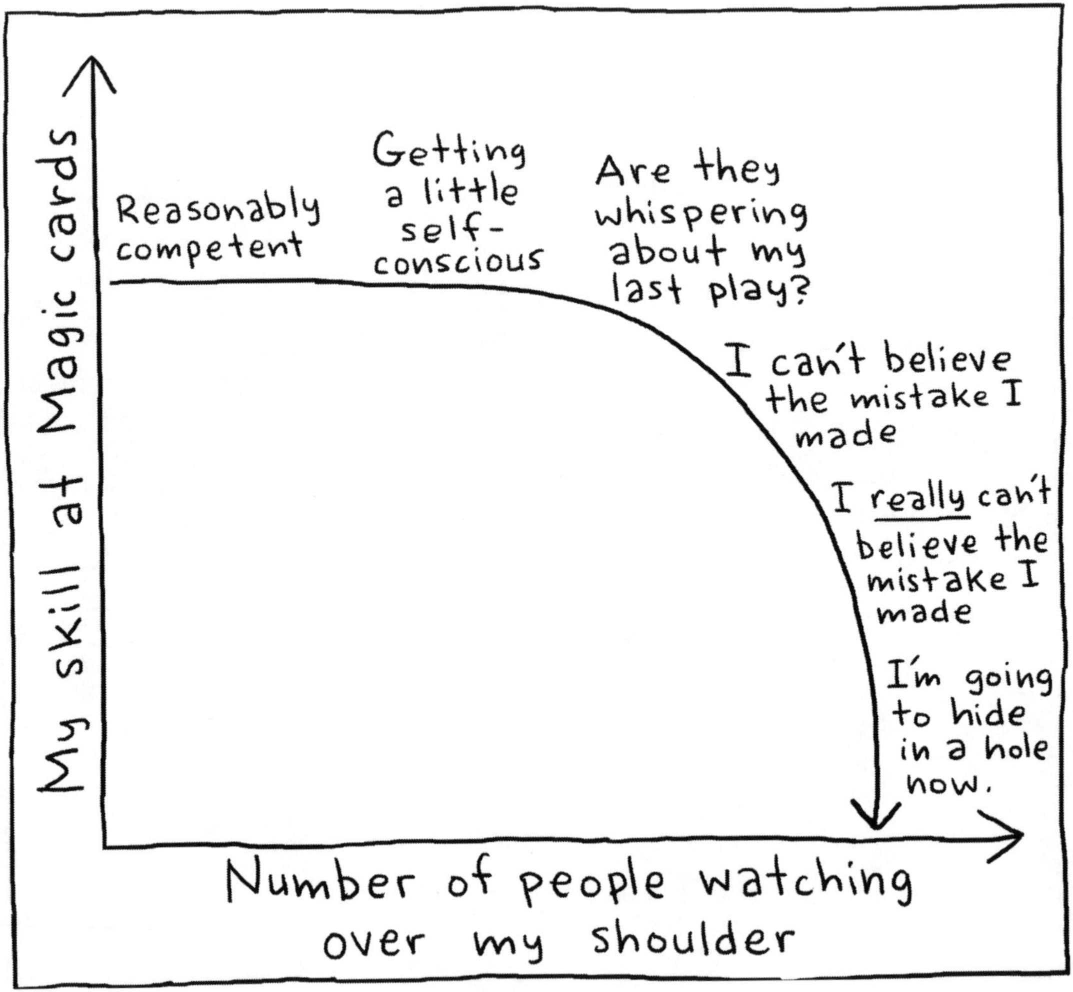
My skill at Magic cards
Reasonably competent
Getting a little self-conscious
Are they whispering about my last play?
I can't believe the mistake I made
I really can't believe the mistake I made
I'm going to hide in a hole now.
Number of people watching over my shoulder

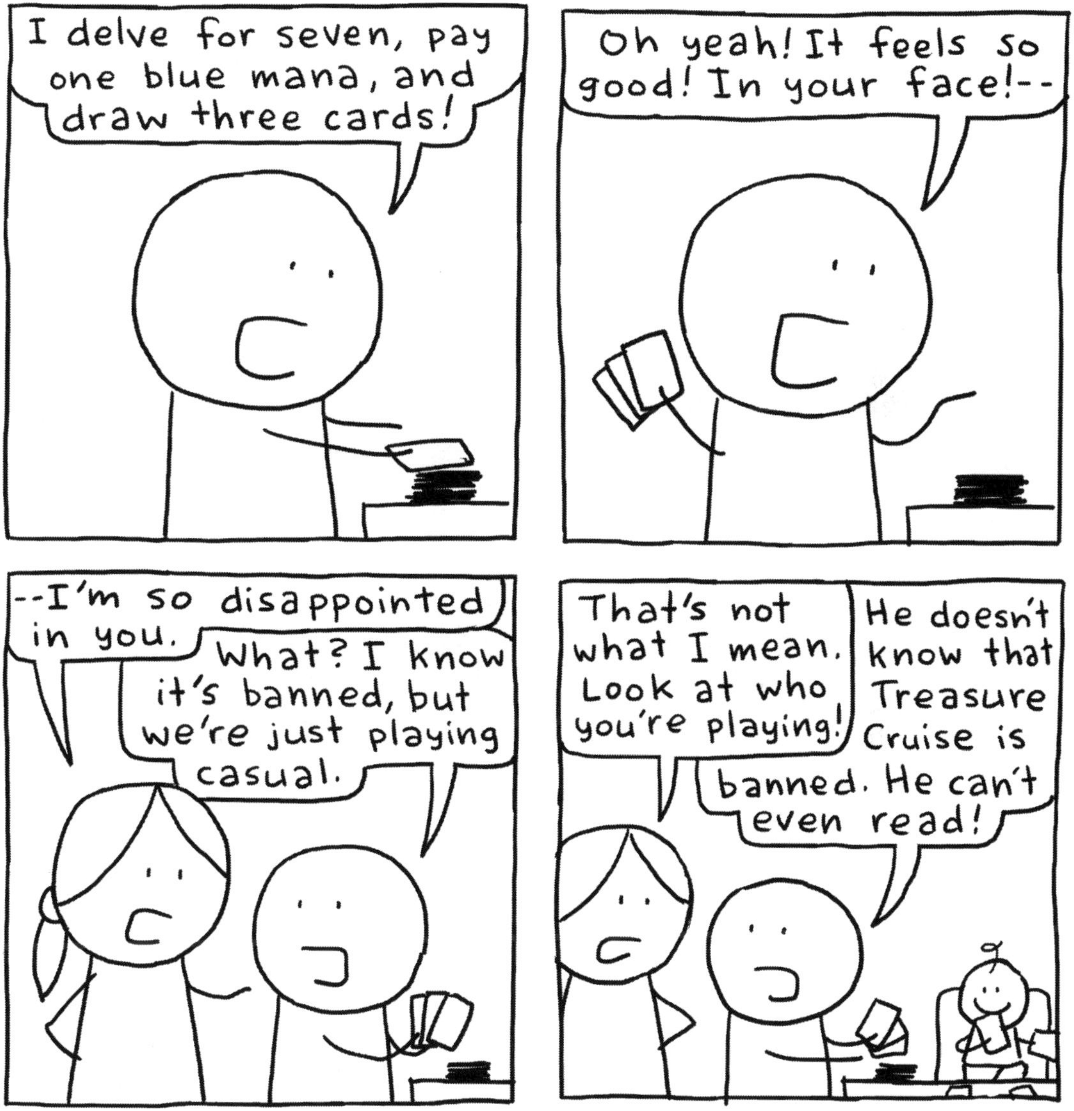
I delve for seven, pay one blue mana, and draw three cards!
Oh yeah! It feels so good! In your face!--
--I'm so disappointed in you.
What? I know it's banned, but we're just playing casual.
That's not what I mean. Look at who you're playing!
He doesn't know that Treasure Cruise is banned. He can't even read!

Cardboard Crack has been online since March 2013, featuring comics exclusively about the world's most addictive game, Magic: The Gathering. Since that time, the Cardboard Crack website has gained many thousands of followers and many millions of page views. It has received links from a wide variety of prominent personalities in the Magic community, from Aaron Forsythe (current director of Magic: The Gathering R&D) to Jon Finkel (widely regarded as one of the greatest Magic players of all-time). Cardboard Crack is also featured in the weekly newsletter of StarCityGames.com (the world's largest Magic store).

New comics can be found regularly at:
cardboard-crack.com
facebook.com/CardboardCrack

Check out these other Cardboard Crack books:
Cardboard Crack
I will never quit Cardboad Crack
Cardboard Crack anytime, anywhere
Cardboard Crack until the day I die

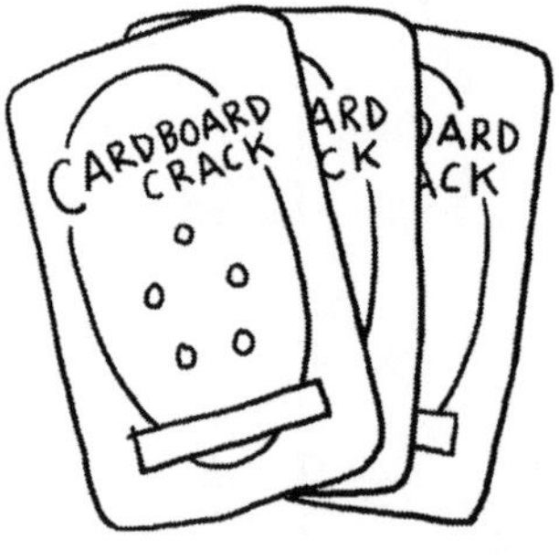
CARDBOARD
CRACK